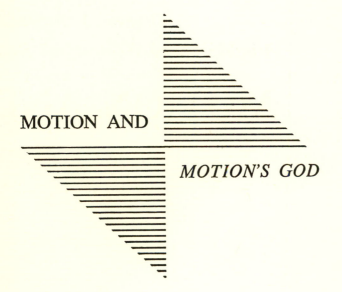

MOTION AND MOTION'S GOD

Thematic Variations in

Aristotle, Cicero, Newton, and Hegel

MOTION AND

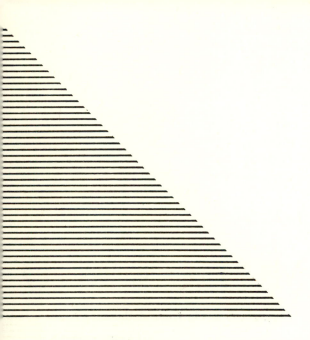

MOTION'S GOD

BY MICHAEL J. BUCKLEY, S.J.

PRINCETON UNIVERSITY PRESS 1971

LC Card: 73-132234

ISBN: 0-691-07124-1

This book has been composed in Linotype Granjon

Printed in the United States of America by

Princeton University Press, Princeton, New Jersey

For My Brother Jesuits

CONTENTS

CONTENTS

MOTION AND

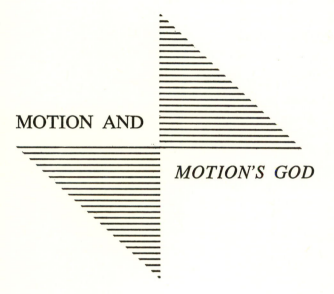

MOTION'S GOD

INTRODUCTION: *Problem and Procedure*

WHEN Moses Maimonides purposed to justify Jewish revelation to thinkers versed in the cosmological and scientific sophistications of the twelfth century, reconciling scriptures with the demands of philosophy, he proposed to found a continuity between human and divine wisdom upon a doctrine of God demonstrated from the evidences afforded by motion. Following the lead of Ibn Daoud of Toledo, he vindicated belief in the God of Abraham, Isaac, and Jacob through an illation to a moving cause, an unmoved mover, whose agency ultimately explains all changes and movement and whose demonstration occupies the initial books of the *Guide of the Perplexed*.[1] Ibn Rochd (Averroes), in the Islamic tradition, made no attempt to conjoin reason and revelation, the teachings of the Koran with the conclusions of the philosophers. Yet, even content with the doctrine of threefold interpretation, he coined a formula in which faith, theology, and philosophy would merge, summing up the ascent of the human mind to the divine: "The cause of motion is the cause of the world."[2] Aristides, the first ecclesiastical writer to style himself "Christian philosopher," attempted in his *Apologia* to the Emperor Hadrian a conjunction of the new evangel with the wisdom of the Hellenistic civilization, appealing to the effects of divine

[1] Moses Maimonides, *The Guide of the Perplexed*, trans. Shlomo Pines (Chicago: University of Chicago, 1963), i. 71. "It is the greatest proof through which one can know the existence of the deity—I mean the revolution of the heavens—as I shall demonstrate. Understand this" (p. 174); cf. ii. 2, pp. 175-254. For a description of the audience to which the *Guide* was directed, cf. Etienne Gilson, "Homage to Maimonides," *Essays on Maimonides*, ed. Salo Wittmayer Baron (New York: Columbia, 1941), pp. 23-33.

[2] Averroes, *Tahafut Al-Tahafut* [The Incoherence of the Incoherence], trans. Simon Van Den Bergh (London: Luzac, 1954), D. iv, No. 264 (I, 156).

3

causality and using his conclusions as norm for judging and rejecting revelations other than the Christian: the barbarians worship elements and men; the Greeks endow their gods with bestial passions; the Jews destroy the supreme transcendence with petty rules of external observance. Only in the religion of Jesus, he contended, did the native force of the demonstration tell. And how is God demonstrated? "Seeing that the cosmos and everything within it is necessarily moved, I understood the mover and master to be God."[3]

But the assertion that the God of revelation could be known from the data afforded by natural motion; that there were two manners of attaining the divine, one by natural knowledge and the other by religious doctrine; and that these two ways were distinct—these comprised but one position in each of the three religious traditions. A second position, of equal importance, asserted that there were not two ways, but only one: theology is the guide of all natural knowledge, divine revelation includes all true science and opinion, and even the authentic grasp of the science of physics depends upon the knowledge of scripture. In Europe this tradition was Augustinian, and Roger Bacon would found the justification for his coincidence of science and theology in Augustine's *De Doctrina Christiana*: "If elsewhere there is truth, it is found here [in the Bible]; if there is any hurtful thing, it is here condemned."[4] Both positions could demonstrate the existence of God from motion, but the difference between them is that the second will in time

---

[3] Aristides, *Apology* I. The translation is mine from the Greek text as in *The Apology of Aristides on Behalf of the Christians*, ed. J. Rendel Harris (Cambridge: University Press, 1893), p. 100. For the later tradition of this argument through the Christian fathers, cf. *ibid.*, pp. 52-53.

[4] Roger Bacon, *Opus Majus* ii. 1. Cf. *The Opus Majus of Roger Bacon*, trans. Robert Belle Burke (Philadelphia: University of Pennsylvania, 1928), vol. I, p. 36. "I wish to show in this second part that there is one wisdom that is perfect and that this is contained in the Scriptures. From the roots of this wisdom all truth has sprung. I say, therefore, that one science is the mistress of the others, namely theology, to which the remaining sciences are vitally necessary, and without which it cannot reach its end. The excellences of these sciences theology claims for her own law, whose nod and authority the rest of the sciences obey. Or better, there is only one perfect wisdom, which is contained wholly in the Scriptures, and is to be unfolded by canon law and philosophy."

4

add a more satisfactory proof, one which will purify or color the others or one which will be less unworthy of the transcendence of God. Anselm, after the three a posteriori demonstrations of the *Monologium*, would undertake in the *Proslogium* a higher, an a priori inference; for so unique a concept as the divine demands a correspondingly unique demonstration.[5] In the former position, only the a posteriori proof works. In the second, both are made to tell; and the ontological purifies the a posteriori, related to it as perfect to imperfect. But in both positions the demonstration of the existence of God can be done from motion.

A third position, in contrast to both, found lodging in each of the three religious traditions: a sharp rejection of all natural knowledge which purported to bear upon the divine. Philosophic knowledge was neither a distinct manner of knowing God nor an incompletion brought to fruition in theology; it was a corruption. "Obeying the precepts of God and following the law of the Father of immortality," wrote Tatian, the contemporary of Aristides, "we repudiate whatever rests upon human opinion."[6] In Islam, the Mutakallimoun, especially in the converted Al Ash'ari, repudiated Greek philosophy and science in an effort to preserve the freedom of God and the purity of the Koran.[7] Judah Halevi in his *Kuzari* pleaded against the introduction of pagan philosophical devices into the

[5] Anselm, *Proslogium* 1. "For I do not seek to understand that I may believe, but I believe in order to understand. For this also I believe—that unless I believed, I should not understand." *Saint Anselm: Basic Writings*, trans. S. N. Deane (La Salle, Ill.: Open Court, 1966), p. 7. For the central texts used in the continuing debate on the ontological argument, cf. Alvin Plantinga (ed.), *The Ontological Argument* (Garden City, N.Y.: Doubleday, 1965). For an analysis of the career of the argument, cf. Herbert Lamm, "The Relation of Concept and Demonstration in the Ontological Argument," unpublished Ph.D. dissertation, Department of Philosophy, University of Chicago, 1940.

[6] Tatiani *Oratio ad Graecos* 32, translation mine, from the Latin text as in *Corpus Apologetarum Christianorum Saeculi Secundi*, ed. Joann. Carol. Theod. Otto (Jenae: Prostat Apud Frider. Mauke., 1851), VI, 126.

[7] Etienne Gilson, *History of Christian Philosophy in the Middle Ages* (New York: Random House, 1955), pp. 182-185. Gilson maintains that the conversion of Al Ash'ari from the Mutazilite school was of pivotal importance in the history of Arabian thought in identifying orthodox Islam with a repudiation of Hellenic philosophy.

5

exegesis of the Torah and for a cleansing of biblical theology from its non-Jewish elements—a return to the God of Abraham and Moses who had acted in the history of his people.[8] No demonstration of his existence was required; none was possible; faith alone was necessary.

Three distinct religious traditions, then, came to deal with a problem of great philosophic import: a demonstration of the existence of God from motion. Within these traditions three positions would be taken: federation, subsumption, rejection. Each position would entertain discussions of the meaning and value of the demonstration. Whether one denied the pagan arts, or asserted a natural theology as effect of the internal inspirations of grace, or distinguished the way of reason from the way of faith, the complicated lines of inquiry, debate, proof, and discussion wound around the knowledge of God from movement and change. Yet the fixities of vocabulary and the apologetic needs of the community often disguised serious ambiguities within the new elements. The proposition, the existence of God can be known from motion, is one upon which many thoroughly divergent philosophies would insist, but the concord would be linguistic rather than real. Each of the terms and their resulting statement are systematically ambiguous, understood differently in distinct philosophical structures and applied to contrasting, if not contradicting, realities. So deeply rooted into the coordinates of system are divergencies in the meanings of the terms, the interpretation of the evidence, the movement of the inferences, and the sources of the doctrine that no simple series of definitional clarifications could hope to distinguish them adequately. The ambiguity results from an identity in philosophic statement and persists throughout the transformations effected by religious context. This ambiguity can only be clarified and the statements differentiated through an understanding of the philosophical enterprise of which they are the product.

---

[8] Julius Guttmann, *Philosophies of Judaism*, trans. David W. Silverman (New York: Holt, Rinehart and Winston, 1964), pp. 120-126. The influence of the Asherites reached into Judah Halevi's thought through Al Ghazali (*ibid.*, p. 122).

The following work is an attempt to do precisely that, to clarify the *theme* that God can be demonstrated from motion as it runs through the four philosophic systems of Aristotle, Cicero, Newton, and Hegel.[9] Each of these major philosophers has posited an illation from motion to God, but so ambiguous has the statement become in its differing contexts that the thematic unity hides a divergence of meaning and application. Even the peculiar problem to which each addressed himself was not univocally common to all: Aristotelian inquiry treated the definitional structures and varieties of motion, demonstrating that each movement must have a first cause and finding the relational unity of the universe in God as moving and final cause. Balbus, in Cicero's dialogue, sets forth his argument to justify the religious beliefs which undergirded Roman political life and fell back upon the evidences provided by a Stoic analysis of motion. Newtonian universal mechanics found a unified basis for the laws of motion in a universe in which space was necessarily eternal, the sensorium of God in which he acts with the dominance that is his central characteristic. Hegelian logic mounts from the encountered oppositions, essentially factual beginnings, through the reduction of contraries to the dialectical resolving movement that is itself God, defending the ontological insight of Anselm against Kant in this merger of concept and motion. There is, however, an ambiguously common problem which unites them all: How does one infer the existence of God from the reality of motion? What is the relationship between process and the divine?—disjunctive or conjunctive?—and how? But the common problem by which they are joined for the purposes of this book is as ambiguous as the common theme to which each of them would assent.

The study of a theme, like the evidence of God in motion and the motions of the world, requires the examination and use of the philosophic arts by which philosophic *inquiry*, i.e., the solution of philosophic problems, is related to philosophic *semantics*, i.e., "the examination of different solutions of phil-

[9] For an understanding of the nature and use of "theme," cf. Richard McKeon, *Thought, Action and Passion* (Chicago: University of Chicago, 1954), pp. 5ff.

osophic problems."[10] The thrust of philosophic semantics is not towards a single or preferred answer to a common problem, rejecting alternatives as inadequate or partial or false and asserting a particular solution as true; much less is it towards a philosophical relativism which obviates any questions of truth or falsity through the reduction of all knowledge to cultural conditionings or perspectival discriminations. If one were doing philosophic inquiry instead of philosophic semantics, unambiguous coincidences of conclusions rather than ambiguities of terms and themes would be sought. In inquiry these conclusions would be sought in the various systems and brought to bear upon the problem of the divine existence so that the arguments of one system could be translated, transformed, or modified in working towards the problems of another. The medieval commentaries, for example, often turned into essays in philosophic inquiry, using the particular author not for the study of the formalities of his inquiry but for the material contributions he could offer or allow in the solution of one's own inquiry. This is to study substantive questions and to judge the truth or falsity of suggested conclusions. Philosophic semantics, in contrast, is an attempt to understand the working inquiries of others and to relate them in a structure of meanings—not to criticize their propositions, using one's own position as norm, but to consider their operations and their unambiguous problems individually and to compare, distinguish, and relate these operations collectively. This is a formal analysis of divergent inquiries, not a judgment or evaluation of the solutions in which they issue. Philosophic semantics, then, is a peculiar kind of effort to understand, to trace a literal series of meanings for each system; it is to so situate a theme in terms of its philosophical coordinates that its one or several meanings comes through, that it becomes an unambiguous proposition.

There are four basic coordinates of philosophic semantics, four factors in terms of which any discourse may be understood and through which many different systems interrelated. Inquiry must be brought to bear upon some area, some subject-

---

[10] Richard McKeon, "Philosophic Semantics and Philosophic Inquiry" (mimeographed, Chicago, 1966).

field which will provide the basic terms of the discussion, and this concentration constitutes the author's "Selection"—whether that focus is directly upon the nature of things (metaphysical selection) or upon the processes of thought as criteria for things (epistemological selection) or upon human expression in deed and speech (pragmatic or semantic selection). Secondly, the basic composite of discourse is the proposition. That in terms of which a predicate can be ultimately attributed to a subject indicates the author's "Interpretation." "Interpretation" discloses the "really real" within the system, that which allows for truth or falsity in statement and action—and interpretations differ as reality is said to transcend phenomena ontologically or to underlie them entitatively or to structure the phenomena essentially or to be superimposed arbitrarily through an existential perspective. The third coordinate, "Method," provides the pattern by which one proposition leads into another. It is the manner of procedure in discourse—whether it be through the dialectical resolution of opposites or the logistic additions and divisions of basic unities or the problematic movement towards each problem on its own terms or the operational elaboration and application of a matrix to yield the most fruitful results. Finally what unites each system is its "Principle," that through which the disparate propositions achieve unity and final justification—whether that "Principle" be comprehensive of all problems or reflexively commensurate with a peculiar set of problems or constitute the basic simple out of which the whole is constructed or form the initial action through which the whole is begun and explained. Selection, Interpretation, Method, and Principle—these four coordinates of the schematism of philosophic semantics will be clarified and developed as they enter instrumentally into the subsequent analyses of arguments. They are supremely useful for understanding the efforts of the authors we study. With their aid, contrasts or corroborations can be asserted and the real issues of disagreement can be separated from verbal contradictions or philosophical complementarities. Thus philosophic semantics prepares for philosophic inquiry and, in turn, is furthered by it.

As the common problem is that of the relationship between

"motion" and "God" in contrasting philosophies, so the authors have been chosen because they exhibit sharply divergent *methods* by which this conjunction is achieved: the problematic method of Aristotle, the operational method of Cicero, the logistic method of Newton, and the dialectical method of Hegel. What is here the subject of the semantic analysis are four "proofs" of the existence of "God" from "motion." The quotation marks surround each of the pivotal terms because what is being proved, what is being used as its basis, and the manner of the inference in each case is somewhat or radically different, leaving the application and the meanings of the terms as well as the assertions and realizations of the theme ambiguous. God can be made a principle by any of these methods, and the mobile object is subjected to a variety of interpretations. These four philosophers will agree or disagree in the type of principle, interpretation, and selection, but each uses a distinct method in working through the common problem. To focus upon method is not the only way such a study in philosophic semantics could be made, but it is the way in which the various approaches to a common problem are most clearly apparent as variations on a common theme, i.e., it is the semantics of discursive methods.

Besides the coordinates provided by philosophic semantics in selection, principle, method, and interpretation, certain *terms*, i.e., linguistic variables, will be noted as they recur in each author. The verbal identity of each of these words allows for comparisons of meaning and application, as a single symbol threads its way through divergent resolutions of the common problem. The primary terms have already been noted, "motion" and "God," but these in turn entail any number of secondary terms which function as parameters: cause, nature, art, time, place, thesis, and hypothesis. Hypothesis, for example, forms the necessary initiation of Aristotelian science, the characteristic subject of Ciceronian rhetoric, an unscientific explanation in Newtonian natural philosophy, and a repudiated beginning in Hegelian method. Each of the terms goes through similar changes in meaning and application in the developments of each system, and their understanding is critically necessary if the relationship between motion and God is to be understood.

In addition to the *coordinates* of philosophic semantics and to the *terms* of philosophic inquiries, the clarification of the common *theme* will be aided by the isolation of a set of *questions* and the means of establishing warrantable answers. The theme raises such questions about each author: of the problematic, i.e., what is the immediate context of the inquiry; of the problem, what is the problem peculiar to each; of the devices used; of the sciences which handle the problem; of the attributes and characteristics of the god demonstrated. The interworking of the three sets, *terms* and *theme* and *questions*, correlate with the four *coordinates* of philosophic semantics; and the relationship established among the philosophic systems as a result should be a very delicate and complicated one. But without this complexity the interrelations of philosophic systems become a process of over-simplification and distortion, providing occasion for the reduction of one to another and for the refutation of alien positions which are obviously absurd in their conclusions or nonsensical in their statements.[11]

The authors have been taken in chronological order not because this paper attempts to trace influences. There have been such, but their story is not the burden of this book. Much less is it an essay in the archaeology of an author. Whatever the psychological development of Newton or the strata of the *Metaphysics*, each work contains an argument or a series of arguments relating "motion" and "God." What are these arguments, what do they mean in themselves, and how do they relate to each other?—these are the questions which this work hopes to treat. Thus the order of the treatment does not follow the times of redactions nor the psychology of discovery, but the properly philosophical order of ideational sequence. The attempt is not for the date of composition nor for the moments of invention, but for the internal conjunction of arguments and

[11] For a total failure to situate philosophic assertions and arguments within their proper systems, cf. Wallace I. Matson, *The Existence of God* (Ithaca, N.Y.: Cornell, 1965). Only Professor Matson's refusal to take radical philosophical pluralism seriously could allow the massive over-simplification of all theistic argumentation to his manageable list.

the thematic connection between systems. This is to treat each work philosophically and to deal with the history of philosophy as thematic variation and development rather than as contradictions or absurdities. The isolation of term, theme, and question is not an effort to erect an artificial structure into which the inquiry of each of the authors is to be fitted. On the contrary, the effort will be to follow the argument peculiar to each as it evolves in his investigation. But the focus during this sequence will be upon the meanings given to the ambiguous terms, the sense which the theme achieves, and the methods and principles through which it is argued and established.

Any effort to link such divergent wisdoms as those of Hegel and Aristotle, Cicero and Newton immediately enters into the arena of clashing interpretations—an unhappy fact, but nevertheless a fact. The muster in each camp is a long one, and their lists have not yet drawn to a close. But debate does not necessarily spell disaster, and perhaps this addition to the ongoing controversies will not be without its contribution to that continuing meditation upon the meaning of the masters of Western thought—a meditation which promotes the education of the West and whose continuity forms much of its richest traditions.

This book owes so much to the deeply generous drudgery of Mr. Michael Czerny, S.J., who both proofread its galleys and compiled its indices. Nor could I close an introduction to the problems and procedures of this study without acknowledging my indebtedness to Professors Clifford Kossel, John Wright, and Herbert Lamm. So much of this work was occasioned by their conversations, suggestions, and encouragement. Above all I stand in grateful debt to Professor Richard P. McKeon, whose classes introduced me into the possibilities of philosophic pluralism, whose guidance supervised the inquiry of this essay, and whose friendship is among my most treasured possessions.

MICHAEL J. BUCKLEY, S.J.
Jesuit School of Theology
Berkeley, California

PART I

ARISTOTLE

I.

Problematic Method

THE PROBLEM which initiates the Aristotelian inquiry into a single principle beyond sensible form is that of the endless perdurance of natural motion. That motion is eternal is not a given of observation and experience; it is a conclusion obtained through an investigation whose methods and devices have been specified by the character and attributes of motion and whose alternatives are framed within its opening question:

> Whether motion became once, not having been before, and will perish again so that there will be nothing moved,
> Or it neither became nor will perish, but always was and always will be, and this deathless and pauseless (reality) inheres in beings, being a kind of life to all those things which are constituted by nature.[1]

The dialectical structure of the sentence focuses the general problem of endless motion through the immediate issue which it generates: Is natural motion eternal or not? This is a ὅτι question, the first of the four which Aristotle lists as propaedeutics of scientific inquiry and the particular one which examines the composition or division of a subject and a predicate, i.e., the affirmation or the denial of a fact.[2] It is an either/or ques-

---

[1] *Ph.* viii 1. 250^{b}11-16, translation mine. Hereafter (m) will indicate that the translation is either entirely or partially the author's. Otherwise the Oxford translation has been used as in William David Ross (ed.), *The Works of Aristotle* (Oxford: Clarendon, 1908-31). The writings of Aristotle are cited with the abbreviations used by Liddell and Scott, *A Greek-English Lexicon* (Oxford: Clarendon, 1940), Vol. I, p. xix.

[2] *APo.* ii. 1. 89^{b}24-29. One must be very careful in his selections from the Aristotelian corpus to substantiate an interpretation. Aristotle's problematic method and reflexive principles isolate certain areas for unique methodological treatment, and individual propositions can only be understood in terms of the

tion: Is eternality to be affirmed or denied of motion? Its resolution closes the first phase of the investigations of *Physics* viii.

Once such a connection between a subject and an attribute has been established, the search turns for the reason that it is so. It is a second inquiry, begun by a διότι question and terminated in the reasoned fact.[3] Granted such-and-such a synthesis of subject and predicate, why is it so? What is the principle of their conjunction? Thus the second moment of the general problem follows hard on the heels of the first; it is a question about principle and cause: Because of what (διὰ τί) is motion eternal?[4] Unlike the previous question, this can be neither posed in simple alternatives nor answered in composition or division.[5] The inquiry is for a middle term, for a cause which will scientifically explain the fact because it has really effected the fact.[6] And each of the four causes can be the middle term of such a demonstration. The fact (τὸ ὅτι) has indicated that a principle must exist; the reasoned fact (τὸ διότι) shows what this principle is.[7] The phases of inquiry follow the pattern of questions: The endless duration of natural motion is first to be established as a fact; then it must be understood in terms of the principle which has authored the fact.

The simplicity of this formula, however, belies the enormous difficulties inherent in the terms of the questions. The problem of the eternality of motion cannot even emerge until the definition of the terms has been established, until "nature," "mo-

---

entire tractate. Here the attempt is to relate the questions of inquiry which Aristotle discusses in the *Posterior Analytics* to the particular inquiries made in the physical and metaphysical works, not to give a "comprehensive picture" of Aristotle's philosophy through a pastiche of citations, taken irrespective of their context. It was this latter method which Bernard Weinberg scored as the "tradition of fragmentation and of methodological insouciance" which characterized the habit of Renaissance interpretation. Cf. "From Aristotle to Pseudo-Aristotle," in *Aristotle's Poetics and English Literature*, ed. Elder Olson (Chicago: University of Chicago, 1965), pp. 194-195.

[3] *APo.* ii. 1. 89^{b}29-31.

[4] *Ph.* viii. 3 begins this causal inquiry into the eternality of motion, joining it to an inquiry into the principle which explains why some things are now at motion and then at rest. For both, the question is διότι.

[5] *APo.* ii. 1. 89^{b}29-31.   [6] *Ibid.* ii. 2. 89^{b}37-90^{a}7; 11. 94^{a}20-24.

[7] *Ibid.* ii. 2. 90^{a}5-7.

tion," and "eternal," as well as the plurality which enters the subsequent questions and resolutions, have been understood. This determination of crucial terms is the task belonging properly to the prior question, τί ἐστι.[8] Aristotle uses a "problematic method," a method whose discursive processes and analytic instrumentalities are directly determined by the subject under investigation and by the principles proper to that subject.[9] The content of the terms is of critical importance in↓ working out the intelligibility of a problem. Consequently, definition is not accomplished in the problematic method through an initial imposition of meaning and its arbitrary application nor through a matrix of precisely formulated symbols and formal relationships. The significance of the important terms which compose the problem of eternal motion has been the product of the painstaking inquiry of the previous books of the *Physics*. Critical definitions have come as results of investigations and as clarified through inductions, not at the beginning of either.[10] There is no single method with which to obtain definition; it depends directly upon the principles employed and the thing to be defined. For to define a

---

[8] *Ibid.* ii. 1. 89ᵇ31-35.

[9] There is an ambivalence to the Aristotelian μέθοδος which is lost in its English transliteration. Μέθοδος can denote the manner of scientific procedure, the way of investigation, the formal structures of the movement of inquiry; and Aristotle uses ὁδός and τρόπος as equivalent variants. Or μέθοδος can mean the method and its product. Most frequently, it is this blend of both meanings that μέθοδος signifies, for the Aristotelian scientific tractates were not a collection of conclusions reached, with the final propositions reduced to the perfect figure of the syllogism. They are progressive moments in the ongoing progress towards definitions, causes, and properties; they are literally "methods" of obtaining the same conclusions. For the use of μέθοδος and its variants, cf. *APr.* i. 30. 46ᵃ3, 28, 31. 46ᵃ32. For the various uses and critical texts for their interpretation, cf. Hermannus Bonitz, *Index Aristotelicus: Aristotelis Opera* (Berolini: Georgii Reimeri, 1870), V, 449-450. For a discussion of Aristotle's use of μέθοδος, cf. Richard McKeon, "Rhetoric and Poetic in Aristotle," in *Aristotle's Poetics and English Literature*, p. 220, n. 29. Also Richard McKeon, "Philosophy and the Development of Scientific Methods," *Journal of the History of Ideas*, XXVII, No. 1 (January-March, 1966), 5-8.

[10] Thus *Ph.* ii initiates an inquiry into the definition of nature by noting the common feature possessed by animals and their parts, plants and the simple elements, while *Ph.* iii begins the investigation of the definition of motion by calling attention to the three states in which things exist.

17

word problematically is at the same time to define the reality for which it stands.[11] Whether this "reality" is in the order of things or thoughts or words, is a question of selection; but that the scientific definition of the term is accomplished only through the definition of that to which it is applied, whether thing, thought, or word, is a characteristic of the problematic method. The method of definition of poetic reality is quite different from the one traveled in defining a natural thing,[12] and even among natural things, "If there is no single or general method for solving the question what it is (τί ἐστι) . . . for each subject, we shall have to grasp what is the method."[13] The method is specified by the subject and its principle and cannot pass from one subject to another. So, for example, physics cannot take up questions of mathematical infinity because "we are examining sensibles and it is concerning these that we construct the method [περὶ ὧν ποιούμεθα τὴν μέθοδον]."[14]

This specification of method by the problematic proper to a particular subject obviates any single "scientific method" appropriate to all reality. The distinction of subjects provides for a radical particularization of methods. Even if the definitional question, τί ἐστι, is always identical in form, the manners of its revolution will be as different as the subjects at

---

[11] *APo.* ii. 10 distinguishes the nominal formula (τί σημαίνει τὸ ὄνομα) from the definition which exhibited τί ἐστι. The latter gives the reason for the thing's existence in exhibiting its essential nature. It is for this reason that *APo.* ii. 8 (93ᵃ18-20) insists that the answer to the question of inquiry, τί ἐστι, could only occur after or simultaneously with the answer to the question εἰ ἔστι. The nominal formula answers the question τί τὸ λεγόμενον ἔστιν. Cf. *ibid.* i. 1. 71ᵃ13.

[12] For the process of natural definition, cf. *Ph.* ii. 2. 193ᵇ22f.; *Metaph.* vii. 10. 1035ᵃ22f. For the collective method of poetic definition, cf. *Po.* i-vi, especially 1449ᵇ23-31. For a contrast of these two methods of definition, cf. Elder Olson, "The Poetic Method of Aristotle: Its Powers and Limitations," in *Aristotle's Poetics and English Literature*, pp. 181-186.

[13] *de An.* i. 1. 402ᵃ16-18. (m)

[14] *Ph.* iii. 5. 204ᵃ35-ᵇ3. (m) Cf. *Metaph.* xiv. 3. 1091ᵃ18-22: "But since they [the Pythagoreans] are constructing a world and wish to speak the language of natural science, it is fair to make some examination of their physical theories, but to let them off from the present method [ἐκ δὲ τῆς νῦν ἀφεῖναι μεθόδου]; for we are investigating the principles in the unmovables, so that we must examine the generation of numbers of this kind." (m) Cf. *APo.* i. 12. 77ᵃ40-ᵇ15. For the radical difference between mathematical and physical methods, cf. *Ph.* ii. 9. 199ᵇ34ff. and *Metaph.* ii. 3. 995ᵃ15ff.

which it is leveled.[15] Though all four lines of dialectical investigations, predicables dealing with "property," "genus," "accident," and "definition," can be called "definitory," neither singly nor together do they offer a unique method by which definitions are obtained:

This means, to use the phrase previously employed, every manner [ἅπαντ᾽ . . . τρόπον] we have enumerated might in a certain sense be called "definitory." But we must not on this account expect to find a single method [μίαν . . . μέθοδον] applicable universally to them all. For this would not be a very easy thing to find; and even were one found, it would be very obscure indeed, and of little service for the treatise before us. Rather a special method [ἰδίας . . . μεθόδου] must be laid down for each of the genera we have distinguished . . . The way through the subject [ἡ διέξοδος τοῦ προκειμένου] will be easier if we begin from the things proper to each.[16]

There is a reflexive relationship between the principles, the methods, and the subject of a science, a relationship of interdependence by which the province and procedure of each science is established. The sciences can be distinguished from one another by their ultimate principle, their final cause: the theoretical sciences aim at knowledge; the practical, at action; the productive or poetic, at making.[17] Physics, mathematics, and theology form the most general divisions of the speculative sciences, each of which admits further specification as the subjects treated are further refined.[18] And each will have its own

---

15 de An. i. 1. 402ᵃ10ff. APo. i. 28. 87ᵃ37-39: "A single science is one whose domain is a single genus, viz. all the subjects constituted out of the primary entities of the genus—i.e. the parts of this total subject—and their essential properties." Thus "we cannot in demonstrating pass from one genus to another. We cannot, for instance, prove geometrical truths by arithmetic." Ibid. i. 7. 75ᵃ36-37. A source of sophistical reasoning or scientific error lies in not using the method proper to each subject. Cf. Top. viii. 12. 162ᵇ3-11; SE 11. 171ᵇ10-11.

16 Top. i. 6. 102ᵇ33-103ᵃ1. (m) Cf. ibid. i. 5. 102ᵃ9-10. Thus the question of the method appropriate to each subject becomes of pressing importance: cf. APo. ii. 1. 53ᵃ1; 23. 68ᵇ13; de An. i. 1. 402ᵃ10ff.

17 Metaph. vi. 1. 1025ᵇ19-28; EN vi. 4. 1140ᵃ1-24.

18 Metaph. vi. 1. 1025ᵃ22; xi. 7. 1063ᵇ36ff.

19

method. One can speak properly of the "physical method"[19] or "political method"[20] or "dialetical method."[21] In all of these subdivisions, the problematic method insists upon the priority given to the subject of inquiry: one does not set up an intelligible structure and bring it to bear upon the object of inquiry, as one would with nominal definitions or formal matrices. Rather intelligibility is brought out of the subject, is actualized, through the methodological operations proper to each. One does not bring meaning to the subject; the meaning of the subject is realized. And it is precisely for this reason that the definition of terms must be worked out of the subject as a prior task of inquiry.[22]

Thus neither the meaning of the "motion," "nature," etc., nor the order of the inquiry is an arbitrary one; the definition of terms must precede questions of further conjunctions or predications. But even the understanding of terms is subsequent to the assertion of the existence of the subject to which they are applied. One cannot first define and then search for a subject in which the definition might be realized. Just as the fact (τὸ ὅτι) must be known prior to or simultaneously with the reasoned fact (τὸ διότι), so "we cannot apprehend a thing's essence [τὸ τί ἦν εἶναι] without apprehending that it exists, since while we are ignorant whether it is [εἰ ἔστιν] we cannot know what it is [τί ἐστιν]."[23] Εἰ ἔστι takes a certain priority over the other three in scientific procedure as it asserts the existence of its generic subject-matter.[24] It is here that the Aristotelian selection of terms becomes of operative importance.

---

[19] IA 2. 704ᵇ13.   [20] EN i. 1. 1094ᵇ11.

[21] Rh. i. 2. 1358ᵃ4. Cf. Top. i. 1. 100ᵃ18; 101ᵃ29; i. 3. 101ᵇ5; ix. 11. 172ᵇ8.

[22] "The objective of the method of inquiry is neither the resolution of contrarieties into more inclusive or posterior dialectical unities nor the organization of more and more sciences into systems of deductive consequences from primitive principles, but the discovery of solutions of problems and the advancement of knowledge. The method of inquiry, therefore, is a plurality of methods: a general logic common to all the sciences and particular methods adapted to the problems, the subject-matters, and the principles of the particular science." Richard McKeon, "Philosophy and Method," The Journal of Philosophy, XLVIII, No. 22 (October 25, 1951), 664.

[23] APo. ii. 8. 93ᵃ18-20 (m); cf. ii. 7. 92ᵇ17-18.

[24] Ibid. ii. 7. 92ᵇ17-18; ii. 1. 89ᵇ31-35.

When Aristotle claims a science to be "of nature" or "of being," he does more than title his work.[25] He selects a simple term to indicate what he is talking about; he gives the subject of investigation through the single term or phrase.[26] One term involves many others: "nature" is an internal principle of "motion"; "being" is primarily realized in "substance" or is distinguished into states of "act" and "potency."[27] Each method has a limited number of critical terms, the least units of its propositions and arguments, which mark off a certain area for subsequent affirmations or denials. But just as the subject and principles of investigation specified Aristotle's problematic method, so the known took a priority in the selection of simples for argument and discourse. The term is a word with the meaning of a thing.[28] The three are identical: the meaning of the word is the same as that of the corresponding concept or of its correlative reality.[29] The three are made intelligible simultane-

[25] As, for example, in *Ph.* i. 1. 184^{a}15; iii. 1. 200^{b}12; *Metaph.* iv. 1. 1003^a 21-22; xi. 3. 1060^{b}31.

[26] Father Joseph Owens correctly notes that "Aristotle does not speak of the 'object' of a science. He merely names what the science treats, either in the accusative case after a verb, or in the genitive after a noun; or more frequently, with the preposition 'about.' The Arabians—in accord with their general usage of the passive participle for the object of any activity—employed the participle MAWDU, meaning 'that which is posited.' This was the same term which they used for the *subject* of predication. . . . The Latins translated the term in both cases by *subjectum.* They spoke accordingly of the 'subject' of a science. At *Metaph.* xi. 4. 1061^{b}31, Aristotle uses the corresponding Greek word ὑποκείμενά, in the plural, for the things which a science treats." *The Doctrine of Being in Aristotelian Metaphysics* (Toronto: Pontifical Institute of Mediaeval Studies, 1951), p. 304, n. 10. This naming what the science treats, as well as the critical predicates which will enter into its examination and explanation, is a question of selection.

[27] *Ph.* iii. 1. 200^{b}12-14: "Nature has been defined as a 'principle of motion and change' and it is the subject of our inquiry. We must therefore see that we understand the meaning of 'motion'; for if it were unknown, the meaning of 'nature' too would be unknown." A similar introduction precedes the discussions of potency and act, as being is predicated (λέγεται) of substance, quality, and quantity, and in another way of potency and act. Cf. *Metaph.* ix. 1. 1045^{b}30-36.

[28] For the mutual involvement of word, thought, and thing, cf. *Cat.* 1. 1^{a}1-16; *Int.* i. 1. 16^{a}1-18; *APr.* ii. 10. 93^{b}28-94^{a}19.

[29] The examples with which Aristotle illustrates the movement from the general whole-of-experience to the particular principles, causes, and properties, serve also to exemplify the simultaneous clarification of the meaning of the word, the determination of the concept, and the explanation of the reality:

ously: the selection of terms does not give linguistics a priority over judgment nor make thought a criterion for extra-mental natures and dispositions. The term cuts through all three: the verbal, the mental, and the real, for the term is a word whose meaning is the significance of what is apprehended, what is meant, and what is said. Thus Aristotle can study "nature" or "motion" and simultaneously define the reality, clarify the concept, and delimit the symbol. This selection of terms allows him to deal with "motion" in inanimate processes, animal functions, movements of thought, and changes of discourse.

These individual terms are neither true nor false, but true and false propositions are composed of them.[30] They indicate the subject of the science or the object of investigation. They draw in the discussion upon themselves, and they do this by signifying a reality whose definition is in question. The Aristotelian selection answers the initial question, εἰ ἔστι, not by providing a definition of the term, but by indicating the reality of its referent.[31] Selection allows it to be the recipient of conse-

---

"Much the same thing happens in the relation of the name to the formula. A name, e.g., 'round,' means vaguely a sort of whole; its definition analyses this into its particular senses. Similarly a child begins by calling all men 'father' and all women 'mother,' but later on distinguishes each of them." *Ph.* i. 1. 184^b8-14. This selectional coincidence of thing, thought, and word through the term grounds the indispensable importance attributed to experience and to empirical data: "It is the business of experience to give the principles which belong to each subject. I mean, for example, that astronomical experience supplies the principles of astronomical science: for once the phenomena were adequately apprehended, the demonstrations of astronomy were discovered. Similarly with any other art or science. Consequently, if the attributes of the thing are apprehended, our business will be to exhibit readily the demonstrations. For if none of the true attributes of things has been omitted in the historical survey, we should be able to discover the proof and demonstrate everything which admitted of proof, and to make that clear whose nature does not admit of proof." *APr.* i. 30. 46^a17-27. And again: "Lack of experience diminishes our power of taking a comprehensive view of the admitted facts. Hence those who dwell in intimate association with nature and with its phenomena grow more and more able to formulate, as the foundations of their theories, principles such as to admit of wide and coherent development; while those whom devotion to abstract discussion has rendered unobservant of the facts are too ready to dogmatize on the basis of a few observations." *GC* i. 2. 316^a5-10.

[30] *Cat.* 4. 2^a4-10; *Int.* i. 1. 16^a9-18.

[31] *APo.* ii. 1. 89^b34-35: "On the other hand, when we have ascertained the

quent definition or of accidental predication. The selection of terms does not preempt the task of the method; it indicates that there is something to which the method can be conjoined, providing the simples of subsequent assertions and denials and introducing the subject-genus to which they apply.

The structure of the Aristotelian method of attaining the unmoved mover follows closely the demands of the questions of inquiry. The reality of motion and of nature is submitted as the hypothesis of all physical investigation and defended dialectically against Eleatic denials.[32] The proper subject of physical inquiry is what nature and motion are, not whether they are, and it is here that Aristotle joins issue with his fellow physicists.[33] Once the εἰ ἔστι and the τί ἐστι of motion have been established, one can open the questions of motion's duration and its cause. Just as these initial questions drew attention to Aristotle's selection and his method, so the latter focused particular attention to his interpretation and his principle.

Actually all four coordinates of inquiry—selection, method, interpretation, and principle—figure in every discourse responding to any of the four questions. One cannot put together propositions without an interpretation of the evidence or of the criteria for truth or falsity, nor can one justify the interpretation without method and principle. Thus Aristotle joins all four coordinates of inquiry in the initial sentence with which he opens the physical investigations, indicating the pro-

thing's existence, we inquire as to its nature, asking, for instance, 'what, then, is God?' or 'what is man?' " Cf. *ibid.* ii. 2. 89ᵇ36ff; 7. 92ᵇ17-18; 8. 93ᵃ18-20.

[32] *Ph.* i. 2. 184ᵇ25ff. and viii. 3. 253ᵃ32 provide the general dialectical defense of motion against Parmenides and Melissus; the one, at the initiation of the entire tractate; the other, at the beginning of a search for an ultimate moving cause. The defense is subsequently supported as succeeding moments of the inquiry uncover principles which allow for a more thorough discussion. Cf. *ibid.* i. 8. 191ᵃ23ff.; vi. 9. 239ᵇ5ff.; and viii. 8. 263ᵃ4ff. in which Zeno is successively discussed, as the ongoing process of inquiry deals with the premises upon which his denials were predicated.

[33] *Ibid.* ii. 1. 193ᵃ1-4: "*What* nature is [τί μὲν οὖν ἐστιν ἡ φύσις] and the meaning of the terms 'by nature' and 'according to nature' has been stated. *That* nature exists [ὡς δ' ἔστιν ἡ φύσις], it would be absurd to try to prove; for it is obvious that there are many things of this kind." For motion, cf. *ibid.* i. 2. 185ᵃ12-14 and iii. 1. 200ᵇ13-14.

gram of method, the subject of his science, the criteria for knowledge, and the pivotal importance of principle:

> Concerning all methods of which there are principles or causes or elements: Since understanding and scientific knowledge occur through knowing these—for we only think that we know each thing when we know the first causes and the first principles and even the elements—it is clear that the science of nature must first determine what pertains to principles.[34]

A number of assertions are contained in this rather complex sentence. Three factors are listed in order of progressive particularity: principle, cause, and element. A principle is any beginning, any source.[35] A cause is that upon which another depends for movement, state, or knowledge—thus all causes are principles.[36] An element denotes the first component of a thing which remains within it—thus, one kind of cause.[37] There is an inclusiveness about principle, then, which embraces them all and which will justify the primary question to be about principles.[38] Understanding and science, the one referring to a direct grasp of the whole, and the other to an understanding mediated through that which is previously established, result when these questions of principles have been resolved, i.e., when the subject-matter under investigation is finally grasped in terms of all of its sources, the relationships through which it exists in the manner in which it does, and its internal components.[39]

---

[34] *Ph.* i. 1. 184^{a}10-16. (m)   [35] *Metaph.* v. 1. 1012^{b}34ff.

[36] *Ibid.* v. 1. 1013^{a}17.

[37] *Ibid.* v. 2. 1013^{a}24ff.; v. 3. 1014^{a}15-16; xii. 4. 1070^{b}22-23.

[38] For the comprehensive inclusion within "principle" of "cause" and "element," cf. Owens, *op.cit.,* p. 96. Father Owens agrees with Werner Jaeger, *The Theology of the Early Greek Philosophers* (Oxford: Clarendon, 1947), pp. 24-28, that the philosophical uses of ἀρχή date from the speculations of Anaximander (Owens, p. 347, n. 19).

[39] For the contrast between the immediate grasp of definitions which are indemonstrable and the mediated nature of science, cf. *APo.* ii. 19. 100^{a}14-^{b}17; 3. 90^{a}35-91^{a}12. The community of science lies in this mediation: "In virtue of the common elements of demonstration—I mean the common axioms which are used as premises of demonstration, not the subjects or the attributes demonstrated as belonging to them—all the sciences have communion with one another." *Ibid.* i. 11. 77^{a}26-28.

But the principles are said to belong to a method; they are "of a method." And there is an admitted plurality of methods. In sharp contrast to the Kantian transition from one critique to another, an *Übergang* which is made possible by keeping a single, universal method and varying the principle commensurate with each kind of knowledge,[40] every Aristotelian method is covariant with its principle. Change either of these two basics, principle or method, and the other is necessarily altered. Thus "nature" as the internal principle of motion and physical method were so interdependent that to deny the principle was to subvert the entire method.[41] The principles of the various methods or sciences differ among themselves to the degree to which the sciences differ.[42] They are commensurate with their subject-matter and cannot substitute one for the other: "Units, for instance, which are without position, cannot take the place of points, which have position."[43] The principles of each method are not only commensurate with that method, but they are reflexively self-instantiating, as will be seen in the case of nature and the unmoved mover.[44]

The other coordinate to which Aristotle draws attention here is that of the location of intelligibility. First philosophy opens

[40] Immanuel Kant, *Critique of Practical Reason*, trans. Lewis White Beck (Indianapolis: Liberal Arts, 1956), pp. 7-14. Kant, *Critique of Judgment*, trans. J. H. Bernard (New York: Hafner, 1951), p. 12: "There must, therefore, be a ground of the *unity* of the supersensible which lies at the basis of nature, with that which the concept of freedom practically contains; and the concept of this ground, although it does not attain either theoretically or practically to a knowledge of the same, and hence has no peculiar realm, nevertheless makes possible the transition [*Übergang*] from the mode of thought [*Denkungsart*] according to the principles of the one to that according to the principles of the other."

[41] *Ph.* viii. 3. 253ª32-ᵇ6; *Top.* i. 1. 100ᵇ18-21.

[42] *APo.* i. 28. 87ª37-b4: "One science differs from another when their principles [αἱ ἀρχαί] neither stem from one another nor from some common source. The sign of this is whenever one reaches their indemonstrable premises. For it is necessary that their [principles] as well as their conclusions be in the same genus [ἐν τῷ αὐτῷ γένει]. And the sign of this is also whenever their conclusions are in this genus and are homogeneous." (m) Cf. *ibid.* i. 32. 88ª18-ᵇ29.

[43] *Ibid.* i. 32. 88ª32-33. Cf. *Top.* i. 2. 101ᵇ2-3; *Metaph.* i. 3. 984ª28. Thus first principles have no ulterior causes in their own order of inquiry. Cf. *Ph.* i. 6. 189ª30; viii. 1. 252ᵇ4.

[44] "Reflexive principles appear, however, in their purest and perhaps most explicit form in the philosophy of Aristotle, for the major parts of his philoso-

with the acknowledged drive of a man to know,[45] while the initial sentence of the *Physics* asserts as a reflexive awareness that this desire is satisfied only in grasping principles, causes, and elements. These, then, are the criteria of assertions and denials as the method progresses. They are that in virtue of which the subject of investigation is to be understood and that understanding formulated in definition and propositions. They are equally, then, the measure of the truth or falsity of any sentence which purports to make affirmative statements during the method about the subject. This is a question of "interpretation"—that in terms of which any proposition within the method is true or false. An author's "interpretation" is the character of the reality by which he asserts meanings, conjoins or separates subject and predicate, and makes a claim to fact or fiction. In Aristotle, there is a coincidence of these critical criteria with the structure and functions of the objects presented as empirical data. The Aristotelian science of natural motion presupposes that natural things possess their own meaningful patterns, that each of them has its significance identified with itself, a significance which emerges through the methodological operations upon the subject-genus in an effort to determine principles and properties.[46] Thus the legitimacy of the predication of eternal of motion is argued from the structures of the mobile and the formal relationships of "now." The character of the known is the criterion for assertion and denial.[47] The object to be known contributes the formal struc-

---

phy are organized and the interrelations among them are determined by reflexive principles: metaphysics, which is the science of first principles, finds its basic principle in God, the unmoved mover, whose characteristic activity is thinking about thinking; in psychology actual knowledge is identical in human thought with its object, and the soul is in a way all existing things; the bases of politics are laid in the definition of the citizen by his functions of ruling and being ruled; the end of morals is happiness which is found in contemplation since that is most nearly akin to the activity of God; and art is an imitation of action and of character." McKeon, "Philosophy and Method," *loc.cit.*, p. 668.

[45] *Metaph.* i. 1. 980ª21.

[46] *Int.* 9. 18ª27ff.; *APo.* i. 13. 78ª22ff.; ii. 10. 93ᵇ27ff.; ii. 19. 99ᵇ15ff.; *Metaph.* i. 1. 980ª27ff.

[47] *Ph.* viii. 1. 251ª8-252ª4. It is this which lies beneath Aristotle's insistence on the adequate apprehension of the phenomena. Cf. *APr.* i. 30. 46ª3-27;

tures of the known, as it has supplied the referents for the terms and the principles of the subject and has specified the method itself. The human intellect does not contribute the structure, but gives intelligibility through the movement of the thing known from potency to actualization.[48] Thus, understanding—the goal of the desire to know—is a single action, but with diverse relationships. Paradigmatically, it refers back to the object known; in its mode of induction or abstraction, it results from the method of the intellect.[49] What is known, i.e., the "facts" grasped or asserted about the subject-matter, are expressed in propositions, and the "essentialist interpretation" of Aristotle forms or judges these propositions both for their meaning and for their truth by the attributes and principles which are given in the structural content of the phenomenal.[50] The essentialist interpretation resolves the questions of truth or meaning by an appeal to the patterns and intelligibility of the experienced.

The four coordinates of inquiry—selection, interpretation, method, and principles—become in Aristotle a selection of terms, an essentialistic interpretation, a problematic method, and reflexive principles. They are factors which are operative in all methods, controlling any Aristotelian resolution of a scientific question. They are also the operative coordinates of all logical analysis. Here one must distinguish between scientific method and analysis. Every science possesses its uniquely proper principles, method, and subject-matter; and the subject-matter of a science always lies in things, actions, or art-prod-

---

APo. ii. 19. 100ª3ff.; *Metaph.* iv. 3. 1005^b8; vi. 1. 1025^b1ff.; *GC* i. 2. 316ª 5ff.; *GA* iii. 10. 760^b27ff.; *Juv.* 2. 468ª22ff.

[48] *de An.* iii. 3. 429ª19ff.

[49] *Ibid.* iii. 7. 431^b2-17.

[50] *Metaph.* vi. 4. 1027^b17ff. *Ibid.* ix. 10. 1051ª34-^b9: "The terms 'being' and 'non-being' are employed firstly with reference to the categories, and secondly with reference to the potency or actuality of these or their non-potency or non-actuality, and thirdly in the sense of true and false. This depends, on the side of the objects [ἐπὶ τῶν πραγμάτων], on their being combined or separated, so that he who thinks the separated to be separated and the combined to be combined has the truth, while he whose thought is in a state contrary to that of the objects is in error. . . . It is not because we think truly that you are pale, that you *are* pale, but because you are pale we who say this have the truth."

ucts. Analysis, Aristotelian logical inference, is quite different. It is an ὄργανον, an analytic instrument brought to bear on whatever purports to be significant discourse. Unlike method, the analytic studies the components of discourse itself, wherever this discourse embodies itself—in written or oral words or in the progression of reason. Thus, while questions of method might be the definition of motion or the cause of its eternality, the questions of analysis would be those of the validity of a proof or of the kind of demonstration. Aristotle's selection of terms brings method to bear upon things and actions; the orientation towards discourse brings analysis to bear upon any form of intelligent movement which purposed to establish conclusions, assert principles, or define realities. Methods, then, are many, differentiated by subject-matters, principles, and the formalities of their structures; analysis is single and cuts across all scientific, dialectic, rhetorical, or sophistic discourse. Scientific method studies things for intelligibility; Aristotelian analytic studies scientific work for coherences and correctnesses. Thus there are two moments of scientific work: that of method is the obtaining of positive knowledge, the establishment of definitions and principles; that of analysis is the critical appraisal of the knowledge gained through a double resolution into proper demonstrative form and into ultimate premises. Method leads to new knowledge; analysis judges its scientific value and completeness.[51]

Analytic isolates four questions which every inquiry can treat: εἰ; τί; ὅτι; διότι; and the physical methods advance through the problems which these questions pose. The source of the progress of the problematic method lies in laying a further question against the answers provided to a previous one. In Books i and ii the existence of motion is defended dialectically against its denial, and the defense terminates in the internal components which make it possible; the existence of motion is investigated scientifically through an understanding of its principles in nature and art, and the inquiry terminates in nature as the hypothesis of physics. Books iii and iv of the

[51] McKeon, "Philosophy and the Development of Scientific Methods," loc.cit., pp. 5-7.

Physics take up the definition of motion in terms of its formal structure and necessary attributes. The subsequent books establish propositions with motion—the species in which it is realized, the subjects of which it is predicated, and the quantities by which it is modified. Book vii of the *Physics* connects every natural movement with a moving cause. Book viii argues from the subjects and attributes of motion to its eternity, and then to an unique, eternal moving cause whose agency alone can author eternal movement and unite the divergent motions into a cosmos. The *Metaphysics* follows a similar problematic pattern in the dialectical investigations of being, transposing the conclusion of physics to the subject of theology, a transposition in which the moving cause of the *Physics* becomes the final cause of the universe.

II.

Nature: Hypothesis of Physics

"WE PHYSICISTS must take for granted that things that exist by
nature are, either all or some of them, in motion—which is
plain by induction."[1] The existence of motion, εἰ ἔστι, is
properly speaking not a scientific question, for movement is
presupposed by the sciences which study or employ it and the
advance of scientific method is made constantly from that
which is clearer and more known by men to that which is
clearer and more known in itself.[2] These are not polar extremes marking off a single, linear progression, but contraries
between which the method is continuously moving. Paradoxi-
cally what is clearest and most distinct to man is confusion;
Aristotle's Greek here is very strong: τὰ συγκεχυμένα, things
which are poured in upon one another, the undifferentiated

---

[1] *Ph.* i. 2. 185ᵃ12-14; viii. 1. 250ᵇ15-18.
[2] *Ibid.* i. 1. 184ᵃ16-21. Cf. *Metaph.* ii. 1. 993ᵇ9-11. "Perhaps, too, as difficulties are of two kinds, the cause of the present difficulty is not in the facts,
but in us. For as the eyes of bats are to the blaze of day, so is the reason in
our soul to the things which are by nature most evident of all." *Metaph.* vii.
3. 1029ᵃ33-ᵇ12. "It is agreed that there are some substances among sensible
things, and so we must inquire first in respect to them. For it is an advantage
to advance to that which is more knowable. For learning proceeds for all
in this way—through that which is less knowable by nature to that which is
more knowable; and just as in conduct our task is to start from what is good
for each and make what is without qualification good for each, so it is our
task to start from what is more knowable to oneself and make what is knowable by nature knowable to oneself. Now what is knowable and primary for
particular sets of people is often knowable to a very small extent, and has
little or nothing of reality. But yet one must start from that which is barely
knowable but knowable to oneself, and try to know what is knowable without
qualification, passing, as has been said, by way of those very things which
one does know." *de An.* ii. 2. 413ᵃ11-13: "Since what is clear or logically
more evident emerges from what in itself is confused but more observable
by us, we must reconsider our results from this point of view." Cf. *EN* i. 4.
1095ᵃ30-ᵇ13.

whole-of-experience. It is from this phenomenal universal that the elements and principles of the method emerge, as the method moves towards the particulars contained within such a totality,[3] but it is equally to this whole that the forms and meanings are continuously reapplied and instantiated in recognition and induction.[4] To such a whole-of-experience the principle must correspond as commensurate source of its reality and adequate explanation of its existence. It was for this reason that Aristotle joined the defense of the existence of movement with the investigation of its principles.

Against the most radical process theories of his times, the essentialist interpretation of the character and reality of the phenomenal is brought to bear and the problematic method turns to dialectic for an attack on the arguments of the opponents. For the Italian philosophers in general, motion was only appearance, an illusion utterly unreal. Reality, for Melissus, was the infinite, the boundless, and no change was possible within the all that was the infinite. What *is*, for Parmenides, was being, and being could not become more than itself nor could it pass into non-being, while out of non-being, nothing could issue. Both Eleatics employ a comprehensive principle to deny a source of motion and to justify this denial with an ontic interpretation which necessarily underlay or transcended the

---

[3] *Ph.* i. 1. 184ª21.

[4] "What is better known to us is perceived by sense, and the objects of sense are not in themselves particular or universal, but may be said in one context to be particulars, in another context to be universals, and in a third context to be universals in particulars. If it is a question of the stimulation or actualization of sense, actual sensation apprehends individuals, while knowledge apprehends universals which are in a manner of speaking within the soul (*de An.* ii. 5. 417ª18-24). If it is a question of the form of what is perceived by sense, the object of sense is a kind of confused whole or 'universal' and analysis yields from it elements and principles as 'particulars' which constitute its parts, in much the same fashion as the meanings of words are established, by differentiating in definition properties involved in the meanings of unanalyzed words (*Ph.* i. 1. 184ª21-ᵇ14). If it is a question of content, the content of sense perception is universal, although the act of perception is of a particular, for what is perceived is man, not the man Callias, and induction yields from such rudimentary universals an explicit knowledge of true universals (*APo.* ii. 19. 100ª15-ᵇ5)." Richard McKeon, "Aristotle's Conception of the Development and the Nature of Scientific Method," *Journal of the History of Ideas,* VIII, No. 1 (January, 1947), 30. Cf. *Metaph.* ii. 1. 993ᵇ6; *APr.* ii. 21. 67ª29.

phenomena.[5] Heraclitus joined an existential interpretation to an actional fire-principle to assert the precise contrary: there is only endless, chaotic, measureless motion. Process lies at the heart of reality, and all beings are caught up in motion that denies species, kind, and intelligibility.[6] For the Eleatics, movement was only appearance; for Heraclitus, rest was only appearance. For Aristotle, it was precisely the appearance, the phenomena of both motion and rest which spelled the total inadequacy of either theory.[7] His use of the structures given in the phenomena as criterion for the falsity of his opponents' conclusions, indicates the strength of his attachment to the use of reflexive principles in essentialist interpretations, allowing him to assert the existence of motion without reducing all stability to the level of the deceptive. On the contrary, the existence of motion would be impossible were there not an element of stability within the change.

Motion is given, present, obvious in every aspect of human life, operative not only in the transitions evidenced in the extramental but in the internal processes by which these transitions are perceived, in dreams by which they are recalled or exaggerated, in imaginations, in opinions, in all the sciences, and in arts, chance, and fortune.[8] The complexities and varieties of life are seen in the polymorphic movements and functions of living things.[9] Animals are such that some part is always involved in motion, and death is indicated when changes cease.[10] Civil society and its constitutional structures can be moved, can change; and political wisdom consists in knowing the causes,

---

[5] *Ph.* i. 2. 184^{b}25ff.; viii. 3. 253^{a}32ff. While both Eleatics agreed upon the comprehensivity of their principle, Melissus founded it upon an underlying matter (an entitative interpretation) and Parmenides justified it through a transcending definition (an ontological interpretation). *Metaph.* i. 5. 986^b 18-21.

[6] *Top.* i. 11. 104^{b}21ff.; *Metaph.* i. 6. 987^{a}22ff.

[7] *Ph.* i. 2. 185^{a}5-12; viii. 3. 254^{a}35-37: "We have sufficient ground for rejecting all these theories in the single fact that we see some things that are sometimes in motion and sometimes at rest."

[8] *Ph.* viii. 3. 253^{a}22-254^{b}7; *de An.* iii. 7. 431^{a}1-8; *GC* i. 1. 314^{b}12ff. These citations, as well as those given in the next few pages, are selected to give some outline of the range of Aristotelian "motion."

[9] *de An.* ii. 2. 413^{a}23; *PA* ii. 1. 641^{a}11-17.

[10] *Ph.* viii. 2. 253^{a}12-21; *APr.* ii. 27. 70^{b}11.

directions, and advantages of such motions.[11] Motions differ in dreams and in waking not by presence or absence, but by increase or decline; and it is at moments of waking that one can determine that the previous images were "really movements lurking in the organs of sense."[12] Even to assert a conclusion or to suggest an opinion is to move from initial premises to their consequences in thought and speech. Motion occurs in the formation of images by the imagination and in the demonstration of propositions by the intellect.[13] Motion is action in political life, in ethical choice, and in artistic production. Thus even to deny motion is an instance of motion, for "If there is such a thing as false opinion, or any opinion at all, then there is also motion."[14]

There is a constant in these distinct realities which allows the term "motion" to be applied to things, thoughts, and symbols, "if it is the case that anything seems to be different at different times."[15] To experience motion is to experience successive difference, successive heterogeneity, to find that the same is different. This sequence in time of the different by the different is the fundamental reality of motion, that the same thing is different at different periods or that different determinations replace one another in corruption and generation. It is the experience that the one is many, but at different "nows."[16]

It is precisely this heterogeneity that allows "motion" to function not only as a critically important term in physical method, but also as an analytic post-predicament. The *Categories* treats the characteristic of individual words, which enter materially into the discourse of propositions and syllogisms. The incomplex modes of signification are classified and treated in the predicaments. The five post-predicaments give relations among these simple terms not yet joined in the predication of propo-

---

[11] *Pol.* ii. 8. 1268^{b}25-34; iv. 16. 1300^{b}38.

[12] *Insomn.* 3. 462^{a}8-13.   [13] *Ph.* viii. 3. 254^{a}24-34.

[14] *Ibid.* viii. 3. 254^{a}27-28. Even the hypothesis can be the subject of change; cf. *Cael.* i. 8. 277^{a}9.

[15] *Ph.* viii. 3. 254^{a}28-29.

[16] *Ibid.* iv. 11. 218^{b}21-219^{a}1; iv. 10. 218^{a}24; iv. 13. 222^{a}33; vi. 1. 231^{b}10; vi. 6. 237^{b}5-7. For motion belonging to plurality, cf. *Metaph.* iv. 2. 1004^{b}29.

sitions. They deal with terms in pairs—opposition, contrary or contradictory terms; priority and posteriority; simultaneity, two terms in some way coincident; motion, two terms successive. Only motion could allow contrary or contradictory terms to be used as predicates of the same subject.[17]

Thus the Eleatic affirmation that motion is only the deceptive appearance of what is more basically, more profoundly at rest was an irresponsible disregard for the realities of observation and experience, of the "things better known to us," which constitute the initial moment of physical method. Nothing is more known, more obvious, than experienced motion; if it be denied, then all human knowledge is groundless, without certitude or probability. The denial of motion is the comprehensive destruction of science, opinion, and perception:

> Therefore, the motionlessness of all things and the attempt to make this position reasonable by the denial of sense perception is both a paralyzing of the intellect and a denial affecting not just a part, but the whole. For it is not only against the physicists, but against all science, and all opinions, because all of these make use of motion.[18]

A dialectical examination of the history of physics indicated that this experienced heterogeneity led to a general consensus on the principles of motion: "All thinkers, then, agree in making the contraries principles."[19] First principles would be primary contraries, primary in not being derived from anything else and contrary because not derived from each other.[20] Aristotle identified this contrariety as that between privation and its correlative form: movement was from white to non-white, from non-musical to musical, etc.[21] But there must be something that perdures, something that is subject to successive alterations, something that changes. Non-white does not become white; that which was non-white is now white. Privation figures in motion as the *principle out of which* motion originates—the movement going from not possessing a particular

[17] *Cat.* 14. 15ª13ff. [18] *Ph.* viii. 3. 253ª32-ᵇ2. (m)
[19] *Ibid.* i. 5. 188ª18. [20] *Ibid.* i. 5. 188ª26-29.
[21] *Ibid.* i. 5. 188ª35-ᵇ26. Cf. *ibid.* i. 8. 191ᵇ15.

form to its possession. Form is the positive *principle to which* the movement progresses, whose progressive realization constitutes the motion, and at which the motion terminates. The subject in motion passes from a state of privation to a state of form. If the motion is not to be total creation and annihilation, something must remain through the change; there must be a principle of stability, a constant which moves out of privation and into form. It is this which changes, which is the subject of the succeeding predicates, which is the matter of the change.[22] Privation, form, and substrate: the three internal components of every change. These components did not prove the existence of motion, but they undercut the objections of the Eleatics by giving the internal principles which made movement no contradiction.[23] Motion does not issue from what is simply non-being, but from what is non-being κατὰ συμβεβηκός, i.e., from a state of privation: the matter changed was not modified in the manner in which it is to be. Matter is not accidentally what it is to become; privation is not essentially what its contradictory is, but exists accidentally as a state of the matter prior to change.[24]

The components of change explain its internal possibility and answer its dialectical opponents, but they do not explain the sources of change. For this, another differentiation within things in motion is necessary: "Of beings: some are by nature, others through other causes."[25] Just as motion is a given through observation and experience, so also is nature. The uses of language indicate those things commonly accepted as natural: "We say that these things and things like them are by nature."[26] These fall into three kinds: animals and their organic parts, plants, and the simple elements which constitute bodies. Radically diverse in their inner structures and in their external operations, these three exhibit a central characteristic which

---

[22] *Ibid.* i. 7. 189^b30ff.

[23] Thus, referring to the Eleatic denials, Aristotle could write immediately after having isolated the three internal components of motion: "we will now proceed to show that the difficulty of the early thinkers, as well as our own, is solved in this way alone." *Ibid.* i. 8. 191ᵃ23.

[24] *Ibid.* i. 8. 191ᵇ10-27.　　　[25] *Ibid.* ii. 1. 192ᵇ8; 193ᵃ1-3.

[26] *Ibid.* ii. 1. 192ᵇ11-12.

distinguishes them from another entire class of reality, i.e., from the things which are not by nature. These possess within themselves the principle or cause of their own motion and rest. If they increase, alter, or change place "naturally," the root of this change is within. If they are produced "naturally," the source of their generation is another of the same kind. A bed or a coat does not issue from another bed or coat; but a man does come from another man. A natural thing contains within itself—precisely because of what it is—the specifications of how and why it is to move and what it is to generate: it has "an innate tendency towards these changes."

The contrary of nature is art, opposed as the external to the thing moved in one of two ways: either as thing to thing, as in the case of agent and product, or as aspect to aspect, when, for example, the doctor cures himself.[27] Art and nature differentiate motion not by categorical kind, but by the principle of motion. Both nature and art possess purpose and "if the shipbuilding art were in the wood, it would produce the same results by nature. If, therefore, purpose is present in art, it is present also in nature."[28] In nature, moving and final cause merge as different aspects of the natural form; in art, the moving cause is numerically distinct in form from its product and purpose.[29]

This difference can be doubled if one considers chance and fortune: "Chance and fortune are causes of results such as might originate from mind or nature as cause, though in fact they are brought about by some accidental cause."[30] Chance will always involve external causes (and in this, it is like art), but these external causes will always be the result of motions which have nature as a cause. Chance is, therefore, posterior to nature and dependent on it; and in the inter-influence of one natural thing with its environment, anything that is by nature in an individual is also to some degree by chance.[31] Correspondingly, that which could have been projected through antecedent planning but was not is said to happen by fortune.[32] The prin-

---

[27] *Ibid.* ii. 1. 192^{b}12-32.   [28] *Ibid.* ii. 8. 199^{b}26-30.

[29] *Ibid.* ii. 1. 193^{a}30-^{b}18; ii. 7. 198^{a}22-28; *GA* ii. 1. 734^{b}36-735^{a}4.

[30] *Ph.* ii. 6. 198^{a}5-7.   [31] *Ibid.* ii. 6. 197^{b}18-20; ii. 6. 198^{a}7-11.

[32] *Ibid.* ii. 6. 197^{b}21-36; *PA* i. 1. 640^{a}27-33.

ciples of motion, thus, become four: nature, when the principle is internal; art, when the principle is external and in an intelligent agent; chance, the privation of an internal principle in an event which might have possessed it; fortune, the privation of an artistic plan in a movement which could have been effected by it. Nature and chance concur in that neither engages the uses of reason; art and fortune involve the use of reason or its privation. Nature and art agree in being essential causes of movement; chance and fortune, in being accidental causes of events and processes.[33] Nature, art, chance, and fortune—the four are given in experience, and Aristotle recognizes them as four principles of motion, incorporating mutually exclusive relationships and as comprehensively inclusive of all motions as they are exhaustive of all logical possibilities—internal or external source, substantial or accidental causes:

> Each substance comes into being out of something that shares its name. (Natural objects and other things both rank as substances.) For things come into being either by art or by nature or by fortune or by chance. Now art is a principle of movement in something other than the thing moved; nature is a principle in the thing itself (for man begets man), and the other causes are privations of these two.[34]

The methodological differentiation of motions in terms of moving principles allows the subject-genus of physics to emerge. No science can deal with the products of chance and fortune, though the meaning of both can be examined and their ethical worth determined.[35] Art is the concern of either the practical or of the productive sciences: the former determine its product, the latter its use.[36] Nature emerges as an internal principle of motion, justifying the assertion that motion is and necessitating an examination of motion's definition. In the initial chapter of Book ii of the *Physics*, both the εἰ ἔστι and the τί ἐστι questions about nature itself had been answered:

[33] *Ph.* ii. 5. 197ᵃ33-35.   [34] *Metaph.* xii. 3. 1070ᵃ4-8. (m)
[35] *APo.* i. 30. 87ᵇ19.   [36] *EN* vi. 4. 1140ᵃ10-16.

What nature is, then, and the meaning of the terms, "by nature" and "according to nature," has been stated. That nature exists, it would be absurd to try to prove; for it is obvious that there are many things of this kind.[37]

In the analytic discussion of demonstrative premises, Aristotle had distinguished a *thesis* from an *axiom*; the latter must be known to be true before any inquiry is instituted, the former need not. *Thesis* admits of two sub-divisions—*hypothesis* and definition. *Hypothesis* asserts the existence or the non-existence of something; definition, as such, does not.[38] In the metaphysical investigations of the classification of the sciences, each science accepts both the existence and the definition of its subject-genus as its initial hypothesis, either assuming the existence or making it plain by an appeal to sense perception. In either case, *hypothesis* involves both questions of existence and of formal structure. If one begins with the question εἰ ἔστι, and conjoins to its answer the further question τί ἐστι, the answer is an *hypothesis*. Thus, the fundamental "real definition" in Aristotle is an *hypothesis*: defining the structure of something that exists. Properly speaking, then, scientific method begins with hypothesis.[39] For the particular sciences neither "offer any discussion of the essence of the things of which they treat," nor do they entertain "the question whether the genus with which they deal exists or does not exist, because it belongs to the same kind of thinking to show what it is and that it is."[40]

The hypothesis of physics is that "nature is a principle of motion": ὑπόθεσις γὰρ ὅτι ἡ φύσις ἀρχὴ τῆς κινήσεως.[41] The hypothesis sets up the subject and principle of the method of physics as nature, asserting the definition and the existence of nature together with the existence of motion.

[37] *Ph.* ii. 1. 193ª1-5.
[38] *APo.* i. 2. 72ª7-24. Cf. *Metaph.* iv. 3. 1005ᵇ16.
[39] *Metaph.* vi. 1. 1025ᵇ1-18. For the "hypotheses" of syllogism, cf. *APo.* i. 19. 81ᵇ14.
[40] *Metaph.* v. 2. 1013ᵇ20; *Ph.* ii. 3. 195ª18.
[41] *Ph.* viii. 3. 253ᵇ5-6.

III.

The Definition of Motion

THE CORRELATION of motion with nature as its reflexive principle turns the method of nature towards a definition of motion.
The question is now τί ἐστι. In problematic inquiry, movement enters into the very intelligibility of nature; the principle
is only understandable in terms of that which it authors.[1] But
the determination of the general meaning of motion poses
peculiar difficulties: "There are as many kinds of motions or
changes as there are of reality (τοῦ ὄντος)."[2] Just as "is" can be
divided into substance, quantity, and quality or into potency
and act,[3] so it provides the devices both for the definition of
motion and later for the categorical determination of its species: potency and act will be used to elaborate the formal
structure of motion; the categories will allow for distinctions
within motions and what moves, these being questions not of
definition but of propositions and predications.

What, then, is motion? The buildable is precisely a potency
—in this case, a passive ability. The fulfillment of this potency,
its actualization, is either the house or the process of being-
built. This latter is the act of the buildable qua still in potency;
it is the motion, being-built, the passage of the potency from
a state of privation to a state of fulfillment. This transition is
an actualization of the potency in so far as it is in potency to
further actualization; motion is the act of being in potency
in so far as it is in potency. Before the motion, the modifica-
tion-to-be is just in potency; at the end of the motion, it exists
in act. Motion itself is a process between these two extremes,
a transition from potency to act through the actualization of

---

[1] *Ph.* iii. 1. 200ᵇ12-14.   [2] *Ibid.* iii. 1. 201ᵃ4-9. (m)
[3] *Metaph.* ix. 1. 1045ᵃ34-35. Cf. *Ph.* iii. 1. 201ᵃ9 and *Metaph.* ix. 10.
1051ᵇ34ff.

the potency. Before motion: "Not yet." After the motion: "Already." The motion itself: a fluid synthesis of "already" and "not yet." The actualization of the buildable in so far as it is buildable is the "being-built." The actualization of the alterable in so far as it is still further alterable is qualitative alteration. The actualization of that which can be increased or decreased in so far as it can be further increased or decreased is quantitative motion, etc. In each case, movement is the act of a being in potency to further actualization.[4]

Motion can also be defined in terms of the moving cause and its subject. Movement is a fulfillment of potency *within the mobile*, i.e., within the thing changed or moved, *by the influence of a mover*. The actualization is single, but with distinct relationships. When the mobile passes from privation to determination, it does so under the influence of something imparting this new form. Diverse relationships are actualized in the same movement: the actualization of the mobile qua mobile, and, in the same motion, the actualization from the mover qua mover. A mover is only a mover when something is being moved, just as a cause is only causing when something is being effected. The moving of one is the being-moved of another. The motion of the cause and the motion of the caused are not two distinct events, not two different motions as they are for Hume. They are one and the same motion, a single event but with distinct relations: *in* the mobile but *from* the mover. In so far as this single motion is from the agent or mover, it is called action; in so far as it is in the patient or mobile, it is termed passion. But the terms, action and passion, denote the identical motion according to different relations.[5] The cause and effect are bound together in a single actualization, a single event which is from the moving cause and in the mobile:

The solution of the difficulty that is raised about the motion —whether it is in the movable—is plain. It is the fulfilment

---

[4] *Ph.* iii. 1. 200^{b}12-201^{b}15.

[5] *Ibid.* iii. 2. 202^{a}2-3; 202^{b}22. The moving cause was "the cause vaguely dreamed of by all our predecessors, definitely stated by none of them." *GC* ii. 9. 335^{b}8-9; cf. *Metaph.* i. 3. 984^{a}16-22.

of this potentiality, and by the action of that which has the power of causing motion; and the actuality of that which has the power of causing motion is not other than the actuality of the movable, for it must be the fulfilment of *both*. A thing is capable of causing motion because it actually does do this. Hence there is a single actuality of both alike.[6]

The salient characteristic of Aristotelian mover and moved relationships are brought into bold relief through the sharp contrast offered by Hume. On almost every point there is flat divergence between the Aristotelian essentialistic differentiation of cause-effect in terms of relationship and the entitative causality which Hume presents and attacks. For Hume, cause is one event, effect another.[7] For Aristotle, cause-effect signify the single event under different aspects—action, as from the agent; passion, as in the patient. For Hume, the causal event must precede its effect in time as the motion of one billiard ball precedes the motion of the other it hits.[8] For Aristotle, actual cause and effect are simultaneously relations of the single movement; the cause is only causing the motion of the moved when the moved is being moved, i.e., essential, particular causes in act:

> Causes which are actually at work and particular exist and cease to exist simultaneously with their effect, e.g. this healing person with this being-healed person, and that house-building man with that being-built house; but this is not always true of potential causes—the house and the house-builder do not pass away simultaneously.[9]

Hume attacked any physical inquiry which pretends to discover the effect in the cause and if this fails, no causal determination is established, only customary succession. Only mathematics permits this type of causal analysis.[10] For Aristotle, the characteristic methods of physics and mathematics are diamet-

---

[6] *Ph.* iii. 3. 202ᵃ12-19. (m)

[7] David Hume, *An Enquiry Concerning Human Understanding* (New York: Washington Square, 1963), p. 40.

[8] *Ibid.*, p. 39.

[9] *Ph.* ii. 3. 195ᵇ17-21. Cf. also *ibid.* vii. 1. 242ᵃ24.

[10] Hume, *op.cit.*, pp. 39, 156-158.

rically contrasted on this point of procedure. Just as physics and mathematics obtain their subject-matter and principles by different methods,[11] so they contrast in the necessity which relates principle to conclusions. Both follow the necessity of their principles, and the error of the previous physicist was to collapse this distinction logistically and reduce all necessity to the antecedent necessity of mathematics.[12] Thus, if the straight line is such by definition, the triangle must have a particular sum to the degree of its angles—antecedently determined to be such by its linear composites. In mathematics, the necessity lies with the antecedent, with the premises. Granted these premises or these components, the conclusion follows with absolute necessity, and mathematics works from cause to necessary effects and properties. The direct opposite is the method of physical speculation. The hypothesis is given, and one works back to its essential causes and its material antecedents. The result is given through perception and experience and focused upon through induction. The necessity is here, in the given result, in the hypothesis of the sciences. Granted such-and-such a result, what must necessarily be its causes? Thus, physical method establishes the meaning of natural realities by tracing them from their characteristic functions and operations back to their causes, irrevocably linked as their actualization is the same.[13] The actualization by the moving cause is the identical reality which has been experienced as the movement of the mobile.[14]

The devices of potency and act allowed for a definition of movement as the act of a being in potency qua potential; those of action and passion delimited motion through its source and subject. But the full definition of motion must include considerations of its characteristic properties; this would bring in such attributes as continuity, infinity, place, and time. Like motion itself, infinity is only a potential being, existing successively in the operations of addition and proportional division.[15] Locomotion indicates the reality of place and the ficti-

---

[11] *Ph.* ii. 2. 193^{b}5-194^{a}11.
[12] *Ibid.* ii. 8. 198^{b}10-32; ii. 9. 199^{b}34-200^{a}1; *PA* i. 1. 640^{a}1-27.
[13] *Ph.* ii. 9. 200^{a}15-^{b}11.   [14] *Ibid.* iii. 3. 202^{a}12-19.
[15] *Ibid.* iii. 6. 206^{a}25-207^{a}14.

tious character of the Democritean void, place being only the surfaces of the containing bodies.[16] The most characteristic attribute of motion, however, was time, and "we perceive time and motion together."[17]

For one subject to possess contraries or contradictories, there must be a succession in time, a "now" at which one contrary exists and a "then" at which its opposite exists. Transition, whether in the movements of discourse, the operations of the mind, or the processes of things, demands a "before" and an "after" which constitute the continuum over which the transition moves as contrary replaces contrary and serves to measure out the transition itself. "Before" and "after," "now" and "then" are intrinsic to every motion, and the measure of motion according to these intrinsic units is time.[18] Motion does not measure out time for Aristotle as it did for Plato. In sharp contrast, time is the measure of motion, and the definition of time is accomplished only through an analysis of movement of which it is the intrinsic number. Just as motion is perceived by the difference which occurs between a "now" and a "then," so rest was discovered when no such difference emerges.[19] There can be no motion without time, and there can be no time without motion.[20] The truth of this proposition is pivotal for the Aristotelian consideration of the origin of motion.

[16] *Ibid.* iv. 1. 208^{b}1-26; iv. 4. 212^{a}20. For the impossibility of the void if there is to be locomotion, cf. *ibid.* iv. 8. 214^{b}13-216^{b}20.

[17] *Ibid.* iv. 11. 219^{a}4.   [18] *Ibid.* iv. 11. 220^{a}23-24.

[19] *Ibid.* iv. 12. 221^{b}6-13.   [20] *Ibid.* viii. 1. 251^{b}10-14.

IV.

Motions, Mobiles, and Movers

As it was to counter the Eleatic denials that Aristotle defended the existence of motion, so it was against the patternless process of Heraclitus' existential interpretation that he asserted the kinds of change and movements.[1] This was to progress from problems of definition to those of propositions, from questions of τί ἐστι to τὸ ὅτι. The previous treatment had been a methodological development and determination of the terms involved in nature as a principle of motion, concluding to the definition of each. That motion is and what motion is have both been established. Now the question is, What are the varieties or kinds of motions? The components of change provide the devices with which to distinguish, for "every change is from something to something," between opposites which may be either contraries or contradictories, and the categorical classification of terms allows for a specification of the name and the meaning of the motion. In changes in quantity, quality, and place, there is a transition from contrary to contrary within a subject that perdures; only such changes are motions. In changes in substance, the transition is from non-subject to subject or from subject to non-subject, generation and corruption of the thing itself. In these latter, the substance does not become something; it becomes. Thus motion becomes a species of change and its opposite; change in the former case is used to denote any transition from potency to act, and in the second to indicate that species of change which is between contradictories.[2]

[1] Cf. résumé offered in *Ph*. viii. 3. 253^{b}7ff.

[2] *Ibid*. v. 1. 224^{b}6-225^{b}9. Aristotle charged that the natural philosopher reduced this variety of kind to a single type. The Ionians resolved all change into qualitative modifications of the single substratum (*Metaph*. i. 3. 983^{a}10;

The internal components of change serve not only to differentiate its species, but to specify its subject, i.e., to determine
in both cases the kind of thing of which any motion can be
predicated: "The subject of change is necessarily divisible."
For every change is from "this" to "that." At the former, the
change has not yet begun; at the latter, it has terminated. If
the mobile is changing, then, it can be neither at the first stage
nor at the last completely. It must be partly at one and partly
at the other, or at an intermediate. Thus the mobile must be
divisible, not necessarily with the actual division of distinct
organic parts, but with the continuity which possesses a potentiality for endless proportional division.[3] Whether this divisibility occurs in the operations of nature, in the processes of
reason, or in the movement of discourse, motion receives its
own continuity through the continuity of the mobile. Thus
Aristotle could assert a double divisibility of every motion:
"Motion is divisible in two ways: (1) According to time; (2)
According to the motion of the parts of the moved."[4] This
double divisibility will found a rejection of a temporal origin
of motion, for the continuity afforded motion by its subject
is such that there can be no first part of movement which is
not further divisible, and the continuity of time prevents any
division of duration into indivisibles.[5]

The species in which motion is realized and the subjects
of which it is predicated lead to a question of principle. Nature, art, chance, and fortune were established as principles to
explain the existence of motion. Now the question is, How
explain the conjunction of motion and the divisible, of process and its subject? How can there be motions? It is a διότι
question, a question about the reasoned fact, and it brings the
Physics to an affirmation of a first mover unmoved for every
motion:

Everything that is in motion must be moved by something;
for that which is in motion [i.e., the subject of movement]

<hr />

4. 985^{b}11), Empedocles and Anaxagoras to quantitative additions and sub-
tractions (*ibid*. i. 3. 984^{a}10), and the atomic scientists to locomotion (*ibid*.
i. 4. 985^{b}17).

[3] *Ph*. vi. 4. 234^{b}10-20.   [4] *Ibid*. vi. 4. 234^{b}21-23. (m)

[5] *Ibid*. vi. 5. 236^{a}7-26; 237^{b}23.

will always be divisible, and if a part of it is not being moved, then the whole is at rest.[6]

The distinctions of nature and art differentiate the areas in which the proposition must be proved: artistic motion is obviously dependent upon something other than the mobile. But, "if the mobile has the source of its movement within itself," this dependence upon another is not so evident, but it is none the less affirmed. First the dependence must be explained:

1. Negatively: That which is not moved by something does not necessarily rest by the rest of the other.

2. Positively: If something rests because an other stops being moved, the former is necessarily being moved by the latter.[7]

Then the dependence must be demonstrated, and this is done in two ways: first through an example, and then through a middle term. First, then, the example:

1. Set up example:
   (a) When the moved is taken as AB
   (b) AB must necessarily be divisible
       (1) For every moved thing is divisible.
   (c) Therefore, let AB be divided at G.
2. Alternatives:
   (a) If GB is not in motion, AB will not be moved; or
   (b) If AB were moved: AG would be moved; BG would not.
3. Rules out (b):
   If (b), then AB would not be moved essentially and primarily, which is contrary to our supposition.
4. Conclusion:
   Therefore it is necessarily that if GB is not moved, AB must be at rest.
   But that which is at rest because something else is not moved, it is agreed, is moved by something.

---

[6] *Ibid.* vii. 1. 242ª13-16. (m)　　　[7] *Ibid.* vii. 1. 241ᵇ33-36. (m)

Therefore, everything that is moved is moved by something.[8]

Then, through a middle term: "For the moved is always divisible, and if a part of it is not being moved, then the whole is at rest."[9] In order to move, the whole-in-motion depends upon the part-in-motion. But this moving part is itself continuous and divisible. How explain its motion? These parts of the mobile, whether organic actual parts or continuous potential parts, will always be *moved movers*. Each part can author the motion of the whole in some way, but only because it is itself in motion through the movement of its sub-parts. And these sub-parts? Continuous or distinct, they are dependent upon their parts. Can one proceed endlessly?

The series in question here is not the Humean logistic causal chain of antecedents in time. It is the series of causes, essential and particular, actually at work to effect this particular movement. It is not a search for a temporal principle, into the "after" and "before" sequence from which an origin in time will emerge. The question is rather about the causal influences actually responsible for, joined to, and simultaneous with any particular motion: Can one proceed endlessly through moved movers or must one reach a first mover unmoved? Aristotle proves the necessity of the latter by showing the impossibility of its alternative: an infinite series of moved movers would mean that the motion itself would be infinite, the motion being co-extensive with the multitude of the movers. This would mean an actual infinity, yet one that is accomplished in a limited time. The movement of a natural body takes place within a finite time. But if the motion of the moved movers, called upon as explanation, were infinite, it would be measured by the finite time, within a limited "before" and "after." The supposition of an infinite series leads to a flat contradiction between motion and its measure; "therefore it is necessary to come to a stop; there must be a first mover and a first moved."[10]

[8] *Ibid*. vii. 1. 242ª5-14. (m)   [9] *Ibid*. vii. 1. 242ª15-16. (m)
[10] *Ibid*. vii. 1. 242ª21-ᵇ34. (m)

The full structure of Aristotle's argument, that every motion must have a first mover, is brought out by an example:

> Since everything that is in motion must be moved by something—let us take the case in which a thing is in locomotion and is moved by something that is itself in motion, and that by something else, and so on continually—then the series cannot go on to infinity, but there must be some first mover.[11]

The mobile cannot autonomously move itself because it is divisible, dependent for its motion upon its parts, etc. The moved movers cannot proceed infinitely because their motion is numbered intrinsically by a finite time. The propositions lead to a single conclusion: for every motion, there must be a first mover unmoved. It is only a first mover unmoved that can explain any single one of the varieties of movements or the motion of any single divisible subject.

There has been widespread dissatisfaction with Book vii of the *Physics* among Aristotelian commentators. Eudemus ignores it. Simplicius indicates that the inquiries of the subsequent book are more precise. Themistius handles it almost in passing.[12] Both Galen and Avicenna object to the proof for the first proposition, that whatever is moved is moved by something, though Averroes and Aquinas argue in its favor. Averroes contends that it is a *demonstratio quia*, while Aquinas contends that it is a *demonstratio propter quid*, that "it possesses the reason that it is impossible for any mobile object to move itself. . . . For there cannot be a primary mobile object whose movement does not depend upon its parts."[13] Werner Jaeger maintains that it obviously issues from an early period in Aristotle's development, while Philip Wicksteed attributes it to a subsequent follower of the master![14] Joseph Owens finds

---

[11] *Ibid.* vii. 1. 242ª17-21. (m)

[12] Cf. Philip Wicksteed and F. M. Cornford (ed. and trans.), *Aristotle: The Physics* (Loeb Classical Library; London: Heinemann, 1952), II, 204.

[13] Thomas Aquinas, *In Octo Libros De Physico Auditu Sive Physicorum Aristotelis Commentaria*, ed. A. M. Pirotta (Taurini: Marietti, 1953), Lib. vii. lect. 1. sec. 887-89. (m)

[14] Werner Jaeger, *Aristotle*, trans. Richard Robinson (London: Oxford, 1962), pp. 297-98. Wicksteed and Cornford, *op.cit.*, II, v-vi.

it a "treatise quite detached from the main groupings."[15] The interpretation offered in the above pages contends that Book vii of the *Physics* occupies a pivotal position, that it depends directly upon the previous books, and that its purpose is to demonstrate that no subject of motion can account for its own motion. This necessitates a doctrine of a first mover for each motion, natural or otherwise, and one which is not itself a subject of motion. *Physics* vi provided the middle term for the first proposition in the established divisibility of every mobile and *Physics* iv the second proposition in the structures of time. This means that to explain all the motions and mobiles within the universe, an unmoved mover will be necessary. *Physics* viii asks whether it is one or many, whether all of these principles are one principle, joining the problems of the diversity of motions to the questions about temporal origin. The question ὅτι of *Physics* v and vi is explained by the διότι of *Physics* vii. To this Aristotle joins the question ὅτι of the subsequent book, the eternity of motion, and explains both the varieties and eternality of motions through the διότι of *Physics* viii.

[15] Owens, "The Conclusion of the Prima Via," *The Modern Schoolman*, xxx, No. 1 (November, 1952), 38.

V.

The Eternality of Motion

Physical science, no matter how divergent its methods or contrasting its conclusions, was essentially concerned with the making-of-a-cosmos (κοσμοποιεῖν); this was the interest, contended Aristotle, which had induced a general consensus on the existence of motion, and which in turn led to speculation on the principles and properties of generation and corruption.[1] The problematic of a cosmos was that of a world order, and the theories which were advanced to establish this order had been those which clashed on the principle by which it was to be explained: Was there a principle, a beginning, which initiated all movement? The question is a problem of temporal principle, and its answer can only be given in response to a question of fact: Is motion eternal or not?[2] The first problem of the cosmos, then, is a question ὅτι, and so divergent have been the physics that the positions taken are formally exhaustive of the possibilities. The basic alternatives are to affirm or deny a temporal origin of motion, and this contradiction is doubled in so far as substantiation is sought through the devices of nature and art.

Anaxagoras and Empedocles deny that motion always was, but disagree on the number of motionless periods which existed, and, thus, on the number of cosmoi; these could be one or successively many. Anaxagoras held for a single rest, an infinite duration which antedated movement, and the subsequent beginning of motion through the influence of Mind upon inert matter. His was a theory of the single universe, issuing from a single dispersal (διακρῖναι), a "big bang"

[1] *Ph.* viii. 1. 250^{b}15-17. Cf. *Metaph.* xiv. 3. 1091^{a}18-22.
[2] *Ph.* viii. 1. 250^{b}11-14.

50

which occurred once (ἄπαξ), in which intelligence differentiated the congested and motionless mixture and compounded the diversified ingredients anew into separated beings. This was to posit a universe and its natures as originating in a creative art.[3]

In contrast, Empedocles argued for a "pulsating universe," one in which attraction and repulsion, love and strife, regularly and naturally allowed for intermediate periods of rest through their operational balance. These conflicting principles do not resolve one into the other. There are, rather, moments of check in which they cancel each other out and others in which the cyclic (περίοδος) evolution of a world moves on to its internal unity or destruction. There are many cosmoi successively and their principles lie deep in things of necessity (τοῖς τράγμασιν ἐξ ἀνάγκης). It is nature, not art, which explains the origin of motion—a nature identified with necessity and whose products are differentiated by chance.[4]

Of the corresponding alternatives, the Atomists represent one. Motion was everlasting, without beginning or end. Democritus had proved this by arguing from the eternality of time.[5] But this was a motion not within one world, but of many worlds—cosmoi continuously coming into being and passing out of existence in a "continuous creation" made logistically possible by an identification of all generation and corruption with the endless recombination and disjunction of the indestructible atoms. It was like Empedocles' world, one of necessity but the relation was reversed: necessity followed upon the chance combination of atoms. What had been a plurality of succeeding worlds in Empedocles expanded to include plurality of simultaneous cosmoi in Democritus. The motion was eternal and the motion was its own explanation.[6]

---

[3] *Ibid.* viii. 1. 250ᵇ27-251ᵃ5; 252ᵃ7-24. Cf. *Cael.* iii. 3. 302ᵃ28ff.; *Ph.* i. 4. 187ᵃ23ff.

[4] *Ibid.* viii. 1. 252ᵃ9; *ibid.* i. 4. 187ᵃ23ff. Cf. *Metaph.* iii. 4. 1000ᵇ12ff.

[5] *Ph.* viii. 1. 251ᵇ16. This turn contrasted with the nuanced position of Plato according to the interpretation of Aristotle. Plato held for eternal motion, but for beginning of orderly motion whose product was time. Cf. *Cael.* iii. 2. 300ᵇ8-19; *Ph.* viii. 1. 251ᵇ12-19; *Metaph.* xii. 6. 1071ᵇ31-33.

[6] *Ph.* viii. 1. 250ᵇ18-22; i. 1. 184ᵇ21; *Metaph.* i. 4. 985ᵇ5-19; *Cael.* iii. 7. 305ᵃ33ff.

Last in contrast, the final position will be that of Aristotle, agreeing with Democritus that motion is eternal, but a motion within a single universe—a universe which does not disappear and reappear, but one which remains in a "steady state" of internal changes and endless motion. The ultimate dynamic source of this movement is not the nature of Democritus, but the subsistent intelligence—far removed from any artistic, Anaxagorean influence upon matter and seen as reflexively identified with itself in object and operation.

Just as the devices of nature and art serve to differentiate the four possibilities of motion and eternality, so they offer means for the criticism of the three erroneous positions and combine with the four questions of inquiry to point out failures in method and principle. Anaxagoras' Mind destroys all nature. For the infinite is not followed by anything; there is a complete disproportion between the infinite and the finite. To posit an infinite rest, then, is to destroy all proportion and, thus, all order, "for every order is a proportion." This destruction of order, in turn, denies all nature, for "nature is the cause of order among all things." Posit disorder as the basis of all reality, and there is nothing that is natural. Further, even if it were possible to have this infinite, undifferentiated period of rest, why would Mind determine upon this period rather than another for its action? There could be no reason for its choice and thus no cosmos could result from its action.

Conversely, Empedocles' love and strife keep an order, at least one of succession, but proceed irrationally. The fault is a fault in method: Empedocles simply posited a pulsating universe. But unless this proposition is established either by induction or demonstration, it remains an irrational axiom (ἀξιοῦν . . . ἄλογον), asserted without justification. The synthesis of subject and predicate, if not given within the extra-mental world, must be a demonstrable consequent of that which is. While Empedocles failed to prove the fact, asserting it as if it were a given, Democritus failed to determine the reasoned fact. He terminated his investigation with the conclusion that movement was as eternal as time, but did not ascertain why this was so. He did not feel obliged to find the principle to explain this "always." But any conjunction of subject and predicate remains arbitrary unless it is coincident with the principle which explains it or unless within the subject or predicate is found the complete explanation for their conjoining, as would be the case when "the angles of a triangle are always equal to two right angles." But here we have "a cause that is other than this eternal truth."[7] The only truths which are not problematic are the first principles themselves, reflexively true and self-instantiating.[8]

Aristotle founds his own inquiry into the duration of motion upon its already established characteristics: "We must begin from the things already concluded in the *Physics*."[9] Two conclusions of the previous work are of operative importance: the definition of motion as an actualization of the mobile and the interpretation of time as an intrinsic attribute. Thus, the essentialist interpretation decides the duration of motion by arguing from the structures within the given.

Motion always presupposes a subject, a mobile. This subject can either "have become," not having been previously—and thus every motion would presuppose an antecedent motion with which its subject came into being; or the subject can be eternal. If eternal, the subject can be either moving—and thus motion would be eternal; or the subject can be inert. If the latter, then some motion must have occurred to release it from rest. Thus, even in this case, every motion would presuppose an antecedent motion. So also, one can argue prospectively that any "final motion" must be followed by a motion whereby the power to move or be moved is corrupted. Thus any motion would be followed by a subsequent motion. The subject of motion, then, demands both a prior and a posterior motion—and through this demand motion is seen to be necessarily eternal.

Similarly one can argue from time to the eternality of motion. First, a "before" or an "after" are only possible in motion; a period of rest "before" motion, then, would be a contradiction in terms. Moreover, just as time measures and presup-

[7] *Ph.* viii. 1. 252^{b}2-3.   [8] *Ibid.* viii. 1. 252^{a}6-^{b}5.
[9] *Ibid.* viii. 1. 251^{a}8.

poses motion, so "now" measures and presupposes existence. Every "now" is a middle-point, a conjunction of two continua. No matter how far back one traces the moment of existence, its "now" will always point to a time prior as it does to a time to come; no matter how far one projects the future, the "now" reached will demand a subsequent time, a future period. There is an "actual infinity," but every subject of motion and every "now" of existence point to an antecedent and a subsequent, to a past and a future event. As such, both the mobile and the intrinsic measure of its movement conclude to a motion that is eternal.[10]

[10] *Ibid.* viii. 1. 251^{a}9-252^{a}6.

VI.

The Unmoved Mover: The Principle of Motion

EVERY variety and each subject of which motion is predicated possesses the principle which explains this conjunction in a first mover unmoved. None of the particular motions and none of the individual mobiles is absolutely first in time; movement always was and always will be, and this eternal movement is related to the individual, finite movements "like a certain kind of life to all those things which are constituted by nature."[1] Whatever is the principle of eternal movement, then, is responsible for all natural motions, and this allows the inquiry into the eternal mover to begin with a causal question of the basic facts of physics: "The beginning of the inquiry will also be about the above-mentioned question: Because of what are some beings now in motion and now at rest?"[2] The question is a διότι question, and it conjoins in a single search for a principle of the cosmos the most diverse and yet fundamental motions, the motions which open and close the *Physics*. That some things pass from motion to rest is of everyday experience. These motions are the most fundamental as they are the most immediately evident to human observation.[3] That motion is eternal, in contrast, is the most fundamental fact in the very reality of motion itself, a fact which makes all other motions possible. Aristotle founded physical inquiry upon the first and moved gradually to establish the second— as from facts more known by men to more knowable in themselves because necessary. Now the question "why" is leveled at both—not to ask why men think that motion is eternal and things are sometimes in motion and sometimes at rest. The

[1] *Ph*. viii. 1. 250^{b}14.　　　[2] *Ibid*. viii. 3. 253^{a}22-24. (m)
[3] *Ibid*. viii. 3. 253^{a}32-254^{b}7.

55

latter is given through perception and clarified through induction; the former, through argumentation.[4] Rather the question initiates inquiry into that which is ultimately responsible for motion and which will found a distinction within the entire cosmos among those beings which are never moved, those which are always moved, and those which pass in and out of motion. This distinction will function both as solution (λύσις) and as purpose (τέλος), "the solution of all of our difficulties and the purpose of this scientific inquiry."[5]

Physics vii had established that each motion must be traced to a first mover unmoved, but the objections leveled against eternal motion and the problems posed by intermittent motions occasion a fresh division of the subject.[6] For the problematic method responds to and is determined by the new problem under investigation. The problematic specification of the procedure is indicative of Aristotle's method, and the differences between the distinctions and processes of Books vii and viii might be methodologically better understood in terms of a problematic method whose structures are determined by the subject, than by an earlier Aristotle or a later disciple. The precise point here to be determined is the relation between the subjects of movement and their moving causes. And the devices of nature and art are correspondingly modified to provide the basis of a new schema.

Of those things which are moved essentially, i.e., not moved because they belong to something else, some are determined to

---

[4] *Ibid.* viii. 3. 253^{b}35-37: "We have sufficient ground for rejecting all these theories in the single fact that we *see* some things that are sometimes in motion and sometimes at rest." *Ibid.* i. 2. 185^{a}13-14: "We physicists, on the other hand, must take for granted that the things that exist by nature are, either all or some of them, in motion—which is indeed made plain by induction."

[5] *Ibid.* viii. 3. 253^{a}28-32. (m)

[6] *Ibid.* viii. 2. 252^{b}6ff. offers three objections against eternal motion, and Aristotle three times indicates that subsequent method must deal with these new problems (viii. 2. 253^{a}1, 21; 3. 253^{a}21). The more telling are those which claim that a natural non-living mobile can initiate its own motion (objection 2) and that a living being can exhibit movement unpreceded by previous motion (objection 3). Both of these objections affect the demonstration that whatever is moved is moved by something, and the means of solution must be adjusted to the problems presented.

motion by themselves (ὑφ' ἑατοῦ)—and some are determined
to motion by another (ὑπ' ἄλλου)—the distinction lies in the
location of the moving cause, within or without. Cutting
across this distinction is that of the specification of the motion:
some things are moved naturally (φύσει) and others are
moved violently and contrary to their nature (βίᾳ καὶ παρὰ
φύσιν). The schema furnishes four possibilities, but only three
of them are realized motions. It is obvious that all things
which are moved by themselves are also moved naturally; and
these are living things. It is equally obvious that all movement
contrary to nature issues from a moving cause that is other
than the thing moved.[7] It is the final type of motion which
occasions the most difficulty: the natural movement of the
non-living, specifically of the elements. In living things, one
can distinguish the moving cause, the soul, from the resulting
changes which it effects in bodily location, modifications, and
size; but in the case of elemental motion, "these are the ones,
such as the light and the heavy, which would present the
question: By what (ὑπὸ τίνος) are they moved?"[8]

The simple elements are obviously moved violently when
forced to places contrary to their natural tendency, but they
are moved naturally to their proper places. When fire is kept
from ascending or earth is lifted up, the motion is a violent
one; but when they are moved to their proper places, by what
are they moved? Aristotle gives four reasons to substantiate
his contention that it is impossible for the natural elements to
be moved by themselves (αὐτὰ ὑφ' αὑτῶν φάναι ἀδύνατον).[9]
First, to be moved by oneself is indicative of life, is proper
to animated beings. Secondly, whatever moves itself can also
stop itself. There is the question of to move or not to move;
living things can initiate their own motion and can bring
it to an end. Fire, on the other hand, does not cause itself
to rise; it is determined to do so by its very nature. It is
not at rest outside of its proper place unless some extrinsic
cause prevents this movement. Thirdly, it would be irrational
(ἄλογον) to assert that things which possess only a single,

[7] Ibid. viii. 4. 254b6-36.   [8] Ibid. viii. 4. 255a1-4.
[9] Ibid. viii. 4. 255a6.

determined motion move themselves—for that which moves itself does not have its motion determined by another, but determines its own motion; it has the power to determine that its motion be this or that. If fire moved itself up, it should be able to move itself down; but the heavy and the light do not have a variety of motions; only a single motion occurs when it is not hindered. Lastly, none of the simple elements is organically distinguished so that one part might move another; they are one in perfect continuity, and no continuous thing qua continuous can originate its own motion—there must be something to ground the distinction between agent and patient, as in animals there is a distinction of actual parts. Thus the elements neither author the exercise and the type of their motion nor are they physically constituted to be able to; the heavy and the light are nothing more than the internal orientation to a sole and definite movement:

> And so it is asked: Because of what (διὰ τί) are the heavy and the light moved to their proper place? The cause (αἴτιον) is that they are so natured (πέφυκέ) and that this is the being (τὸ . . . εἶναι) of the light and the heavy, the former is determined to up and the latter to down.[10]

If the movement of the heavy and the light is not from themselves, though natural, what is the moving cause responsible for their motion? The heavy and the light are the very determination to motion up or down; what is responsible for this motion? The answer is twofold, built upon the previous distinction between essential and accidental cause. Essentially, whatever generated the determination, whatever made this thing light or that thing heavy, is the cause of its motion, for to impress the determination is to author the movement. This corresponds literally to the previous definition of a moving cause: the one from which (issues) the first principle of the change or of the rest (ὅθεν ἡ ἀρχὴ τῆς μεταβολῆς ἡ πρώτη ἢ τῆς ἠρεμήσεως). The first examples Aristotle gave are instructive: the one who gives advice is the moving cause, for he gives a form through which the subsequent agent acts.

---

[10] *Ibid.* viii. 4. 255ᵇ14-17. (m)

Or, the father is the moving cause of the child, because it is he who introduces the substantial form in generation.[11] So also, the essential moving cause of the natural motion of the non-living elements is that which generated them, which gave them the peculiar, internal determination to a single motion.

Secondly, the one who removes whatever obstacle may be preventing this motion is also a moving cause, but a cause κατὰ συμβεβηκὸς responsible for the movement in the indirect manner that one who removes a column from beneath the roof is responsible for the consequent crash to the ground. The heavy naturally falls. If it is sustained violently at a distance from its proper place, it will fall when this hindrance is removed. To remove a hindrance, then, is to author natural movement, but indirectly. In either case, then, the moving cause is other than the thing moved.

The importance of this consideration of the relationship between the subjects of movement and their moving causes is not just to confirm the proposition of Book vii within the problematic of Book viii, that whatever is moved is moved by something. It also isolates a kind of motion which is eternal—a non-living natural motion—and indicates the two ways in which such a movement will be dependent upon a first moving cause. It further allows for the basic distinction which will figure in all natural movements, for "It is clear that none of these things [the non-living natural beings] move themselves, but they have a principle of motion—not of moving or of making [οὐ τοῦ κινεῖν οὐδὲ τοῦ ποιεῖν], but of undergoing [τοῦ πάσχειν]."[12]

Having established that all things in movement demand an author of their actualization, can one extend this authorship infinitely? Must there be a first or commensurate cause of each movement? As the bifurcation between art and nature provided the basic division between the kinds of motion, so autonomous and dependent agencies distinguish fundamentally the kinds of moving causes. The movement may effect the motion either directly (δι' αὐτὸ) or through another (δι'

---

[11] *Ibid.* ii. 3. 194ᵇ29-33.   [12] *Ibid.* viii. 4. 255ᵇ28-31. (m)

ἕτερον), as for example a stone may be moved by a pry which is wielded by a hand in the control of a man.[13] The distinction serves not only to differentiate independent from instrumental causality, but provides the basis for a causal sequence. When Aristotle insists that "there is a principle and the causes of beings are not infinite, neither in direct sequence [οὔτ᾽ εἰς εὐθυωρίαν] nor in species,"[14] he is merely applying the general conclusion of the physical investigations that there can be no infinite in act.[15] Motion is eternal and time is infinite, but both are realities which exist successively; their infinitude, like their being, is potential. What actually exists of time, the "now," and what actually exists of the motion, the modified mobile, is limited; but both point to a beyond, either that has been or that will be.[16] This series of antecedents and consequences which follow each other in succession is endless in either direction.[17] But the causality of the temporally antecedent is κατὰ συμβεβηκὸς and is in sharp distinction from another type of causality: causes which "are actually at work and are particular exist and cease to exist simultaneously with their effect."[18] These are the causes which the scientist seeks: "in investigating the cause of each thing, it is always necessary to seek what is most precise."[19] Of these causes there can be no infinity for they involve existents in act. All dependent causes, all those which are used by something else for a particular effect, move only because of this use and constitute an intermediate between the principal cause and its effect. Whatever causality they possess is derived. The series of ordered causes can be composed of both kinds of causes, but the entire series operates because of the influence of the independent cause. This autonomous cause is thus a "first cause" for its causal activity is initiated within itself, is not due to some further or higher influence. It is equally an ultimate cause, for as one traces effects back to cause, the independent cause terminates the investigation. In such a simultaneous sequence of

---

13 *Ibid*. viii. 5. 256ᵃ4-5.
15 *Ph*. iii. 5. 206ᵃ7.
17 *Ibid*. viii. 1. 251ᵃ8-252ᵃ4.
19 *Ibid*. ii. 3. 195ᵇ21-22.

14 *Metaph*. ii. 2. 994ᵃ1-2.
16 *Ibid*. iii. 3. 208ᵃ20-21.
18 *Ibid*. ii. 3. 195ᵇ17-18.

causes and effect, the intermediate causes are equally susceptible of a double designation. As one moves back from effect,
they are moved movers; as one moves forward from the first
cause, they are instrumental causes.

The first or ultimate cause necessarily, then, limits any actual series. If the causality of the moved movers is essentially
derived from the first, there must be a first cause. And it is
precisely this fact which makes an actually infinite series impossible. An infinite series is a denial of a first, and would,
thus, comparably be a denial of any causality—for whatever
causality is possessed by these secondary causes is derived from
the first. Without a first, independent cause, there could be
nothing upon which the other causes depend and by which
they would be used. Causality would be intelligible without
instrumentality or without dependent causes—if such a case
de facto exists; it would be absurd, however, without a first
cause. This latter is, then, both principle and limit: the source
of motion and the limit of any simultaneous and ordered
series of dependent and independent causes. The necessity of
a first cause is true of every kind of cause: final, formal, material, and moving; but the precise point at issue here is the
moving cause, although the causal analysis of eternal motion
will ultimately demand an inquiry into all four causes.[20]

Aristotle works the argument both ways, ascending from
the motion to the moving cause or descending from the moving cause to the motion. In the former case, the intermediates
are looked upon as moved movers; in the latter, as instru-
ments of the principal agent. The force of the inference is
identical in both; only the order of procedure is different. It
is precisely this difference of order which will in time, through
a modification by Avicenna's vocabulary, provide a structural
basis for the distinction between the "*prima et manifestior via*"
and the "*secunda via*" of Saint Thomas—the first "*sumitur
ex parte motus*" and working back through moved movers to
a prime mover; the second, "*ex ratione causae efficientis*,"

[20] *Metaph.* ii. 2. 994^{a}1ff. outlines the task of any ultimate causal inquiry
in its conclusion that the actual causes responsible for a single effect are
limited in number and in kind.

advancing from the first cause, which is the *"causa medii"* through the instrumental causes to the effect.[21] Aristotle's procedure is:

I. Ascending:
   If whatever is moved is necessarily moved by something and either by something moved by another or not, and if moved by another,
   It is necessary that there be a first mover which is not moved by another:
   (1) If the first is such, there is necessarily no other.
   (2) For it is impossible that mover and moved-by-another go into infinity. For there is no first of the infinities.

II. Descending:
   Every mover moves something by means of something. The mover moves by means of himself or another. It is impossible for the "by means of which" to move without the mover himself.
   If, however, it moves by means of itself, it is not necessary for there to be another by which it moves.
   If there is another by which it moves, there is that which moves by itself and not by something else.[22]

---

[21] Thomas Aquinas, *Summa Theologiae*, Cura et Studio Petri Caremello (Taurini: Marietti, 1952) I. ii. 3c. In his *Metaphysics*, Avicenna distinguished between a moving cause and a creating cause; the first corresponded to the moving cause in Aristotle, the second to the creating cause of Genesis i. "Creating cause" lent itself to *"causa efficiens"* in the Latin translations of Avicenna, as "Augustine constantly used the word *facere* in order to signify what we now call *creare*." Saint Thomas was not ignorant of Avicenna's distinction, as Gilson noted, but seems to have identified the two types of causes: "The assimilation of the two notions of *causa movens* and *causa efficiens* is completed in the *Commentary* on *Metaph.* V, lect. 2, no. 765: '*Tertio modo dicitur causa unde primum est principium permutationis et quietis; et haec est causa movens vel efficiens. . . . Et universaliter omne faciens est causa facti per hunc modum, et permutans permutati.*'" Etienne Gilson, *Elements of Christian Philosophy* (Garden City, N.Y.: Doubleday, 1959), p. 322, n. 7. Cf. *ibid.*, pp. 184-187, 321-324. Saint Thomas uses the verbal distinction between *causa movens* and *causa efficiens* to denote two different *viae*, but the structure of each seems taken from *Ph.* viii. 5. How much that structure is modified by Thomas' ontological interpretation is another question.

[22] *Ph.* viii. 256ª12-16, 21-28. (m)

In either case, that of moved mover or that of used instrument, a first moving cause is necessary, one which will impart movement to the secondary movers or which employs an instrument distinct from itself. Both proofs have τὸν αὐτὸν τοῦτον λόγον; it is just a difference in ἐπελθεῖν.[23] Both conclude to a moving cause which is first, independent, and which begins or terminates any causal sequence.

The prior considerations of Chapter Three established the scientific validity of the proposition that whatever is moved is moved by something;[24] these subsequent arguments concluded to the proposition that there must be a first cause (here, a first mover) and that one cannot proceed to infinity in a series of simultaneously active causes.[25] One more question must be answered before Aristotle brings these to bear immediately upon the eternality of motion: Must the first mover itself be moved? Again, the devices of nature and art are adapted to allow for a distinction and a consequent double resolution: If the mover must be moved himself, this "being moved himself" can issue from a cause other than or identical with himself.

If the motion were artistic, that is, issued from a cause other than the moved, the connection between the mover and its "being moved" could be one of two: incidental or necessary. When the connection is incidental, the mover happens to be moved but it is not through this motion (οὐ μέντοι διὰ τὸ κινεῖσθαι) that it moves another. The conjunction between the mover and its own "being moved" would be de facto, but not flow from the very nature of the mover. The mover would happen to be in motion, and this occurrence would allow him to effect movement. If this were true, it would be quite possible for this "being moved" of the mover to cease, and, as it is a necessity for a mover, all motion would cease. But this consequent contradicts the manifested necessity of motion's eternality. Therefore, since the consequence is false, the antecedent is false.

The alternative is that the connection between the mover

---

[23] *Ibid.* viii. 5. 256ᵃ23.
[24] *Ibid.* viii. 4. 254ᵇ7-256ᵃ3.
[25] *Ibid.* viii. 5. 256ᵃ3-ᵇ3.

and its "being moved" would be a necessary one. Now what kind of motion would its "being moved" be? The same kind, so that every geometrician would be learning precisely what he is teaching simultaneously? Absurd. A different kind? But the kinds of motions have already been seen to be limited: one would come to the end of the series and terminate with a mover which was not moved. This is precisely how an actual series must terminate; the first mover must be unmoved or the series would be infinite and causality denied.[26]

If all "artistic motion" must terminate in a first mover which is not dependent for its motion upon another, can the first mover be a self-mover? How does a self-mover move himself? How can one be the subject of his own motion? The subject of motion has been previously demonstrated as the divisible,[27] and the basic division of the divisible is between whole and part. Whole and part, then, provide the formal possibilities for an answer. The whole cannot move itself nor an entire part move itself for identical reasons: the same reality would be simultaneously in act and potency in the same manner; the agent would be the patient and the patient, the agent. Relationships which are mutually opposed would become coincident. Could one part move another, and vice versa? Mutual causality of the identical motion would equally deny a first cause; neither part would be prior to the other as each would depend upon its "being moved" by the other in order to effect motion itself. Thus even in self-movers, one must arrive at an independent, immobile first. Even animals must have two "parts": an unmoved mover and a part which is moved. That which is ultimately responsible for a kind of movement must be itself unmoved by the kind of motion which it communicates.[28] This allows for a hierarchy of causes of motion:

For there must be three things—the moved, the movent, and the instrument of motion. Now the moved must be in motion, but it need not move anything else; the instrument

26 *Ibid*. viii. 5. 256b4-257a33.   27 *Ibid*. vi. 4. 234b10ff.
28 *Ibid*. viii. 5. 257a33-b9.

of motion must both move something else and be itself in motion . . . ; and the movent—that is to say, that which causes motion in such a manner that it is not merely the instrument of motion—must be unmoved. . . . So Anaxagoras is right when he says that Mind is impassive and unmixed, since he makes it the principle of motion: for it could cause motion in this sense only by being itself unmoved, and have supreme control only by being unmixed.[29]

Through the devices of nature and art, Aristotle set up distinctions through which he proved that motion was eternal and that whatever was moved was moved by another. The same instrumentalities were adapted to demonstrate the necessity of a first mover, responsible for its causality and independent of external influence in its action. Secondly, since the subject of motion is always divisible, the distinction between whole and part provided a schema by which Aristotle showed that self-movers were composite, made up of an unmoved mover and the part essentially passive to its influence, and that the first moving cause was essentially immobile. Finally, the entire pattern of the inquiry fits together into a summary line of reasoning: "Since it is necessary [δεῖ] that motion always be and not cease, it is necessary [ἀνάγκη] that there be something eternal which first moves, be it one or many, and that this first mover be eternal."[30]

What kind of mover is responsible for eternal movement? The basic choice is between a mover eternal or intermittent, and this choice cut through by another distinction: one or many. The argument advances from the duration and continuity of the motion to the eternality and unicity of the unmoved mover.

The non-eternal, whether one or many, cannot author eternal motion. Whether one speaks of natures, generated or corrupted, or of temporary existents which come into being and perish without generation and corruption; whether one speaks of one such existent or the successive sum of them—he has not explained eternal motion. The abiding motion of the universe

---

[29] *Ibid*. viii. 5. 256ᵇ15-27.   [30] *Ibid*. viii. 6. 258ᵇ10-11. (m)

is a necessity, an eternal necessity. One must find a cause for
its necessary eternality, a cause which is simultaneous with
the motion and whose influence explains its necessity. To posit
endless generation and corruption or the stream of temporary
existents is simply to underline the need for such a cause, a
cause which will explain their eternal coming into and passing
out of being:

> The eternality and continuity of the process cannot be
> caused either by any one of them singly or by the sum of
> them, because this causal relation must be eternal [ἀίδιον]
> and necessary [ἐξ ἀνάγκης]. . . . It is clear that though
> there may be countless instances of the perishing of some
> principles that are unmoved but impart motion, and though
> many things that move themselves perish and are succeeded
> by others that come into being, and though one thing that
> is unmoved move one thing and another move another,
> nevertheless there is something that comprehends them all,
> and that as something apart from each of them, and this it is
> that is the cause that some things are [τὰ μέν εἶναι] and that
> some things are not [τὰ δὲ μὴ] and of the continuous
> change. And *this is to those as they are to the others, causes
> of motion.*[31]

What Aristotle is arguing from is the necessary eternality of
motion. The principle demanded by such a fact is a necessary
and eternal moving cause. There can be three kinds of such
unmoved movers: living things, subject to generation and
corruption; problematic beings which might come into being
and pass from it, but without dependence upon corporeal
generation; necessary beings, eternal in being and in causing
motion. Neither of the former will explain motion; indeed,
they need this eternal cause as much as any effect within the
universe. For the necessity of the eternality of the moving
cause is cotemporaneous with the motion itself, and nothing
whose being is not intrinsically necessary can justify such a
characteristic of movement. One can argue from intermittent
motions to natures responsible for such movement; but the

[31] *Ibid*. viii. 6. 258ᵇ28-259ᵃ6. (Last line, italics and translation: mine).

eternal generation and corruption of these natures as well as the eternality of motion itself raises a problem that forces the inquiry beyond. Even if one posits beings beyond corruption and generation, non-corporeal beings, this is not enough. They must be necessarily eternal, beings that always have been and always will be.

The only motion which could be eternal would be a continuous one, neither broken by internal changes nor terminated by external limits. One mover would be sufficient to explain the eternality of such a movement; one and only one mover would be able to explain its unbroken continuity. If various eternal movers were involved, movers not interdependent, the motion would be, at best, successive, not continuous. Aristotle's line of reasoning is a steady one: eternality is only possible if the motion is continuous; continuity is only possible if the mover is one.[32]

The advance of the argument through natural, living movers to a single unmoved mover has done more than differentiate the former from the latter. It has concluded with a proportion which gives the subjects of the eternal motion as well as furnishes a cosmos for the motions within the universe; the last line of the above quotation stated that the eternal mover is to non-eternal movers as they are to others, i.e., causes of motion. In terms of the previous schema, all non-eternal but natural movers are moved movers. They are the subjects of the eternal motion and thus able to move others. This is what it means for the deathless and pauseless motion to be "like a life for all those things that are constituted by nature."[33] In causing eternal motion, the moving cause moves all movers and thus possesses a relation to them parallel to their relation to their own effected motions.

The subjects of eternal motion, of continuous and endless movement, are all other moving causes; and this gives a dynamic order to all movement as proceeding directly or indirectly from an ultimate and eternal moving cause. Whether it

[32] *Ph.* viii. 6. 259^{a}14-19.

[33] *Ph.* viii. 1. 250^{b}15. Cf. *ibid.* ii. 2. 194^{b}14; viii. 2. 253^{a}7ff.; 6. 259^{b}7ff.; *Metaph.* xii. 5. 1071^{a}14; *GC* ii. 10. 336^{a}15ff.

be the local motion of the elements through which they contact, interact, and generate new substances or the primitive movements of the living organisms or the most sophisticated human processes—all are possible only because each of these independent movers is caught up in an eternal movement. Intermittent motion is possible only because there is eternal motion; natural living things can move themselves only because they are themselves the abiding products of endless motion. Thus the animal is not dominant (οὐ κυρίως) even over the local motion he authors: "For the cause is not from themselves [οὐ γὰρ ἐξ αὐτοῦ τὸ αἴτιον]." Their growth or decline and their breathing are the result of their "environment or of many things such as food which enter into the animal." Even in the most rudimentary movement, animal life is dependent upon other sources for its movement, so that "the first principle is outside of them [τῆς πρώτης ἀρχῆς ἔξωθεν οὔσης]." The animal does author its own motion, but is able to do this only because sustained and moved itself by other motions, motions for which it is dependent upon another mover. "And it is for this reason that they do not maintain continuous and unbroken self-motion. It is something else which moves them."[34]

The list of attributes which Aristotle established for the unmoved mover of eternal motion is thus: unmoved, eternal, one. The interpretation of the characteristics of the eternal mover are taken from the necessities of endless movement itself. But there is a reflexive influence of one upon the other. Thus Aristotle, having established the unicity and eternality of the first mover, turns back to examine the kind of immobility which would make this possible, distinguishing it sharply from the immobility of animal souls. Even this accidental movement, indicating the dependence of the soul upon the body, must be removed from the eternal mover, for anything unmoved which moves itself *per accidens* cannot give rise to continuous movement. Essential and accidental immobility not

---

[34] *Ph.* viii. 6. 259[b]3-20. Cf. *ibid.* 2. 253[a]10-21.

only is established, but provides devices with which the first unmoved mover can be distinguished from animal souls and the principles of planetary movements. Animal souls are moved accidentally by themselves in moving their bodies; "certain first principles of heavenly bodies" move themselves neither essentially nor accidentally, but are moved accidentally by other movements in the complex orbits which make up Aristotelian astronomy. Only the ultimate cause of the physically necessary movement is essentially and accidentally unmoved, either by its own action or by the influence of another.[35] Aristotle has introduced discussions of the possibility of a plurality of first unmoved movers three times in this argument: (1) initially, as an open question;[36] (2) subsequently, finding it sufficient to posit one as principle for eternal movement and necessary to posit only one as principle for the continuity of this movement;[37] (3) now he relates other unmoved movers to this first unmoved mover, distinguishing their movements as dependent *per accidens* upon the influence of the first.[38] These threefold considerations will re-appear within the context of the metaphysical inquiries, with the causality in question transferring from that of moving to final cause.[39]

Generation and corruption in an eternal and necessary cycle have demanded a cause other than their products. Even if one claims problematic beings, ungenerated but passing in and out of being, these cannot explain eternal generation and corruption. The argument is basically that whatever is generated or corrupted or whatever is only temporary in being does not possess the necessity that will account for the necessary eternality of motion. Aquinas will take the structure of this argument as the basis for the *tertia via*, arguing "ex possibili et necessario":

For we find in things certain ones which are possibilities for being and for no-being (*possibilia esse et non esse*); because certain ones are found to be generated and corrupted, and consequently are possibilities for being and non-being.

---

[35] *Ph.* viii. 6. 259^{b}22-31.
[37] *Ibid.* viii. 6. 259^{a}6-13.
[39] *Metaph.* xii. 8.

[36] *Ibid.* viii. 6. 258^{b}11.
[38] *Ibid.* viii. 6. 259^{b}28-31.

It is impossible, however, for all things like these to be forever. . . . It is necessary to posit something which is intrinsically necessary.[40]

It was precisely for this reason that Aristotle joined the initial hypothesis of physics with the problem of eternal motion: the former was only possible by means of the latter. The ultimate principle for both would be the same. The eternal motion would be the immediate effect of the eternal mover. Things which are affected by this movement will themselves become and become movers; the motions which moved movers impart are necessarily intermittent, if only by their own generation and corruption. Thus it is that "other things are moved by a movent that is in motion and changing, so that they too must change."[41] The motion of the first mover is eternal and unvarying for it is always imparted in the same way; because of his unicity and eternality, it will be one and the same. But the subjects affected by this movement will differ in kind, in position, in periods of time. Their manner of receiving the eternal motion and the motions which they consequently author will be radically different.

To resume a bit: the inquiry into the eternality of motion had first established the fact (τὸ ὅτι) and then begun the analysis of the causes of the fact (τὸ διότι). The moving cause was itself unmoved, eternal and one; the subject of its influence were all other movers, the "matter" of its motion. What each of these movers was and the peculiar nature of its characteristic motion would provide the subject of the physical and psychological tractates, but an order of moving causes had been established which gave a unity and a development to their causality. Just as there had been a first moving cause and a first moved, so there must be a first in the order of definition and in the order of final cause.[42] The former remains a physical question, and "What is the primary natural motion?" conjoins with "Which motion alone can be eternally continuous?" to lead into its answer. Just as the considerations of moving causes established an order of dependence, so the investigation of the

---

[40] *Summa Theologiae* I. ii. 3c. (m)   [41] *Ph.* viii. 6. 260ª14-15.
[42] *Metaph.* ii. 2. 994ª1-b30.

primary motion concluded to an intrinsic relationship of motions: an order of dependence, time, and perfection; and in each of these, locomotion was primary. All other motions depend upon locomotion to conjoin the cause with the matter of its operation, and each of the others involves locomotion, though locomotion may be present without generation, alteration, or increase. Locomotion was prior in time even to generation, otherwise all things would be susceptible to generation and corruption and nothing would be eternal. Finally, what is last in the order of genesis is the full perfection of the natural object, and the motion which appears last among the animals is that of self-movement. It is a characteristic of the more developed species and takes less away from its subject than any of the other motions or changes.[43]

The changeless invariance of eternal motion argues to its continuity, and only locomotion can be eternally continuous. The principles of all other motions are mutually opposed and the movements between them differ in species; each of them has a product at which the motion terminates and which may serve for another movement which differs from its predecessor in kind. Only circular locomotion obviates this terminal destruction of continuity, for its movement away from any point is identically its movement towards this point; to leave is to approach in a continuous circularity which joins beginning and end into a motion that is always perfect and complete. Just as one argued from the eternality of motion to an eternal moving cause, so one argued from the same eternality to the kind of motion which alone could make that endless duration internally possible, to a circular motion which was simple, imperishable, more complete, and primary in the order of motions by independence, time, and definition.[44]

The effect of the moving cause is then an infinite and eternal one: eternal, in that the motion it effects is without beginning and end; infinite, in that the concomitant time is a magnitude without terminations, though always finite in act. From this Aristotle argues to one further characteristic of the eternal mover which will place further inquiry beyond physics and

[43] *Ph.* viii. 7. 260ᵃ27-261ᵃ27.   [44] *Ibid.* viii. 7-9. 260ᵃ28-266ᵃ8.

astronomy.[45] To accomplish the necessary eternality of move-
ment, the unmoved mover must have infinite power ($\check{\alpha}\pi\epsilon\iota\rho\sigma\nu$
$\delta\acute{\upsilon}\nu\alpha\mu\iota\nu$), and no finite magnitude can possess infinite power.
"In no case is it possible for an infinite force to reside in a
finite magnitude."[46] Any actual magnitude, including the entire *cosmos*, will always be limited, because as such it will al-
ways limit the forms which have an extension $\kappa\alpha\tau\grave{\alpha}$ $\sigma\upsilon\mu\beta\epsilon\beta\eta$-
$\kappa\acute{\sigma}\varsigma$ through their connection with it.[47] Thus, the unmoved
mover must be separate from magnitude not only in defini-
tion, as any substance, but in subject. For this reason, Aristotle
—unlike many of his commentators—never calls the unmoved
mover of the *Physics* a celestial soul. Any soul would be the
act of a limiting body, and the unmoved mover must be infinite in power. The animation of the fixed stars or of various
planets is an astronomical question, not one of general physics,
and is treated as such.[48] But the general moving cause of eternal motion comes as the conclusion of physics, not astronomy
—one that must be unconnected with magnitude in any way,
one that takes possession of the circumference of the moved,
but without being its soul.[49] The last line of the *Physics* asserts
the negative requirements which make further physical inquiry
impossible: "The eternal mover must be indivisible ($\grave{\alpha}\delta\iota\alpha\acute{\iota}\rho\epsilon\tau\acute{\sigma}\nu$)
and without parts ($\grave{\alpha}\mu\epsilon\rho\grave{\epsilon}\varsigma$) and have no magnitude ($\sigma\grave{\upsilon}\delta\grave{\epsilon}\nu$
$\check{\epsilon}\chi\sigma\nu$ $\mu\acute{\epsilon}\gamma\epsilon\theta\sigma\varsigma$)."[50] The last physical assertion that is or can be
formed of the eternal mover is simplicity and utter transcend-
ence. To study such a substance is the task of a theology, of a
first philosophy.

[45] *Ibid*. ii. 2. 194^{b}14-15; *GC* i. 3. 318^{a}1-8; *Metaph*. vi. 1. 1026^{a}27-31.
[46] *Ph*. viii. 10. 266^{a}25; 266^{b}25-27.   [47] *Ibid*. viii. 10. 266^{a}13-^{b}27.
[48] *Cael*. ii. 12. 292^{a}18-21; 292^{b}1-2; 292^{b}28-30. Cf. *Metaph*. vii. 11.
1037^{a}10-17.
[49] *Ph*. viii. 10. 267^{b}7. What could such a moving principle be? Aristotle
has hinted at it in his use of Anaxagoras, but the limits of physical inquiry
do not allow such a question to be pursued. "So Anaxagoras is right when
he says that Mind is impassive and unmixed, since he makes it the principle
of motion: for it could cause motion in this sense only by being itself
unmoved, and have supreme control only by being unmixed." *Ph*. viii. 5.
256^{b}25-27.
[50] *Ibid*. viii. 10. 267^{b}25-27. (m)

VII.

The Unmoved Mover: The Principle of Being

To HAVE demonstrated an indivisible being as the moving principle of eternal movement concludes the general physical investigations, but this conclusion not only indicates the task of the subaltern sciences as the determination of moved movers, specific forms, and ultimate material cause, but directly initiates further inquiry by providing the subject for an entirely new science.[1] The explanation of natural motion has led to a cause that is above nature, neither subject to the generation and death of the perishable forms nor to the locomotion of the eternal heavens, and the problems which such a transcendent being posits merge with the general examination of being as being and with the dialectical defense of principles of all knowledge in an architectonic wisdom which Aristotle called first philosophy or theology and which succeeding generations have followed early Peripatetics in titling metaphysics.[2] If there had been no substances other than those formed by nature, physics would have been first philosophy and the causal investigation of being would have terminated in natures; but an immovable mover had been established—thus substance must be broader than nature, and causes must go beyond those things which have within themselves the principles of their own activity.[3] The new science would be most properly called

[1] *GC* i. 3. 318ᵃ1-13; *Metaph.* xiii. 1. 1076ᵃ8-12; *Ph.* viii. 1. 251ᵃ5-8.

[2] For the history of the title "Metaphysics," cf. H. Reiner, "Die Entstehung und Ursprüngliche Bedeutung des Namens Metaphysik," *Zeitschrift für Philosophische Forschung*, VIII (1954), 210-237, and "Die Entstehung der Lehre vom Bibliothekarischen Ursprung des Namens Metaphysik," *Z. Ph. F.*, IX (1955), 78-99. Reiner has sufficiently indicated that (contrary to Buhle) the title was a doctrinal rather than simply an editorial designation, and owes its origins to Aristotle's immediate disciples, rather than to Andronicus of Rhodes.

[3] *Metaph.* vi. 1. 1026ᵃ27-32; ix. 7. 1064ᵃ28-ᵇ12; *Ph.* ii. 7. 198ᵃ27-32.

"wisdom" because it proposed to examine all things in terms of their first principles and ultimate causes.[4] Since the God himself figured among such causes, this knowledge was divine, a theology which held the highest place among the theoretical disciplines.[5] It was the most universal, for no other science took for its subject matter being as being, reality as such, nor reached in analysis those influences which were the most pervasive in their causality.[6] Thus, metaphysics was first philosophy, establishing the axioms common to all subsequent sciences and dealing dialectically with thinkers who denied their principles.[7] It was as a theology that it took up again the ultimate source of eternal movement, a theology geared to discuss its own problems through a new set of metaphysical terms and distinctions, proper devices and methods, and which transposed the conclusions of natural philosophy into propositions about reality itself.

Just as motion had been distinguished into natural and artistic through the external or internal location of its principle, so first philosophy would differentiate the intrinsic possession of existence from its modifications, with the consequent effects this would have in reasoning and in predication; "Some things can exist apart and some cannot, and it is the former that are substances."[8] This was the categorical division of being, a division accomplished by a new selection of terms proper to first philosophy and one which would underline the primacy given to substance both in autonomy and in causality:

> We have treated of that which *is* primarily and to which all other categories of being are referred—i.e. of substance. For it is in virtue of the concept of substance that others are said to be—quantity, quality, and the like. For all will be found to invoke the concept of substance.[9]

[4] *Metaph.* i. 1. 981^{b}27-982^{a}3; 2. 982^{a}21-^{b}10; xi. 1. 1059^{a}18.

[5] *Metaph.* i. 2. 983^{a}6-10; vi. 1. 1026^{a}10-32; xi. 7. 1064^{a}28-^{b}6.

[6] *Metaph.* i. 2. 982^{a}21-25; iv. 1. 1003^{a}21-32; vi. 1. 1026^{a}30-32; xi. 7. 1064^{a}7-13.

[7] *Metaph.* vi. 1. 1026^{a}16; xi. 4. 1061^{b}19; iv. 3. 1005^{a}33; *Ph.* i. 9. 192^{a}36; ii. 2. 194^{b}14-15.

[8] *Metaph.* xii. 5. 1070^{b}36.

[9] *Ibid.* ix. 1. 1045^{b}28-32. Cf. *ibid.* iv. 2. 1003^{b}6-10.

It is basically a distinction between being in itself and being in another.

The distinctions among substances indicate the orientation of Aristotelian metaphysics towards a consideration of things and "what is," in sharp contrast to the physicism of Democritus and to the Platonic forms, while the correspondence between natural things and substances in their divisions provides an easy comparison between the interest of physics and the dialectical considerations of first philosophy. Elemental bodies, plants, animals, and their parts can be considered equally well as natural beings or as substances.[10] As natural, they possess the source and determination of their movement within rather than without; as substances, they exist in themselves rather than exist as modifications of another. Thus even the proof from motion changes in direction: in physics, it was to account for natural motion by accounting for its endless duration; in the metaphysics, it was to explain the existence of differences in beings by explaining eternal generation and corruption.

Motion had allowed a further, elemental break-down in terms of matter, form, and privation; being also permitted a second, corresponding division into the broader classifications of potency and act, broader "for potency and act extend beyond the cases which involve a reference to motion."[11] Being, then, could be divided through the categorical distinctions, but realized primarily in substance, or it could be predicated of potency and actuality, but realized primarily in act. Thus, questions of the τί ἐστι of being, of the structure of being as being, are treated in the *Metaphysics*, Books vii through ix. In the discussions of unity, first philosophy introduces the real predication which responds to the question ὅτι, for unity is a predicate convertible with being itself.[12] Just as the *Physics* had obtained from these questions of fact the varieties of motions, so first philosophy leads a further inquiry through the kinds of substances: substance is predicated of elements, plants, and animals. There is real predication here, not simply the explica-

---

[10] *Ibid*. vii. 2. 1028; viii. 1. 1042ᵃ6; *Ph*. ii. 1. 192ᵇ9ff.

[11] *Metaph*. ix. 1. 1045ᵇ27-1046ᵃ1. Cf. *ibid*. xii. 2. 1069ᵇ15; 5. 1071ᵃ5.

[12] *Ibid*. x. 1. 1052ᵃ15ff. Cf. *ibid*. x. 2. 1054ᵃ12.

tion of the definitional structures of being. The inquiry into the what of being and the establishment of a unity with which it is convertible and the substances in which it is realized produces the devices with which first philosophy can join the problems of motions to questions about the sources of substances in a διότι investigation which terminates in imperishable, eternal substance.

Three kinds of moving causes have been uncovered in natural philosophy: nature, in the case of natural things; art, in the products of making; and "besides these there is that which as the first of all things moves all things."[13] However, if first philosophy is not to depend upon physics for its subject matter, the existence of the eternal mover will have to be transmuted into the terms of being and demonstrated anew. The argument falls into three moments, and the divisions are made according to substance and accident, potency and act, and final cause. This last stage is only substantiated through the convertibility of being, intelligibility, and goodness. Then, the demonstration of the eternal mover passes into questions of the one or the many. When the arguments for the existence and unity of the unmoved mover are outlined, it will be seen that the stages of development correspond closely to the order of the previous books of the *Metaphysics*: substance, potency and act, and unity. Just as the discussions of the *Physics* had first to concentrate upon questions of definitions and propositions before establishing their ultimate explanation in an unmoved mover, so the endless production of different substances could not be explained theologically until the terms which were involved in its definition and the propositions of which it was subject had been explored in depth. There is this radical difference between the two theoretical sciences: physics begins with the hypothesis of nature; first philosophy has to establish its full subject through argument. It is in the heart of the theological question that all of these discussions are brought to bear, explaining the existence of divergent substances and establishing the proper subject of metaphysics.

[13] *Ibid*. xii. 4. 1070ᵇ30-35.

Now to trace the argument as carefully as possible in its three steps:

First step.—The establishment from the necessary existence of certain attributes the being of an eternal and necessary substance. Substance holds an absolute priority in being; it is prior to any attribute or motion; whatever is, is either substance or dependent upon substance in order to be, for "without substance, modifications and movements do not exist."[14] If, then, every substance is perishable, everything is necessarily perishable. But this conclusion is impossible— neither motion nor time is perishable, as was proven in the *Physics*; both are necessarily eternal. Therefore, some substance must exist which is equally imperishable, and, thus, eternal. The argument mirrors the previous argument from generation and corruption in Book viii of the *Physics* and bears even stronger resemblance to the Thomistic *tertia via*.[15]

Second step.—The inference to the simplicity of the eternal substance in terms of potency and act. If this eternal substance were not actually causing movement, but only in a state of potency, it could in no way account for the eternality of motion. What is needed is an actually moving cause that is endlessly active, simultaneously effecting an eternal motion. This is why the Platonic forms fail to explain change and motion; the substance must be a moving cause, eternally in a state of actuality. What is more, the eternal substance must be that actuality; it cannot be merely a potency actualized. When the human intellect knows or when an eye sees, a potency has been actualized, and whatever is by its very nature a potency will possess its act by composition. This is the reason that "it is possible for that which is by potency [δυνάμει] not to be."[16] But the substance of the eternal mover cannot be potential in any respect, cannot be in any way a composition of potency and act. It must be only actuality, for this uncomposed act can alone explain its absolute autonomy, its total independence of another cause, its

---

[14] *Ibid.* xii. 5. 1071ª1. [15] *Ibid.* xii. 6. 1071ᵇ3-12.
[16] *Ibid.* xii. 6. 1071ᵇ19. (m)

necessity. Actuality, as such—it is without matter, without any ability to be changed, destroyed, altered, or moved in any way. Such a substance is, thus, absolutely necessary in that it cannot be other than it is, cannot be changed. Further, what the *Physics* had described negatively as being without magnitude and without parts, as indivisible, now becomes, in the selection of first philosophy, actuality, the uncomposed act whose known effect is eternal movement and infinite time.[17]

Third step.—The assertion that this unmixed actuality effects movement as its final cause. The *Physics* had established the indivisible cause as moving cause of the eternality of motion; the physical tractates had investigated natural movers, each first in its own order and each responsible for a kind of natural motion unique and proper to its species. Now inquiry has come full cycle, and summary is made in terms of the same and the different. If there is anything which moves eternally and invariantly, and thus, necessarily circularly, it must be the effect of the eternal mover. If, on the other hand, there is also eternal variance within motions, it is caused by the combined influence of the unmoved mover and of one whose nature is changeable. "Both together are the cause of eternal variety."[18] The same and the different are exhaustive, corresponding in the problem they pose to the endless motions of the *Physics*: What accounts for it? Even observation re-enforced the question, for the endless circular motion of the first heaven was taken as an instance of motion eternally invariant, evident not only by reason (λόγῳ) but by observation of its activity (ἔργῳ).[19] (One point must be stressed here: Aristotle is not saying that the "first heaven" is the only existent which moves eternally and circularly, but that it seems an evident case of one. Eternal, circular motion was the result of a painstaking investigation of the properties of motion, an investigation concluded in natural philosophy not in astronomy. In subsequent astro-

---

[17] *Ibid.* xii. 6. 1071ᵇ13-22. [18] *Ibid.* xii. 6. 1072ᵃ15-18.
[19] *Ibid.* xii. 7. 1072ᵃ21.

nomical observation, Aristotle would treat both the invariant motion of the first heaven and the variant motion of the sun, but he insisted sharply on the irreducible distinction between astronomy and first philosophy.[20] The former could furnish examples to illustrate or principles to be defended, but Aristotle does not reduce his entire metaphysics, especially at the climax of its inquiry, to astronomical probabilities. To maintain that he did is to ignore not only the actual assertions in which he made these distinctions, but also the problematic method with which he worked and the commensurate, reflexive principles which outline proper provinces for the distinct sciences.)

The basic question is, then, irrespective of the examples and of the instances: What is that which moves without in any way being affected by the motion it sets going? "The object of desire [τὸ ὀρεκτὸν] and the object of knowledge [τὸ νοητὸν] move in this way; they move without being moved."[21] The known is not affected by being known, otherwise men would never know things as they are; the loved is not changed by being loved. The changes are in the will that is loving and in the intellect that is knowing. "The intellect is moved by the known,"[22] rather than vice versa. The known is the final cause of knowledge as is the loved of the will. Final cause is not only essentially unmoved, but moves all the other causes to their causality. If the ultimate principle of all motion, both invariant and variant, is to be utterly unmoved—and this is demanded by the very definition of its actuality—it must be final cause and final cause not as the formal product of generation but as the specifying object of knowledge and love.[23]

Granted that the known and the loved are necessarily unmoved, can they, in their highest forms, identify with the unmixed actuality of the eternal substance? In other words, would substance as simply act be the first intelligible being

---

[20] GC ii. 10. 336ᵃ22ff.; Metaph. xii. 8. 1073ᵃ12ff.

[21] Ibid. xii. 7. 1072ᵃ26. (m)

[22] Ibid. xii. 7. 1072ᵃ30. On the priority of final cause in both art and nature, cf. PA i. 1. 639ᵇ14-20.

[23] Metaph. xii. 7. 1072ᵇ1-4.

and primary good? The question is not what is most directly known by the human intellect, but what is most knowable by its very nature. Just as Aristotle had inferred that the first mover must necessarily be simple act, so now he reaches the same conclusion about the first intelligible being and principal good, passing as he does through the same stages marked off by the four terms which had distinguished the previous argument and laying out a hierarchical structure which Saint Thomas will later employ for the *via quarta*. The line of inference, as in the transposed demonstration from eternal motion, is through various kinds of beings or types of unity—substance, accident, potency, act—and the relational unity of the universe will be found in its orientation to the undifferentiated unity of the pure act.

Substance is more intelligible than accident, both in definition and in knowledge. For substance enters into the very definition and understanding of accidents, but not vice versa, and "we think that we know each thing most fully when we know what it is . . . rather than when we know its quality, its quantity, or its place."[24] For the same reason a simple substance is prior to a composite and act is prior to potency; in both cases, the prior enters into the definition and knowledge of the posterior. It follows, then, that the primary intelligible entity φύσει would be a substance whose reality was simple act. This also corresponds to his previous claim that the first principles are always the most knowable φύσει "for by reason of these and from these, all other things come to be known, and not these others by means of the things subordinate to them."[25] A similar ascent can be made through accidental and mixed goods to the substance that is simply good in itself (τὸ καλὸν καὶ τὸ δι᾽ αὑτὸ). This is not an adumbration of the ontological argument. Rather it is to assert that if there is a substance coincident with its actuality, it will be the highest intelligibility and the greatest good (ἄριστον). In this way "the primary objects of desire and of

[24] *Metaph.* vii. 1. 1028ª36-ᵇ1. For the distinction of things better known by nature and things better known by men, cf. *ibid.* vii. 3. 1029ᵇ1-10.
[25] *Ibid.* i. 2. 982ᵇ2-4.

thought are the same."²⁶ Since the previous moments of the argument have demonstrated the antecedent, the consequent follows. Thus the third moment of the argument closes with an eternal substance, pure actuality, whose goodness and intelligibility are the motive of the universe: "On such a principle, then, depend the heavens and the world of nature."²⁷

Now the focus of the inquiry turns from the existence of such a substance to ask what it is—from εἰ ἔστι to τί ἐστι. If the eternal mover moves as the object of thought and of desire, whose is the thought and whose is the desire? The question has already been partially answered in the location of intelligences within the universe, but its commensurate answer cannot be given until the life of the eternal mover has been established as intellectual.

As the final cause is the ultimate good, "the course of his life [διαγωγή] must be like the very best which is ours for a short time."²⁸ The argument is from analogy, whatever man possesses as best must be realized in a supreme degree in the highest good. This is understanding. And this activity of understanding is further specified in its worth by the value of the thing known; there must be a coincidence between the object and "that which is thinking in the fullest sense." In every act of knowledge, there is some reflexivity and the intellect is in-formed by the object of thought in order to know it. But here, in the case of the eternal mover, total reflexivity is required: his activity must be best and its object must be best.

---

²⁶ *Ibid.* xii. 7. 1072ª26-31. The argument is somewhat like the first which the "early Aristotle" is recorded to have used in his lost dialogue *On Philosophy*: "In general, wherever there is a better there is also a best. Now since among the things that are, one is better than another, there is also a best thing, and this would be the divine." (Frg. 16.) Jaeger maintains that this is the "root of the ontological argument," which Ross softens to "what may be called an anticipation of the ontological argument." (Jaeger, *op.cit.*, p. 158; Ross, *op.cit.*, p. 179.) One might maintain that it is almost exactly the opposite of the ontological argument. In the classic statements of this argument, whether in Anselm, Descartes, Spinoza, Leibnitz, or Hegel, the illation goes from a concept to a reality. In Aristotle's argument, the illation is from the fact that there is a series of varying goods to the conclusion that there must be a best—the movement is from reality to reality.

²⁷ *Metaph.* xii. 7. 1072ᵇ13-14.   ²⁸ *Ibid.* xii. 7. 1072ᵇ14-15.

This is only possible in understanding, in an action in which the object and the activity are identified: ταὐτὸν νοῦς καὶ νοητόν.[29] Mind (νοῦς) is introduced as reflexively identifiable with its object, and of this total reflexivity of supreme goodness and intellection, Aristotle predicates for the first time the term, God:

> If then God is always in that good state in which we sometimes are, this compels our wonder; and if in a better, this compels it yet more. And God is in a better state. And life itself also belongs to God; for the actuality of thought is life, and God is that actuality; and God's self-dependent actuality is life most good and eternal. We say, therefore, that God is a living being, eternal, most good, so that life and duration continuous and eternal belong to God; for this *is* God.[30]

The long journey from eternal motion has reached God, a living God whose life is understanding and whose goodness is the infinite power with which the universe moves. Earlier in the *Metaphysics*, Aristotle had praised Anaxagoras' contribution to the discussions on moving cause. Nature, chance, and fortune had proven "inadequate to generate the nature of things." No element of luck could "be the reason why things manifest goodness and beauty both in their being and in their coming to be." Thus, when Anaxagoras introduced Mind (νοῦς), contending that it was as present in the universe as the cause of all order and of all arrangement, "he seemed like a sober man in contrast with the random talk of his predecessors."[31] But Aristotle scores Anaxagoras' unscientific use of this principle, maintaining that Anaxagoras turned it into explanation only when no other cause is forthcoming.[32] Now Mind is reintroduced, but with a twofold purification: no longer as moving cause, but as final cause; not related to its activity as actualized potency, but identified with it. God is the actuality of thought, not an intellect which is a mere capacity for thinking. Mind identifies with contemplation as the divine nature, for contem-

[29] *Ibid.* xii. 7. 1072ᵇ21.
[30] *Ibid.* xii. 7. 1072ᵇ24-30.
[31] *Metaph.* i. 3. 984ᵇ7-22.
[32] *Ibid.* i. 4. 985ᵃ18-22.

plation is the actuality of thought. Since God is his thought, he is his life.[33]

Is such a principle singular or plural? Motion must be eternal, and "the first principle or primary being is not movable either in itself or accidentally."[34] But observation and astronomical theories indicate other eternal movements and other spheres. Each of these movements must—as previously indicated in the *Physics*—be caused by a mover "both unmovable in itself and eternal."[35] The causality here is final, but the same distinction obtains: the first mover is not moved accidentally by another, while the other movers are only unmoved essentially.[36] These movers are—like the movements they author— in a certain order of priority and posteriority, but the first unmoved mover is unique: "For the primary essence has not matter; for it is complete reality. So the unmovable first mover is one both in definition (λόγῳ) and number (ἀριθμῷ)." He is single because utter actuality, and the universe is one because of the uniqueness of its principle.[37] However many subordinate movers and moved spheres there be, they achieve an internal unity to each other in virtue of their further and more radical order to the supreme goodness of God. Thus, the good of the universe is both its intrinsic order and the self-subsisting goodness of its principle: "for all things are ordered together to one."[38] It is in this way that Aristotle's earlier claim was realized: "On such a principle depend the heavens and the world of nature."[39] The alternative to a single principle to which the

[33] *Ibid*. xii. 7. 1072ᵇ15-31. For God referred to simply as "Mind," cf. *ibid*. xii. 9. 1074ᵇ15.

[34] *Ibid*. xii. 8. 1073ᵃ24.   [35] *Ibid*. xii. 8. 1073ᵃ33-34.

[36] Cf. *Ph*. viii. 6. 259ᵇ28-31.   [37] *Metaph*. xii. 8. 1074ᵃ33-38.

[38] *Metaph*. xii. 10. 1075ᵃ11-19: "It must be considered how the nature of the whole possesses the good and the best, whether as something separate and autonomous [αὐτὸ καθ' αὐτό], or as the order, or in both ways—as an army does. For its good [τὸ εὖ] is both in the order and the leader. And especially the leader. For he is not for the sake of the order, but the order is for him. And all things are ordered together somehow, but not in the same manner— fishes, birds, and plants. And they do not exist in such a way that one thing has nothing to do with another, but there is something. For all things are ordered together to one [πρὸς μὲν γὰρ ἓν ἅπαντα συντέτακται]." (m)

[39] *Ibid*. xii. 7. 1072ᵇ14.

universe is ordered would be no cosmos at all, no unity and no order, no good in virtue of which there is order to the parts.[40] Just as natural philosophy began with the reflexive principle of physics, with nature which was the internal principle of movement and rest, so first philosophy concludes to its principle and terminates in its reflexive identity in knowledge and goodness. Again a correction of Anaxagoras' principle makes this possible, for Anaxagoras had made Mind unreflexive, i.e. a moving principle geared to an end other than itself. Now Mind is made reflexive, and it is indicated that both efficient and final cause can coincide in its reflexivity: "Anaxagoras makes the good a motive principle; for his 'reason' moves things. But it moves them for an end, which must be something other than it, except according to *our* way of stating the case."[41] This allows Mind to function both as moving and as final cause, without diremption. Further, only such a reflexive principle could be self-instantiating and primary.

Much discussion has been spent over the relationship between the mover of *Physics* viii and the final cause of *Metaphysics* xii. Paulus and Nolte relate them as the soul of the first heaven to the final cause of the universe, thus distinguishing the causes into things, distinct one from the other.[42] Ross identifies the causalities: "God is the efficient cause by being the final cause, but in no other way."[43] *Salva reverentia*, both seem to identify thing and causal relationship. The former: if there are distinct causal relationships, there are distinct realities; the latter: if there is only one reality, the causalities must merge. Again the reflexive nature of the Aristotelian principle might cast some light on the discussion. A nature is both moving, formal and final cause of its own movement, an identification that is often numerical.[44] So also, one would expect the reflexive principle of the universe to be one, self-identical even with its diverse causal relationships. It cannot be a world soul for it is moved neither accidentally nor essentially nor is it in any

---

[40] *Ibid*. xii. 10. 1075^{b}25-1076^{a}4.   [41] *Ibid*. xii. 10. 1075^{b}7-10.

[42] Owens, *op.cit.*, pp. 411-413.   [43] Ross, *op.cit.*, p. 181.

[44] *Ph.* ii. 1. 193^{b}8-18; *PA* i. 1. 641^{a}25. For coincidence of causes, cf. *Ph.* ii. 7. 198^{a}22. For the subject-identity of moving and final cause, cf. also *Metaph.* xii. 10. 1075^{b}8 and 1075^{b}37.

way possessive of magnitude. The only way in which an efficient cause can be so utterly unmoved by a final cause is by being identified with it in subject. The Unmoved Movers of *Physics* viii and of *Metaphysics* xii must identify because they are unmoved. They constitute a single act of understanding, of infinite power, which can be distinguished into the source of intellection, the activity of intellection, and the object of intellection. But it is a single reality with diverse relationships to the eternal motion which it authors and by which it is known.

As was noted, Aristotle employed arguments which later provided the basic structures for four of the five ways of Saint Thomas. The fifth alone is missing, and Saint Thomas notes in his commentary on *Physics* ii that the foundation for the proof from providence lies with the Aristotelian discussion of the ordination of nature to a final cause.[45] Aquinas would later use this to infer the guidance of God in the operations of natures, but Aristotle does not. Perhaps this, more than any single fact, illustrates the differences between the Greek philosopher and the Italian theologian. They are one in using a problematic method, reflexive principles, and a metaphysical selection, but they differ radically in interpretation, in the character of the reality of the phenomenally given. For Aristotle, there were not the separated forms of Plato, more real than the empirical which participated in them; there was not another dimension of things other than the forms which existed in matter. And this interpretation of the real has been called essentialist. Saint Thomas, however, allows for the same formal structures of the given as Aristotle, but places the pattern of each nature within the ideas of a creator God. The doctrine of the divine ideas and of the divine governance points to a deeper dimension of the real than is given within experience, an "ontological interpretation" that can ground the ontological truth of existents in their conformity to the creative patterns and can give a transcendent hope for historical movement in the hidden guidance of a wise providence. The difference in

---

[45] Thomas Aquinas, *In Octo Libros Physicorum*. Lib. ii. lect. 12. sec. 250. For something *like* the *quinta via*, however, cf. *Metaph.* i. 3. 984^{b}7-22.

interpretation and the agreement in the other coordinates of inquiry place the metaphysics of both in an ambiguous relationship, one that has been productive of the greatest controversies. And over no subject has this controversy been more vigorous than in the demonstration of the existence of God from motion.

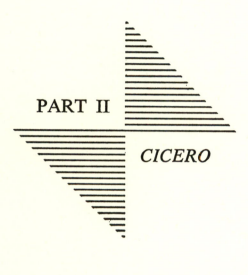

PART II

CICERO

VIII.

Operational Method

IN CICERO's philosophic dialogues as in his textbooks on rhetoric, every serious method of discourse (*omnis ratio diligens disserendi*) was a composite of two moments: invention (discovery) and judgment.[1] The Stoic dialectic failed seriously in its omission of the former, while the preeminence of Aristotle lay in the mastery which he had exercised over both.[2] Each was an art, and both were necessary if the philosophical enterprise was to bring its union of *ratio* and *oratio* to term.[3] Invention, or the topical art, was an ability to discover things or arguments or what might pass for either; it was a heuristic "excogitation," and its function was the construction of argumentation and the uncovering of evidence by which a position might be proved, a case defended, or a cause advanced: "Invention is the excogitation of things which are true or which seem to be true and which will give probability to a case." Its product, then, was the *res* or the *argumentum*, data or a particular line of reasoning by which confidence (*fides*) might be elicited in dubious matters or likelihood obtained in conclusions.[4]

The art of judgment, or dialectics, was geared to the testing or criticism of the discovered, to the verification of the "bright idea." Judgment questioned whether things existed, whether arguments were true, or whether verbal composition was accurate and telling. As such, it was a necessary second moment in

---

[1] *Topica* 2. 6. The text of Cicero's work and the system of references are those of the Loeb Classical Library (Cambridge, Mass.: Harvard; and London: Heinemann). The translations are mine. This chapter was published in the *Journal of the History of Philosophy* (April, 1970) and is republished here with the kind permission of the editor.

[2] *De Oratore* ii. 38. 157-161; *Topica* 2. 6.

[3] *De Finibus* iv. 4. 10.   [4] *De Inventione* i. 7. 9; *Topica* 1. 2.

any discourse. Invention discovered evidence, argumentation, and discourse; judgment weighed the evidence, tested the argumentation, and criticized the discourse. Out of this adjudication issued the correct ordering of the invented or the accurate appraisal of the proffered. Invention and judgment comprised the double periods of creativity and criticism, of originality and experimentation. As such, invention took a priority over judgment, both in the progression through which it was called into play and in the natural dependence of the latter on the former.[5] Both were but distinct moments in the single, ongoing process of thought, and a method of philosophizing would be as thorough as the comprehension which it offered to the arts of topic and dialectic. It is this conviction which induces Cicero to preface almost every major work with an extended history and defense of his scientific method, and the peculiar suitability of the Academic procedure is an assertion with which he opens or closes each of his theological tractates.[6]

In these histories, philosophic method owes its origins to Socrates and its occasion to the dogmatism of the sophists. Gorgias of Leontini had introduced a new practice into the Hellenic assemblies, the procedure of the elicited question and the subsequent extemporaneous lecture. He would appear before his audience, invite a question, and develop the suggested subject into a *schola*, a formal oration on the matter proposed. These elaborate declamations would include any number of assertions, and it was against these that the Socratic method was forged and brought to bear. Socrates followed a pattern of inquiry contrasting sharply with the sophistic at every step. He would first obtain a statement of position from an interlocutor; then, without affirming any positive knowledge himself, he would argue against the position by cross-questioning

---

[5] *De Oratore* ii. 38. 157-161; *Topica* 2. 7.

[6] *De Natura Deorum* i. 5. 11.–6. 14; *De Divinatione* ii. 72. 150; *De Fato* 1. For the unity of these three works, cf. *De Divinatione* ii. 1. 3, and *De Fato* 1. For the most extensive commentary on Cicero's theological works, cf. M. Tulli Ciceronis, *De Natura Deorum*, ed. Arthur Stanley Pease (2 vols.; Cambridge: Harvard, 1955, 1958); and M. Tulli Ciceronis, *De Divinatione*, ed. Pease (University of Illinois Studies in Language and Literature, Vols. VI, No. 2-3, and VIII, No. 2-3; Urbana: University of Illinois Press, 1920, 1923), pp. 159-500, 153-476.

and contention.[7] The essence of wisdom was to know that one did not know, and the purpose of method was the invention of what seemed most likely, i.e., the discovery of the probable. Cicero traced his own methodological heritage back to this antithetical method of the sceptical Socrates: "For this is, as you know, the ancient and Socratic method of speaking against the opinions of another. In this way, Socrates thought that what was the most similar to the truth could be most easily discovered [*inveniri*]."[8] The purpose of his purely negative stance was both to criticize the brash certitudes of the sophists —propositions advanced despite the consensus of Democritus, Anaxagoras, Empedocles, and the vast majority of ancient philosophers that positive, certain knowledge was an illusion[9]— and to discover whatever likelihoods could be uncovered for speculation and action.[10]

In the revolutions which followed the death of Socrates, men began to think of philosophy more in terms of doctrine than in terms of methods and questions, and the antithetical method was allowed to lapse. With the decline of its methodological corrective, dogmatism once more revived.[11] Zeno and the Stoics repeated much of the Platonists' and Peripatetic doctrine, contributing to this dogmatic community little but an originality of vocabulary.[12] It was against Zeno that Arcesilas reinstituted the *vetus et Socratica ratio*, pushing beyond the single Socratic reservation in his assertion that one could not even be sure that nothing could be known. This New Academy employed the antithetical method to argue against any accepted opinion, not just again the Stoics, and the purpose of the practice was again invention—but an invention that the antinomies of any question were so balanced that no assent could be given either side:

He [Arcesilas] acted in a manner that was according to this method, so that, by arguing against the opinions of all men, he led the majority to withhold any consent from either position more easily. And he did this by the discovery [*inveni-*

[7] *De Finibus* ii. 1-2. Cf. *De Divinatione* ii. 72. 150.
[8] *Tusculanarum Disputationum* i. 4. 8.
[9] *Academica* i. 2. 44.   [10] *Ibid*. i. 4. 16.
[11] *Ibid*. i. 12. 44-45.   [12] *Tusculanarum Disputationum* iv. 3. 6.

rentur] that the weight of the reasons on the opposite sides of the same subject were equal.[13]

Thus the method of Socrates was returned to philosophic employment not to discover the probable, but to invent reasons which obviated any conclusions whatsoever.

The full return to the Socratic usages was the work of Carneades. In 155 B.C., Athens sent an embassy to Rome, commissioned to petition against the penalty imposed for the pillage of Oropus and composed of the leaders of the major philosophical schools in the Hellenistic World: Critolaus the Peripatetic, Diogenes the Stoic, and Carneades the Academic. The origins of Roman philosophy date from this legation, though one could trace a tradition back to the Pythagoreans, and Cicero credits Carneades both with the restoration of probability to the Academy and with the introduction of the antithetical method into Roman oratory and philosophizing.[14] It was this method which Cicero owed to Philo of Larissa and which allowed him to draw a simple equation between the practices of Socrates and those of Carneades.[15]

This Socratic *multiplex ratio disputandi* did not function alone; it was essentially two-voiced, depending upon the prior position of the opposite speaker and upon his continual response in the resulting debate.[16] The antithetical method generated the debate, laying a negative cross-questioning or refutation against any assertion whatever, and constituting the properly philosophical treatment of any subject as an argument in which affirmative and negative positions were represented. In a word, the antithetical method begot *controversia*. Some would distinguish this latter from the former, as Piso contrasts in heritage and in usage the debate-method of Aristotle from the antithetical method of the New Academy: "Unlike Arcesilas, who always controverted every proposition, Aristotle, their founder, began the practice of arguing for and against on every subject."[17] But Cicero collapses this distinction, identify-

---

[13] *Academica* i. 12. 45.
[14] *Tusculanarum Disputationum* v. 4. 10-11.
[15] *Ibid.* iv. 3. 5. [16] *Ibid.* ii. 3. 9; *De Oratore* iii. 17. 67-68.
[17] *De Finibus* v. 4. 11. Cf. *De Oratore* iii. 21. 80.

ing the method of the Academy and that of the Peripatetics:
"These considerations have always led me to prefer the custom
of the Peripatetics and of the Academy [*Peripateticorum Aca-
demiaeque consuetudo*], that is, of debating both sides of all
subjects."[18] The antithetical method necessitates that both sides
of any question be heard, and within the resulting disputation,
invention and judgment of truth or of verisimilitude is obtained: "Our disputations have no other purpose than to elicit
and to form in expression whatever is true or seems most likely
to be true—and to do this by speaking on both sides of any
question."[19]

Debate, then, provides a unification not only of the philosophic methodologies of the Platonists and of the Aristotelians,
but of the methods of philosophy and those of rhetoric. In
controversia, there is a merger of the uses of philosophic discourse and of oratorical training: the method is the same and
its product is either the conclusions of philosophy or the command of a polished oration: "My preference," Cicero explained
his choice of method, "is not only because this is the only way
in which verisimilitude can be discovered [*inveniri*], but also
because it provides a superb training in public speaking. Aristotle was the first to employ this, and then those who followed
him."[20] This identification of rhetoric and philosophy in a single universal method is a consequence of the Ciceronian understanding of the interdependence of *res* and *verba*, an understanding mediated and justified through a history of human
culture.[21]

Primitive men wandered bestially about their world, relying
upon physical strength to accomplish the goals set by momen-
tary passions and preying upon one another without justice or
piety. Within this world of human chaos, untouched by the
humanizing influences of family, religion, or civil society, a
genius arose, a great man become aware of the potential of
his fellows and uniting in himself reason and eloquence, *ratio*

[18] *Tusculanarum Disputationum* ii. 3. 9. Cf. *De Oratore* iii. 36. 145.
[19] *Academica* ii. 3. 7.
[20] *Tusculanarum Disputationum* ii. 3. 9. Cf. *De Fato* 3; *De Oratore* 12.
[21] *De Oratore* i. 14. 63; iii. 5. 19; 6. 24. Cf. *Tusculanarum Disputationum*
ii. 5. 7.

93

et oratio. It was he who gathered men into society, who persuaded the strong to respect the weak, who began the instruction and the transformation of men into human beings. His wisdom without eloquence would have been useless, while eloquence without wisdom would have been positively harmful. Only the conjunction of the two in one towering man could have turned rapacious, brute men towards private loyalty and public justice.[22] "It was this method of thinking and expression coupled with force in delivery which the ancient Greeks called 'wisdom.' "[23] This wisdom had marked the great legislators of old, Lycurgus, Pittacus, and Solon of Greece as well as the Catos and Scipios of Rome; in philosophy it distinguished Pythagoras, Democritus, and Anaxagoras—men who had left the study of government to give themselves to theoretical science. Again, the pivotal figure in this history is Socrates, but this time as heresiarch. His aversion from the sophists led him to despise this double wisdom of which they professed themselves teachers. Until his time, the unified knowledge of whatever was most human (*omnis rerum optimarum cognitio*) and its practice was styled "philosophy," but the Socratic "disputations separated the science of wise thought from that of pleasant expression—though in reality they cohere."[24] Socrates, for Cicero, was the hero of philosophic method and the villain of departmentalization. "From him came that separation of the tongue from the heart, a separation according to which some teach us to think and others teach how to speak—a separation which is absurd, useless, and positively reprehensible."[25] Periodically there would be a revolt against this diremption, as Aristotle's contempt of Isocratean education led him into the fields of oratorical training to reestablish once more the conjunction between wisdom and eloquence. The Aristotelian insight into the correlativity of *res* and *verba* gave birth to a scientific methodology in which the knowledge of things was joined to the command over words (*rerumque cognitionem cum orationis exercitatione conjunctionem*).[26] Cicero's Aris-

---

[22] *De Inventione* i. 2. 3.
[24] *Ibid.* iii. 16. 60.
[26] *Ibid.* iii. 35. 141.

[23] *De Oratore* iii. 15. 56.
[25] *Ibid.* iii. 16. 61.

totle has a single method, and the sciences differ only in the subject matter to which this method was applied. Thus Piso would compose the scientific method of the Peripatetics equally from dialectic and the rules of rhetoric.[27]

Cicero envisaged his own career as a recapitulation of the efforts of Aristotle in the reuniting of rhetorical and philosophic excellences.[28] The single method of *controversia* allowed him to move easily from the *studium dicendi* to the questions proper to philosophy, just as it included within its comprehension the heritage of the Platonists and the practice of the Peripatetics:

> This method in philosophy of speaking against all things and making no positive judgments openly was begun by Socrates, repeated by Arcesilas, confirmed by Carneades, and has flourished down to our own times. I understand that in Greece itself it is now almost without adherents, but this I attribute to the dullness of men rather than to the fault of the Academy. For if it is hard to master each discipline, how much more difficult is it to be competent in them all! But this is necessary for those who propose, for the sake of discovering the truth, to argue for and against all philosophers. I do not maintain that I have attained success in a matter so very difficult, but I do claim that I have attempted it.[29]

This method of Cicero, the discursive process by which the thinker moves from the initiations of his inquiry to its conclusions, is an operational one. It is a dialogue in which scientific or practical formulations are situated in their divergent frames of reference, brought into the conflict of irreconcilable debate, and tested according to the views of each auditor for their probability-content. The Ciceronian debate does not move dialectically from communities and oppositions to an assimilation of lesser truths in the greater. It is controversy, and the debate is only resolved insofar as anyone chooses to adopt one of the

[27] *Tusculanarum Disputationum* v. 4. 10.
[28] *De Divinatione* ii. 2. 4; *Tusculanarum Disputationum* i. 4. 7.
[29] *De Natura Deorum* i. 5. 11.

conflicting positions or to modify it or to formulate a new position with elements from the alternatives as components. One begins and ends with perspectival diremptions, and the examination of philosophical positions is not a moment antecedent to and preparatory for the proper work of inquiry (as it would be in problematic procedure), but the properly philosophic method itself. Philosophizing is constituted by this ongoing conversation, the clash of statements and judgments, and the value of the method lies precisely in this discrimination of perspectives and the differentiation of frames of reference. As one cannot think outside of such a reference, the philosophic dialogues attempt to examine the varying products of the divergent schools as devices for invention and judgment. The claim of the author is simply, "I place in your midst the opinions [*sententias*] of the philosophers."[30] The truth emerges from the methodological testing of the arguments by submitting these statements to the differing perspectives. In some cases, the words alone may be really different and by understanding the divergent languages a community of agreement upon a common truth can be discovered. The significance of the Piso-Cotta dispute which opens the theological tractates lies in the Academic identification of the doctrine of the Stoics with that of the Peripatetics, claiming that "the Stoics agree with the Peripatetics on the realities, but disagree in words [*re concinere videntur, verbis discrepare*]."[31] Cicero agreed with Varro that the Platonists also coincided with the Peripatetics in their conclusions about the nature of things, but differed in language [*rebus congruentes, nominibus differebant*].[32] These philosophies which are assenting to the same thing in different terms need a method which will allow for their peculiar coordinate system to be introduced, for the ambiguous terms common to all will only achieve determined significance and translations by reference to their own system. Ciceronian method becomes an attempt to discover what is the case by taking such statements and locating through debate the senses in which they can be asserted and denied.

This is neither an irenicism in which everything that is

<hr/>

[30] *Ibid.* i. 6. 13.   [31] *Ibid.* i. 7. 16.   [32] *Academica* i. 4. 17.

96

asserted is true nor a relativism in which everything that is asserted is indifferently true or false. There are real issues and probable conclusions, but the operational method allows one to distinguish semantic variations from actual disagreement, and the purpose of the dialogues is equally to clarify the former and to resolve the latter. This method can reveal either a common consent underlying the linguistic divergence or a differing understanding underlying a common proposition or term. This allows the controversy both to discover that the different philosophers are stating the same truth in different ways and to judge probabilities by setting one doctrine against its real opponent.

Controversia, then, indicates a universal method for any philosophical or rhetorical enterprise, but this does not argue to an identification of the scientific with the oratorical. These must be distinguished, not in terms of uniquely proper and mutually opposed methods, but in terms of the problems upon which they were brought to bear. Hermagoras of Temnos had extended the province of the rhetorician to include any subject, constituting rhetoric the counterpart not of dialectic but of all knowledge. The Aristotelian distinction of ὑπόθεσις and θέσις, the former originally being a subdivision of the latter, was transferred into the rhetorical hypothesis which furnished the orator with his case and transmuted into a distinction between the special questions, those posed about particular individuals and concrete circumstances, and universal questions, i.e., those not so limited. Hermagoras had contended that both lay within the competence of the orator, tracing the tradition of this universal rhetoric back to Gorgias of Leontini. Cicero translated ὑπόθεσις into *causa* and θέσις into *quaestio*, and used them as devices with which to distinguish the subject-matters proper to philosophy and to rhetoric. The latter dealt with *causae*, cases which involved definite persons or particular events and which stood as subjects for demonstrative, judicial, and deliberate oratory. In its Latin translation, then, ὑπόθεσις no longer denotes the foundations necessary for every scientific inquiry, but rather those subjects which have no place in philosophy. Hypothesis is the proper matter for the lawyer, the statesman, the politician, and the public orator, and it is characterized by its uniqueness and its individuality. The θέσις or *quaestio* indicates "that which is the subject of controversy and which does not involve definite persons."[33] In Aristotelian analysis, one passed from dialectic or rhetoric insofar as the commonplaces became increasingly particular to one subject; in Ciceronian philosophy of science, one passes from the philosophical to the rhetorical insofar as the questions treated become increasingly individualized, the critical differential between *quaestio* and *causa* being located in the "certarum personarum interpositione."[34]

The single *ratio* or method can be laid against the questions posed by the one or against the cases provided by the other; out of this method come four general questions of controversy which can apply to the subject-matters of either philosophic or rhetorical interests. The form and schematism of these four questions proper to the method, whatever its application, echo back the influence of the four questions proper to Aristotelian inquiry—and their mutual differences indicate the changes effected as they are transposed from a problematic to an operational framework:

> Every subject which contains any sort of controversy [*aliquam controversiam*] to be settled by speech and debate, involves a question either of fact [*facti*] or of name [*nominis*] or of kind [*generis*] or of action [*actionis*].[35]

In their philosophic employment, these four are *quaestiones*; in their rhetorical use, they are the *constitutiones*, issues at which

[33] *De Inventione* i. 5. 7.–6. 8. For the relationship between Cicero and Hermagoras on *thesis* and *hypothesis*, cf. H. M. Hubbel (translator), Cicero, *De Inventione, De Optimo Genere Oratorum, Topica* (London: Heinemann, 1960), pp. 18-19.

[34] *De Inventione* i. 6. 8. In *De Oratore* ii. 15. 65, this distinction appears as between the *certa, definitaque causa* and the *infinita, sine tempore et sine persona, quaestio*. Antonius agrees with Cicero that the former constitute the proper province of the orator, that he should be concerned with "those controversies which are characterized by times and by persons." *Ibid.* ii. 15. 66; cf. *De Finibus* iv. 3. 6. There is also a difference in style (*genus dicendi*) between philosophy and oratory; cf. *De Legibus* i. 4. 12.

[35] *De Inventione* i. 8. 10.

the particular *causa* is argued, urged, or extolled. The universality of the method allows the transition between *quaestiones*
and *constitutiones* to be a simple one, and the nature of the
philosophical question is often clarified by its correlative oratorical issue.[36]

The question of fact treats the existence or non-existence of
the subject, and it becomes a conjectural issue in its rhetorical
translation because existence can be asserted or denied of past
and of future events only by conjecture or inference.[37] It is a
problem that deals with *esse*, with the existence of things, and
Cicero defines the criteria according to which it may be asserted or denied: "I say that those things are [*ea esse*] which
can be seen and touched."[38] These real beings are distinguished
from the *notiones*: "I say that those things are not [*non esse
rursus ea*] which are not able to be touched and pointed out,
but which can be discerned by the soul and understood." The
difference between the real beings and the merely notional
beings is that these latter have no sensible body; they are
merely some sort of intelligible impression. To be and to have
a body are identified.[39]

The question of name becomes a definitional issue in its
oratorical use because the controversy turns upon the first noun
which will identify the admitted fact. This is not a question of
essential definitions or of final resolutions into genus and dif-
ferentia—as is the τί ἐστι of problematic inquiry. Rather it
turns about the initial identification by name: By what name
shall it be called? The question turns upon the precise meaning of a term, upon the *vis vocabuli*: "When the controversy
is about the name, it is called a definitional issue because the
force of the term [*vis vocabuli*] must be defined in words
[*verbis*]."[40] Ordinary language-analysis figures here as the principal commonplace in Cicero's forensic manual. The prosecutor
is given as his first topic under the conjectural issue a "brief,
clear definition taken from the sentiment of men [*ex opinione*

---

[36] *Ibid.*   [37] *Ibid.*   [38] *Topica* 5. 27.   [39] *Ibid.*

[40] *De Inventione* i. 8. 10. Cf. *ibid.* i. 8. 11: "There is a controversy about
the name [*nominis est controversia*] when there is agreement about the fact
and the question is by what name [*quo nomine*] the fact is to be called."

hominum]."[41] The definition of the word is to be followed by an exposition and a defense of its accuracy and general acceptability. Only then (*postea*) does one turn from the definition of the word to the nature of the deed: "Then one should join the fact to the established definition."[42] One first defines the meaning of lese-majesty and then shows that his opponent's admitted deed is lese-majesty. In direct contrast to problematic inquiry, the definition of the word is established first in the operational method and then it is shown to fit the reality of which it is predicated. The difficulties here are those of both linguistic differences and divergent appraisals; both stem from the perspectival discriminations in which either is seen: "The deed seems different to different people; and thus they all describe it by a different name."[43] The job of the defense here becomes one of destroying the definitions of the prosecutor, and the principal instrument at his disposal is to show that they contradict the significance of the terms as used by ordinary people in writing or in speech. His initial topic is equally an appeal to ordinary language.[44]

The question of kind becomes a qualitative issue in its rhetorical use. Once a fact has been established and its name affixed, there is further question of predicates which may legitimately be given it. Here again the shifts which obtain in the operational method are stark. These questions of kind do not consist in the predication of attributes of that whose essence has been antecedently established—as in the problematic method—but in the further specification of the named through the additional propositions which can be formed about it. In the Ciceronian schemata of questions, *quid est* had identified the subject; here the interrogatives are *quantum, cujusmodi, et omino quale.*[45] The convertible predicates of the Aristotelian ὅτι propositions would amplify the intelligibility of the subject without altering its specific character, but the propositions of these *quale est* questions do precisely that, i.e., they increasingly specify the subject and can alter its meaning as substantially as the circumstances of a killing can alter its appearance

[41] *Ibid*. ii. 17. 53.   [42] *Ibid*.   [43] *Ibid*. i. 8. 11.
[44] *Ibid*. ii. 17. 55.   [45] *Ibid*. i. 9. 12.

before law.[46] The definitional questions had dealt with the force of the identifying word, the *vis vocabuli*; the qualitative questions treat the force and type of the act itself, *de vi et de genere negotii*.[47] Thus questions about the nature of any granted fact or identified subject fall under the questions of qualitative modifications:

> When it is agreed that an act has been performed, and by what name it shall be called, and there is no question about the procedure, but the *force and the nature and the kind of the act is in question* [*vis et natura et genus ipsius negotii quaeritur*], we call the issue a qualitative one.[48]

In his summary of the devices used to delimit an issue or to determine a subject-matter, Quintilian is content to limit his series of questions to three: *Sitne? Quid sit? Quale sit?*[49] But Cicero himself followed the lead of Hermagoras in listing a fourth and final question: the question of action, or, in its rhetorical location, the translative issue.[50] In a court of law, it became a controversy about judicial procedure: the time and the form of the case, the manner or court in which it is presented, the persons caught up in the suit. In its philosophic uses, it underlines the pragmatic orientation of scientific inquiry in the union that must be effected between philosophy and life. Socrates could be praised for calling philosophy down from the heavens and bringing "her into the cities of men and into their homes also, compelling her to ask questions about life and morality and things good and evil."[51] Philosophy is, for Cicero, "the art of life" or "the guide of life."[52] Each conclusion

---

[46] *Ibid*. ii. 21. 62. [47] *Ibid*. i. 8. 10.

[48] *Ibid*. ii. 21. 62. (Italics mine.)

[49] Quintilian, *Institutio Oratoria* iii. 11. 44, trans. H. E. Butler (New York: Putnam's, 1920-22). For a discussion of the relation between Cicero and Quintilian on the issues and questions of rhetorical method, cf. Richard McKeon, "The Methods of Rhetoric and Philosophy: Invention and Judgment," *The Classical Tradition: Literary and Historical Studies in Honor of Harry Caplan*, ed. Luitpold Wallach (Ithaca, N.Y.: Cornell, 1966), pp. 365-373.

[50] *De Inventione* i. 11. 16.

[51] *Tusculanarum Disputationum* v. 4. 10-11.

[52] *De Finibus* iii. 2. 4; *Tusculanarum Disputationum* v. 2. 5. Cicero's orientation of philosophical interests to practical consequences was a commonly

of philosophy has a practical relevance, and in philosophizing is to be found the remedy for all human imperfections, failings, and serious vices.[53] Familial, social, and civic life were established and are sustained by philosophic wisdom; to devote oneself to these questions is to render an enormously important contribution to the body politic.[54] Conversely, questions dealing with theological subjects gain their human significance because of their influence upon the home and the state. Wisdom fails significantly if it fails to achieve a commanding position over the public and private lives of men.[55] Questions of action, then, dealt with the procedure of the activity which would begin once the reality, the name, and the nature of the subject had been determined.

The four questions of controversy allow for a four-fold division of the Ciceronian treatment of the *thesis* or *quaestio* on the gods. The question of fact deals with the existence of the gods, and the issues into which it subdivides are those of the evidences by which they are indicated, the perspectives by which the data are assessed, and the methods and principles by which the conclusions are established. The question of name becomes that of the initial characteristic by which the gods are identified and fixed as the subject of further predications. The question of kind becomes one of adding these further predications as an operational specification through the increase of attributes. The question of action allows Cicero's own position to emerge from the debates, a series of conclusions which are only possible once all sides have been heard and tested. The question of fact was only in doubt insofar as one attempted to justify the common opinion that the gods existed. The question of name depended more upon the divergent schools for its content and its application. The central question was that of kind: it is a question of the divine activity *ad extra*, of the influence of the divinity upon the cosmic motions and the destiny of men. This question furnishes the three issues according

---

accepted one. Thus Torquatus, the Epicurean, asserts that wisdom, the product of philosophy, is the art of life. Cf. *De Finibus* i. 13. 42.

[53] *De Natura Deorum* i. 3. 7; *Tusculanarum Disputationum* v. 2. 5.

[54] *De Divinatione* ii. 2. 1; *Tusculanarum Disputationum* v. 2. 5.

[55] *De Natura Deorum* i. 6. 14; *De Inventione* i. 1. 2.–3. 5.

to which the three theological tractates of Cicero are distinguished: Are the gods providential? Are they miraculous? Are they deterministic? The three dialogues turn on the questions of providence, divination, and fate. Each of these involves a relation between the actions of men and the nature of the gods:

> By far the majority admit that there are gods—and this seems to contain the greatest probability. It is a conclusion to which everyone is led naturally. . . . But the question which contains the principal issue, the primary subject of dispute, is whether they do not act, whether they are idle and take no part in the administration and governance of things; or—on the contrary—whether they created and ordered all things in the beginning, whether they control and move them for all eternity. There is great disagreement on this point. Unless this particular question is settled, men must necessarily live in the most profound error and in ignorance of matters of supreme moment.[56]

The Piso-Cotta dispute indicates Cicero's position that the differences among the Platonists, the Aristotelians, and the Stoics are more verbal than real—an interpretation which they are often at pains to deny. This agreement on the theologically true allows for a common representation of all three through the Stoics, Balbus or Quintus or Hirtius. Their *magna dissensio* is not among themselves but with the Epicureans, and the Epicureans agree with this division, considering themselves alone in their denials of providence, divination, and fate. Thus the theological schools merge into two. The Academic does not offer a doctrine, but a method of discovery and criticism. Cotta or Cicero will bring this to bear against the positive arguments of either school, generating not only the ongoing process of debate but the probabilities with which Cicero will characterize his own conclusions. Cicero identifies with none of the major interlocutors of the *De Natura Deorum*, as his position is coincident with none of them. His own theology will emerge from the processes of debate and forms the final chapter of this section.

[56] *De Natura Deorum* i. 1. 2.

IX.

The Existence of the Gods

A PIVOTAL presupposition for the Academic method is that the evidences for the existence of the divine—whether this divinity is singular or plural—depend upon the differing standpoints from which men view their world. In a universe that is a commonwealth of gods and men, rationality and its concomitant insights are realized in divergent fashions and distributed throughout the cosmos in distinct philosophical systems. The Ciceronian method uncovers these rational perspectives, and the value of the debate lies not only in the unique lines of argumentation which are invented, but in the peculiar pattern of facts upon which each is built. For the processes of argument depend upon the prior assertions of evidence, and what is observed about nature and movement in the conversations of physics and theology is directly determined by the one who is doing the observing. Each may begin from what might be described as the same phenomenally given experience, but when facts describing this experience are enunciated in a necessarily limited number of propositions, one is immediately involved in the philosophic interpretation by which an attribute can truly or meaningfully be predicated of the subject, the method by which this conjunction can be justified, and the principles from which the method proceeds or to which it finally resolves its conclusions. Whenever one places a subject together with a predicate, he does so in terms of "the character of the real"—and his view of reality already involves a perspective and a commitment.

Since one is dealing here with the evidences of God's existence in terms of the statements of *controversia* and the actions of a body politic, the evidence would take the form of the knowledge about God and the effect of God: How can the changing universe witness the existence of God, and how can God influence either the inquiring intellect or the operations of things? The data, then, with which the antagonists deal is that which broadly and ambiguously centers around the "motions" of the cosmos and the "motions" of the human mind. This distinction realizes in the operational framework of the dialogue the devices which previously figured so prominently in Aristotelian physics: nature and art, together with their correlative privations—chance and fortune. The contrast between the Stoics and the Epicureans on these principles of motion stands as the fundamental opposition between their physical investigations and their theological conclusions.[1]

Epicurus, as his doctrine is mediated through Cicero's dialogues, repeated much of Democritean physics and shared with his master the methodological error of discussing only the material components out of which larger constructs could be made.[2] Democritus has posited indivisible atoms in motion *ex aeterno*, building a plurality of worlds from their intersecting lines of causality and identifying nature with necessity. Aristotle had countered that such an atomic theory merges with chance as its ultimate principle, that each of the subsequent corpuscular combinations is absolutely determined but that the origin of primary combination is placed in chance. In Aristotelian physics, chance was only possible because of an antecedent nature; Democritus reversed this dependency and erred in doing so—chance without nature was an impossibility.[3] Epicurus handled this criticism by keeping the logistic or constructive methods of his master, but by altering his simple principles. Thus the atoms do not simply fall perpendicularly in the void, but make an extremely small swerve

[1] *De Natura Deorum* ii. 32. 81. Richard McKeon has noted this as of crucial importance: "The fundamental opposition between the Epicurean and the Stoic theories of physics, as well as the basic weakness which Cicero found in both, is in their conceptions of 'nature.'" Richard McKeon (ed.), "Introduction to Cicero," Cicero, *Brutus, On the Nature of the Gods, On Divination, On Duties* (Chicago: University of Chicago, 1950), p. 39.

[2] *De Finibus* i. 6. 17-18; iv. 5. 13. Cf. *De Natura Deorum* i. 24. 66; i. 25. 69; i. 26. 73.

[3] *Ph.* ii. 4. 195^{b}35-196^{b}4.

(*declinatio*) which brings them into collision and combinations and allows for indeterminacy and freedom within the worlds of men and things.[4] What Epicurus introduced was an internal principle of change and motion, making the ultimate source of the universe to be within rather than without. The principle was reflexive, the swerve was the cause of the swerve—which causes Cicero to judge it an arbitrary fiction, removing causality from physics and depriving atomic motion of the motion natural to all heavy bodies.[5] But in the physics of Epicurus, the swerve was a self-instantiating equivalent of Aristotelian nature and brought into atomism such concepts as non-determinacy, reflexivity, and self-moved movers.

Epicurean motion remained the locomotion of bodies in the void, and physics studies such atomic motions and their resultants in things, sensations, and thoughts.[6] The theological absurdities of the Stoics stem from their failures in physics: one had to import a divine intervention in the universe only if one failed to understand that this world and innumerable others were effected not by intelligence, but by nature. There is a continuous creation here as "nature will effect, effects, and has effected countless worlds."[7] There is no need to posit an artistry or a divine intelligence behind the creation or direction of eternal motion of matter. Nature suffices, and Epicurean "nature" is sharply delimited in the Stoic attacks as an "irrational force causing determinate motions in bodies."[8] It is this force which Velleius further specifies as "the infinite force of innumerable atoms" moving within the three-dimensional,

---

[4] *De Finibus* i. 6. 17-20; *De Fato* 10. 22-23. The swerve (*declinatio atomi*) was to account both for combination in the physical universe and for freedom in the destinies and choices of men.

[5] *De Finibus* i. 6. 19; *De Fato* 22. 46-48.

[6] *De Finibus* i. 6. 18, 19. *De Fato* 10. 22: "Epicurus thought that by the swerve of the atom, the necessity of fate would be avoided. And so a third motion arises—other than gravity or weight [*pondus*] and impact [*plagam*] —when the atom swerves a little. (Epicurus called this ἐλάχιστον). And he is compelled to confess (in reality, if not in words) that this swerve takes place without a cause." These three types of *motus* are all variations of local motion, the swerve adding circularity to the other two. For the locomotion of atoms which underlies all subsequent reality, cf. *De Natura Deorum* i. 22. 54.

[7] *De Natura Deorum* i. 20. 53.   [8] *Ibid.* ii. 32. 81.

limitless void.[9] This identification of nature with the force inherent in the atoms allowed the Epicureans equally well to speak of "natures," i.e., of the elements out of which larger bodies were constructed.[10] These atoms come together, cohere, and construct the forms and figures of the visible universe, and even the gods themselves are formed by the atomic flux, owing their immortality to the endless replacement of their basic components.[11]

This logistic fixing of motion as the movement of bodies in space not only allows a secular autonomy to the physical universe, but reduces Platonic creation and Stoic providence to absurdity. In *controversia*, each speaker tends to reinterpret the others through the coordinates of his own perspective. Transposition of the myth of the *Timaeus* into Epicurean mechanics turns the analogies of the dialectical method into literal-minded propositions which are patently ridiculous. By the same sort of shift, Stoic physics becomes theater: providence becomes a goddess, and the goddess is either a threatening hag occasioning superstitions and terror or a *deus ex machina* invented to shore up an inadequate science of nature.[12] The underlying objection leveled at both is the argument of nature against art. Both the Platonists and the Stoics located an origin or a governance for the universe in intelligence. The Epicureans repudiated such an explanation in favor of movements which need no other principle but themselves. Physics becomes a discipline whose contribution to the human community was not to found a rational belief in the gods, but to purify religion from divination and fear.[13] In the operational context of the Ciceronian dialogues, the Epicurean charge of a failure in physics becomes a fault in invention as the Platonic theories are "desired rather than discovered [*inventa*]."[14] Within the same context, Epicurean history becomes a rhetorical device by which adversarial positions were translated, listed, and shown to be obviously absurd.[15]

---

[9] *Ibid*. i. 20. 54. [10] *Ibid*. i. 9. 22.
[11] *Ibid*. i. 19. 46. [12] *Ibid*. i. 8. 18-21; i. 20. 53-56.
[13] *De Finibus* i. 19. 63; iv. 5. 11; *De Natura Deorum* i. 20. 54, 56.
[14] *Ibid*. i. 8. 19. [15] *Ibid*. i. 10. 25–15. 41.

Epicurean reflexive principles operate not only for the separation of the physical universe from divine causality, but also for the establishment of the proposition that the gods exist. Here the argument switches from the external motions of the universe to the internal movements of the human mind. It is a given of observation and cultural history that no tribe of people or type of men deny that there are gods; it is a subject of universal consent. So universal an opinion cannot be explained, then, by external forces of authority, the directive powers of law, or the hidden compulsions of cultural conditionings. The agreement stands among men throughout the world, no matter how different their rulers, their laws, or their civilizations. The only factor common within such divergence is man himself, and it is within man that the origin of the belief must lie.[16] So the Epicureans push the causal analysis back to an internal *prolepsis*, a basic concept which underlies all subsequent thought and made it possible. Cicero translated Epicurus' πρόληψις as "antecepta animo rei quaedam informatio," or, more simply, "anticipatio sive praenotio," and Velleius appeals to the *Canon* of his master for the discipline by which such a causal sequence could be maintained and justified.[17]

Epicurus repudiated the Stoic dialectic as superfluous, noted Diogenes Laertius, and constructed a *Canon* or *Criterion* to meet the epistemological problems which dominated the philosophic interest of the Hellenistic period. The *Canon* offered three criteria for truth: sensations, passions, and preconceptions. The sensation is devoid of reason and is the total effect of the atomic influences upon the purely passive subject. The passions indicate infallibly through pleasure and pain the

---

[16] *Ibid.* i. 16. 43–17. 44. The argument to the existence of God from the universal consent of mankind existed in different forms and with divergent values in previous philosophers. In the problematic inquiry of Aristotle, it served as a confirmation of physical theories: *Cael.* i. 3. 270^{b}5-11. In the dialectical method of Plato, it has an initial and a subsequent, purified position: *The Laws* x. 886^a-888^d. As will be indicated below, it will take alternative structures as it occurs within the Stoic argumentations and with the operationalisms of Cicero himself.

[17] *De Natura Deorum* i. 16. 43–17. 45.

direction for a practical course of action.[18] The preconceptions (προλήψεις), as Velleius explains them, are individual, rational notions which underlie all subsequent understanding, inquiry, and disputation.[19] They are the first principles of intellectual activity, and as such are "instinctive or rather innate ideas [*insitas eorum vel potius innates cognitiones*]."[20] The *prolepsis* is a self-justifying concept, a concept which in turn furnishes a criterion by which the adequacy or inadequacy of subsequent concepts can be ascertained. It is thus a reflexive principle of thought, and it is this reflexivity which allows it to function as the "foundation of this question."[21] In summary: universal consensus indicates a preconception underlying human opinion; the preconception is necessarily true itself and the source of all further propositions about god.

The shifts in explanation which Epicurean reflexive principles introduced into atomism are indicated by contrast with the natural theology of Democritus. Sextus Empiricus cited the latter's analysis of religious belief in his work *Against the Physicists*: among the images (*eidola*) which impinge upon every man, some are massively great or evil. These images signify the future beforehand, and they are extremely difficult for a man to dismiss. "The ancients, on receiving a presentation of these images, supposed that god exists, god being nothing other than these images and possessed of an indestructible nature."[22] Democritus had traced the causes of belief back through images and sensations to atomic principles; Epicurus traces the community of belief back to a particular kind of concept, a reflexive concept which guarantees by itself the reality of its referent. The idea of the gods demonstrates its own validity because nothing in the external world could have caused such a concept. It issues from "nature rather than teaching."[23] Epicurus is constructing an ontological argument for

[18] Diogenes Laertius, *Lives of Eminent Philosophers*, trans. R. D. Hicks (London: Heinemann, 1925), x. 31-34.

[19] *De Natura Deorum* i. 16. 43.   [20] *Ibid*. i. 17. 44.

[21] *Ibid*.

[22] Sextus Empiricus, *Against the Physicists*, ed. and trans. R. G. Bury (Cambridge, Mass.: Harvard University Press, 1936), i. 19.

[23] *De Natura Deorum* i. 16. 43.

the existence of god. Like a similar process in Descartes, however, it is the ontological argument done a posteriori, i.e., one argues from the concept to the reality of its correlative, and the existence of the latter is the only possible explanation of the thought itself.[24]

The evidence which the Epicurean found pertinent to theological discourse was twofold: the locomotion of bodies, which offers no data for the affirmation of divinity, but serves for the destruction of false religion and ungrounded terror—and it is this motion which is the subject of the investigations of physics. Secondly, the general agreement of all men that the gods exist, indicating a *prolepsis* grounded in the nature of knowing itself—and it is this sort of criteria which epistemology isolates and justifies. Thus natural theology and religious belief find their foundation in a canonic, not in a physics, and to introduce divinity into the latter is to attribute a causal efficacy to actional principles within the universe that can only author superstition and disbelief. Reflexive principles enter physics with the assertion of the swerve, and they enter epistemology with the self-instantiations of sensation, feeling, and preconceptions. These principles allow for a distinction of nature and art, though the entitative interpretation will locate the motions of either within the substructures of both, and the logistic method will identify these motions ultimately as that movement of atoms which constitutes the reality of nature.

The Stoics also turned to physics for an investigation of the nature of things and distinguished it sharply from a dialectic of statement and from an ethics of human practice. In the Ciceronian version, there is a dependence of the Stoics upon the Aristotelian both in problems treated (*materia*) and in the method by which they are resolved (*ratione*). The Peripatetics surpassed the Stoics in the data they observed, collected, and classified in both botany and zoology and in the causal investi-

---

[24] René Descartes, *Meditationes de Prima Philosophia*, iii, *Oeuvres de Descartes*. Eds. Charles Adam and Paul Tannery (Paris: Cerf, 1904), VII, 40-47. The "classically perfect" ontological argument does not merely argue from the existence of such a concept to the existence of its referent, as above, but from the content of the concept to the necessary existence of its referent, as in the Fifth Meditation of Descartes.

gations and explanations of natural phenomena. In scientific procedure, the Stoics followed the Peripatetics on almost every major point, and so completely were the former indebted to the latter that their physics go under the same proper name. Cicero draws the analogy that Zeno is related to the Aristotelians as Epicurus is to Democritus. And like Epicurus, Zeno also introduced subsequent modifications which became those of principle and interpretation. While he agreed with Aristotle that the "entire world and all of its parts are ruled by the divine mind and nature," still he assimilated into a single nature the principle out of which reason and intelligence issue, and identified this nature with fire.[25] Zeno introduces a single comprehensive principle which will ultimately explain all motion, all life, and all intelligent creation and providence, and merges this principle entitatively—like the Epicureans—with the substructural energy of the universe.

The Stoics of the dialogues follow this problematic identification of their method, even taking their problems from the Aristotelian distinctions. The questions of natural divination are strictly distinguished from those of artificial, and both are defended against explanations which would reduce either to fortune or chance.[26] They could speak of a method that was specifically physical.[27] Living beings had movements which could issue from nature, force, and will, and the problem was to determine which of these applied to the locomotion of the celestial bodies.[28] But as distinct problems are resolved and these solutions nailed down to their principles, chance and fortune merge into a providence which both authors and governs the universe, and this creative and artistic providence becomes the comprehensive fire which energizes the universal nature. The Stoics' method allowed for distinct problems with their proper data, sciences, and procedures; the comprehensive principle permitted their individual solutions an assimilative movement which ultimately resolved them all in a single, all-embracing resolution.

[25] *De Finibus* iv. 5. 11-13.   [26] *De Divinatione* i. 6. 11-12; 18. 34.
[27] *De Natura Deorum* ii. 9. 23; 21. 54; 24. 63, 64; 28. 70.
[28] *Ibid*. ii. 16. 44.

Stoic motion becomes the sympathetic and rational inter-
operation of a single organic whole. Physics studies the movements not only for the Epicurean purposes, but much more
for the correlative ethical growth they offer. The phenomena
of the heavenly motions suggest the powers of self-control, indicate the utility and beauty of order, inspire men to a loftiness
of mind in the contemplation of their sublimity and inculcate
a human justice that mirrors the proportions with which the
cosmic intellect disposes and governs his creation.[29] The heavens are what man can become. It was the *ordo sempiternus*
which one found in the mammoth movements of the great
heavenly bodies which accounted for the benefits of nature,
the significance of portents and auguries, and the worship of
the stars.[30] But this ordered motion is not just in the heavens
nor only a change in place; it is found in every alteration of
every kind. In all parts of the world, there is a harmonious
blending of one process into another: the continuous mutations within plants and animals, the regular fluctuations of the
tides, the predictable changes within government and in the
fortunes of rulers—all of these exhibit a sympathetic conver-
gence, an interconnection so that from the changes in one an
illation can be drawn to another. The world manifests a vastly
intricate but utterly congruous interconnection of changes:
"tanta rerum consentiens, conspirans, continuata cognatio."[31]
Motion was "musical harmony of all parts of the universe,"[32]
and in this essentially organic reality the growth of men from
the earth could be analogized with demonstrative force to the
growth of fruit from a tree.[33] Both were patterned within a
regular and rhythmic unity which caught up divergent elements into design and rationality. The reflexivities contained
within the Stoic method allow for four distinct problematics
from which one can argue to the existence of divinity: organic
movement of natural bodies; the universal consent of all men;
the attested records of theophanies; the proven worth of divi-

29 *De Finibus* iv. 5. 11.   30 *De Natura Deorum* ii. 5. 15–6. 16.
31 *Ibid.* ii. 7. 19.
32 *Ibid.* Cf. *ibid.* ii. 46. 19; iii. 11. 27; *De Divinatione* ii. 14. 34.
33 *De Natura Deorum* ii. 8. 22.

nations. Each of these is a separate argument, and each must be treated somewhat differently, but it is ultimately the doctrine of sympathetic motion which makes all of them intelligible. The parts of the universe are so intimately related that each is symptomatic of the other: physical movements, the expressions of human culture, divine revelations, and superhuman prophecy. All of these draw from a common spirit so that, in contrast to the Epicureans, theology becomes a crucial part of physical inquiry, and the profoundest questions in cosmology are theological.

Cleanthes and Chrysippus homologize the beginnings of physical inquiry and the entrance into an unfamiliar home. Everywhere one finds *ratio, modus,* and *disciplina,* and one spontaneously recognizes the presence of intellect. Some mind had planned and prepared the rational ordinations of these diversities.[34] *A fortiori* a simple attention to the cosmos generates this response: "When we look at the heavens and watch the heavenly bodies, what can be more obvious than that there is some transcendent intelligence by which they are governed?"[35] This *numen praestantissimae mentis* is not so much an object of a labored illation as a given within the immediate experience of the ordered motions—so much so that Balbus contends that one could deny the existence of divinity only with an obduracy equal to the task of denying the sun; one is not more evident than the other.[36] The Stoics made their own the line from Ennius' *Thyestes:* "Aspice hoc sublime candens quem invocant omnes Jovem."[37] This contemplation of the "uniform motion and the revolution of the heavens" figures in Cleanthes as the fourth and most powerful argument for the existence of the gods.[38] Chrysippus reduced these in his reflections to syllogistic expression: if something is accomplished which is beyond human powers, it must result from someone greater than man. But the heavens and their "eternal order" are far beyond human creation or control. Thus, they must

---

[34] *Ibid.* ii. 5. 15; 6. 17.   [35] *Ibid.* ii. 2. 4.

[36] *Ibid.* ii. 2. 4-5. Cf. *ibid.* ii. 37. 94.

[37] *Ibid.* ii. 2. 4; 25. 65; iii. 4. 10; 16. 40.

[38] *Ibid.* ii. 5. 15.

result from some greater power than man. Such a one must be a god, overreaching man in his proudest human trait, intellect.[39]

Each of the Stoic arguments for the existence of divinity contains two moments: evidence is found in the universe which indicates the existence of divinity, and then this divinity is subsequently merged entitatively with the universe itself. *Ratio, modus,* and *disciplina* were discovered not only in natural motion, but in the practices of divination, the messages of portents, and in the universal beliefs of mankind. The evidence was always a harmony between divergent factors, a pattern or design was indicated, and one argued that the intelligible structure was impossible without a functioning intellect. Despite Cicero's insistence, Quintus will not distinguish the questions about the existence of god from those about the validity of divination: "If there is divination, there are gods; if there are gods, there is divination."[40] The universal intelligence demands an abiding control of all motion and a consequent presence that is as intimate as it is directive. So complete and complicated a harmony within the universe indicates the comprehensive and pervasive spirit. Two moments to each argument: one in which the Stoic argued from the world to a divine intellect and the second in which he merged the two into a single being.

Or the process could be reversed. The Stoic could demonstrate that the world was intellectual and then that this intellectual world was divine. Balbus contends that this procedure was used by Zeno and Chrysippus and founded on an organic relationship between man and his world. The universe is the comprehensive whole of which man, animals, plants, and inanimate things are integral parts. The whole is always superior to its parts; thus the crucial proposition: "Nihil mundo melius." One can argue from any positive attribute possessed within the universe to its superior possession by the universe itself, and in the illation the world becomes rational, wise, happy, and eternal. Once these series of predicates had been asserted, it

[39] *Ibid.* ii. 6. 16.
[40] *De Divinatione* i. 6. 10; 38. 82-83. Cf. *ibid.* i. 32. 70.

was a simple task to attribute divinity to this greatest of rational beings.[41]

Both processes work off nature and art: visible nature was found to be the production of a divine art, and this intelligence eventually merged with its product, or universal nature was discovered necessarily intelligent and this intelligence eventually determined as divine. In both, intelligence and nature merge, and this identification is made positively possible through the physical investigations (*rationibus physicis, id est naturalibus, confirmare*) which establish the relationship between fire and life, and negatively tenable through the dialectical attacks on the obvious errors of the Epicurean physics.[42]

The self-motion of every living thing indicates that it lives and points to a source of this movement within. Biological and physiological analysis indicates that the definite, uniform motion characteristic of life issues from an energizing heat within.[43] The equivalence is drawn between this fire and the soul as the source of life, and this heat is found latent in all parts and elements of the world: fire can be obtained by striking two stones together; the heat within water is what prevents its becoming ice; air can be generated by heating water.[44] Fire sustains and permeates the entire world, interfused with every other nature and constituting the ruling principle (ἡγεμονικόν) of the universe.[45] As parts of the cosmos are sensible and rational, their dominant principle must also contain these attributes and in an eminent fashion, for it could not rule its own peers nor elements which surpass it in nobility. Fire, the energizing spirit of the universe, must possess its own rationality and sensibility—identifiable with the nature of fire itself. Since it penetrates the world of things and men, everything must possess a consciousness and a sensibility: "It is therefore the nature which contains the entire world and guards it, and it itself is not without sense and reason."[46] It follows necessarily that the world, the entire cosmos, possesses

---

[41] *De Natura Deorum* ii. 7. 18; 8. 21.

[42] *Ibid.* ii. 9. 23. [43] *Ibid.* ii. 9. 24; 11. 31.

[44] *Ibid.* ii. 9. 25. [45] *Ibid.* ii. 11. 29.

[46] *Ibid.* ii. 11. 29; 12. 32.

in its *principatus* a conjunction of mind and nature which is the comprehensive source of creation and of providence.

This natural science which found fire as the energy of the universe rather than atoms in random movement led Zeno to define nature itself as an artistic or a craftsmanlike fire (*ignem esse artificiosum*): what is done by the human hand is done far more skilfully (*multo artificiosius*) by nature, which is both this artistic fire and the teacher of all the other arts.[47] *Artificiosa* can be predicated of every nature in the sense that it follows a method or procedure (*viam quandam et sectam*) appropriate to achieve a particular end. But the comprehensive nature of the world itself "is styled by Zeno not merely 'craftsmanlike' [*artificiosa*], but actually a 'craftsman' [*artifex*]—a provident one who takes into account the use and possibilities of all."[48] This lodges the divinity of the world as the fourth grade of the orders of natures, possessed of intelligence and creativity and containing all lesser natures as elements or as organic parts. The divine is the source of all movement.

The innate rationality of the world also explains the Stoic acceptance of the telling force of universal consent. For the Epicureans, this consent indicated an internal *prolepsis* which was reflexively self-justifying. For the Stoics, the consent was another instance of the rational universe, a theophany of the thinking world within the consciousness of men. Universal consent was not only the present, de facto concurrence of all men, but a *stabilis opinio* which had been tested by the passage of time. The Stoics stressed the purifying effect which succeeding generations effected upon human belief. No one any longer believed in the hypocentaurs or chimaera; men do believe in the gods even after the lapse of many centuries: "The years obliterate the products of opinion [*opinionis . . . . commenta*] but they strengthen the judgments of nature [*naturae judicia*]."[49] These judgments which come from nature and which are tested by time well up within the human soul to a belief that is beyond any explanation other than that of an underlying rational world spirit: "All have engraved on their souls, as

---

[47] *Ibid*. ii. 22. 57.   [48] *Ibid*. ii. 22. 58.   [49] *Ibid*. ii. 2. 5.

it were, the innate belief [*innatum est*] that there are gods."[50] To challenge common consent on either divination or the existence of the gods is to posit a world removed from reason.[51]

In the Epicurean reflexivity of principle, these two arguments (from the motion of things and the movement of the mind) are distinguished in structure and divergent in value; with the comprehensive principle of the Stoics, they ultimately merge into a single explanation which is equally telling whether it begins problematically with organic motion in physics or with the data offered by chronicles, histories, public religion, and poetry.

The Academic stands within the theological dialogues not to present an alternative position, but to probe those already advanced. The Stoic is not pitted directly against the Epicurean; both are singly engaged by the New Academy. In the operational methods of Cotta or Cicero, one enters directly into the evidences presented or into the argumentations constructed without reducing either to a third system. Any philosophy can be twisted into absurdity by the rephrasings of another school, but the absence of dogma within the Academy persuaded its members of an ability to enter any system and to manifest its inadequacies. The Academic must only address himself "to those things which have been said by you, but in such a way as to affirm nothing and to question everything."[52] Carneades is praised for destroying Stoic divination without affirming Epicurean physics.[53] Cotta confesses that this antithetical method is far easier than the positive demonstrations of propositional truth, and that in no science is this more evident than in physics.[54] Here the Academician found his spirit one with Simonides' reply to the questioning Hiero: "The longer I think the matter over, the more obscure it appears to me."[55] Thus the method of attack for the Academy lay in inserting itself within the structures of its opponents and destroying them, in concluding that "the method [*rationem*] which you bring to bear is not sufficiently strong."[56]

[50] *Ibid.* ii. 4. 12.
[51] *De Divinatione* ii. 12. 33; 33. 84.
[52] *Ibid.* ii. 3. 8.
[53] *Ibid.* ii. 72. 150.
[54] *De Natura Deorum* i. 21. 57-58, 60.
[55] *Ibid.* i. 22. 60.
[56] *Ibid.* i. 22. 62.

The Epicureans had erected their theology upon a statistical survey and had accounted for their conclusion through an underlying concept. The Academy questioned both the adequacy of the sample and the accuracy of its causal explanation. Universal consent had been established in such a sloppy manner as to leave it unfounded and false (*cum leve per se tum etiam falsum*). There were too many divergent civilizations and barbaric tribes of which the Roman world possessed no knowledge to allow any fact to be asserted as of common belief. So vast was the area of human culture, uninvestigated and unknown, that one could contend with equiprobability that many people were too underdeveloped to possess a concept of god. Even within Western civilization, this history of philosophy recorded such positions as the agnosticism of Protagoras of Abdera and the positive atheism of Diagoras of Melos and Theodore of Cyrene. Even more serious, the Epicureans had failed to understand the cause of what assent there was; they had equated external agreement with internal conviction. But the treatment meted out to such figures as Protagoras—exile and obloquy—had made many others reluctant to confess disbelief or religious scepticism openly. While the Epicureans had traced fear and superstition back to religious conviction, Cotta is suggesting the reverse: religious protestations issue from the fear of penalties visited upon the non-conformist by a hostile community. In place of what men say, Cotta proposes the criterion of what they do, a pragmatic test of belief. If men were authentically convinced of the gods, could they conceivably commit temple theft, judicial perjury, or familial impiety? Apply these as criteria, and little is left of this putative universal consent.[57] The Epicureans had founded their theological arguments in the reflexivities of human thought as opposed to a secular physics. The Academy countered that they had neither correctly appraised this thought nor causally explained it: "That method of yours [*ratio ista*] has not been adequately put to the test [*explorata*] to sustain the conclusions you wish."[58]

[57] *Ibid.* i. 23. 62-63.   [58] *Ibid.* i. 23. 64.

The Stoics attempted a theological equation between nature and intelligence, and they did so, contended the Academy, through an apotheosis of the irrational and the unintelligent. To argue from common consent becomes now self-contradictory. The *insani* and the *stulti* become the measuring rod of recondite and difficult matters; the uninformed are made the final judges in science: "And thus you want to judge these major questions by the opinion of the stupid—you especially who contend that the stupid are mad."[59] What the ordinary man thinks is no mark of what things are—these are distinct questions.[60] To appeal to theophanies is equally to call upon the unintelligent, to "old wives' tales," to "common talk rather than to solid argument."[61] This abdication of reason tells especially in divination. The Stoics refuse to consider the causal questions of Carneades demanding to know how such prophecies are possible, and they trot out their stories of successful prediction despite the attested evidence that diviners are usually liars and that these tales originate with the superstitious and the old.[62] In each of these arguments, the Stoics draw conclusions from the irrational and the uneducated to assert an ultimate identification between nature and mind.

Nor is the appeal to the experience of celestial movements as an immediate experience of divinity the less irrational. It is acceptable to neither the ignorant nor the educated: "As if anyone of us really gave the name of Jove to the heavens rather than to the Jove of the Capitol, or as if it were self-evident and universally agreed that those beings are divine."[63] Balbus bitterly complained that this is not an adequate treatment of his arguments from motion, and Cotta agrees. The real investigations of the Stoic arguments from harmonious and sympathetic movement are postponed to the refutations in the definitional and qualitative questions.[64] The shift is deliberate and brings into bold relief the initial objection of the Academy to each: Epicurean theology has failed to understand the extent

[59] *Ibid*. iii. 4. 11.
[60] *Ibid*. iii. 7. 16-17.
[61] *Ibid*. iii. 5. 13.
[62] *Ibid*. iii. 6. 11; *De Divinatione* i. 4. 8.
[63] *De Natura Deorum* iii. 4. 11.
[64] *Ibid*. iii. 7. 18-8. 20.

and causes of religious belief; Stoic theology has constituted the irrational as the criterion of the scientific. The Academy will deal with their basic errors in epistemology and in physics in the subsequent analyses of divine form, happiness, and providence.

X.

The Identification of the Gods

THE DEFINITIONAL issue does not occupy the central position within the operational method that it holds in the problematic. In the latter, it is the final specification of the subject in terms of its proper intelligibility; in the former, it is the initial identification which constitutes a subject apt for the subsequent, qualitative predications which progressively realize an intelligible structure through the restriction and delimitation of attributions. The Ciceronian questions, as also the Aristotelian, make for an ongoing progress within the inquiries of philosophy, but the shift in method has its correlative shift in the location of argumentation. Within the operational context of the Ciceronian theology, the dialogues do not pause on the *quaestio nominis*. The Epicurean moves from the problems of existence to those of nature, rather than of name; the Stoic passes from the demonstrations of the divine existence to those which begin with questions of quality; Cotta follows this structure as the antithetical method takes its initiation from the statements of the opponents.[1]

In the theological tractates, it could not be otherwise. If there had not been antecedent agreement upon and positive identification of a name, no discussion of existence or nature would have been possible. The name, "god" or "gods," gave a community with which the three schools could begin an investigation: the existence of the reality it names forms the conjectural issues, and the nature of this reality functions as the questions of kind. It is this name which gave *controversia* its subject.

But the definitional issue deals not just with a word, but

[1] *De Natura Deorum* i. 17. 45; ii. 17. 45.

with the "force of the word,"[2] and the treatments of the existence have nailed down this further identification. The three schools agree that demonstration is possible through some variant of universal consent: the Epicureans explain this belief in terms of canonic necessities, while in Stoic physics it becomes another theophany of the innately rational world. The Academic, Cotta, founded his own assent upon the common opinions of the statesmen and founders of the body politic. In each there was a universal consent, a consent which differed as epistemological, physical or political justification was given it. This adds a new dimension to the original verbal consent; it gives a new force to the name which it did not bear before the beginnings of the dialogue: god has become a rational necessity for any thought at all. This agreement is only minimal, as its substantiations are divergent. But the conclusions of each treatment of divine existence contain a common element: within the perspectives of man and his thinking, god is. Universal consent injects a common, basic agreement in the use of the word "god," and it is this common denominator which allows the inquiry to proceed to problems about the divine nature itself. There is common agreement that no human being can do any thinking at all, theoretical or practical, without being involved in the notion of god. God has become a rational necessity for thinking.

The definitional issue, then, is solved in the theological tractates partially at the beginning of discussion and partially during the demonstrations of the divine reality. "God" began the dialogue by giving *controversia* a subject. A minimum force was given this name in that the existence of the divine is necessarily posited by human thought. This offers a basic intelligibility to the term which permits the theological focus to be upon questions of nature rather than of name, and which gives a stability to the interchange even during the accusations of ambiguity, denigration, and atheism.

[2] *De Inventione* i. 8. 10.

XI.

The Nature of the Gods

EPICURUS' contribution to theology, Velleius contended, issued from the proficiency with which his scientific work moved through the two moments of philosophy: invention and judgment. His logistic inquiries are reduced, within the rhetorical context of the Ciceronian dialogues, to these two periods: "These have been both discovered very acutely [*inventa sunt acutius*] and expressed very subtly [*et dicta subtilius*] by Epicurus, so that not everyone is capable of understanding them."[1] This conjunction underlies his vital role in the history of thought: he not only understood the abstruse and the recondite, but expressed their significance with the precision and mastery with which one controls tangible realities.[2] Particularly true is this in his discussions of the *vim et naturam deorum*.[3] In these qualitative issues the canonic, physics, and ethics combine to analyze the sources and inferences of theology, the internal composition of the gods, and the nature of divine happiness. The reflexivity in Epicurean principles had allowed for the differentiation of questions of theology from those of physics, while the canon would establish or justify principles of knowledge for either. The sciences do not now merge into a single science of the gods; rather the distinct sciences converge upon the same subject through divergent questions.

---

[1] *De Natura Deorum* i. 19. 49.

[2] *Ibid.* Torquatus, the Epicurean of the *De Finibus*, refers to the master as to "illo inventore veritatis." *De Finibus* i. 10. 32.

[3] *De Natura Deorum* i. 19. 49. This *natura deorum* indicates the principal interest of the dialogues. Cf. *ibid.* i. 6. 13; 7. 17. It is conjoined with *vis* here by the Epicurean, by the Academy in *ibid.* i. 44. 122, by the Stoic in *De Divinatione* i. 6. 12; 7. 13; 9. 15, and by Cicero in *Tusculanarum Disputationum* v. 25. 70.

Reflexivity also characterized the principle of Epicurean ethics in that the source of human action became the attainment of happiness. Negatively, this happiness was described in the initial axiom of Epicurus' κύριαι δόξαι, and Velleius uses it as a preface to his inquiries into the divine nature: "The happy and the deathless can neither receive nor inflict trouble on another; as a result, they can feel neither anger nor favor, for all such things belong to the weak."[4] Positively, the *summum bonum* equates with pleasure. One does not demonstrate this equation. It is evident in the natural attraction-repulsion movement of any animal. Pleasure stands obvious as the real motive for action and self-justifying as an ethical concept. It cannot be proved the true incentive of human choice, for nothing is better known.[5] This is not to posit an indiscriminate hedonism, as a present pleasure may make for a later and greater sorrow. It is a calculated utilitarianism, and great pain may well devolve upon one who fails to pursue pleasure by its method.[6] Granted a correct understanding of human motivation, one can reduce any heroic action to a careful grasp of personal interest. "Do you really believe that they charged an armed enemy or treated their children, their own flesh and blood so cruelly, without thought to their own utility and advantage?"[7] This personal reflexivity peaks in the definition of the greatest pleasure as the total absence of pain; it is an emancipation in which a man reaches through his freedom the highest form of human happiness.[8]

That the gods are happy and eternal is so universal a conviction that it indicates its source within the necessary structures of the human mind. The combination is properly divine. Men might become happy through ethical living, but they are destined for death. Atomic particles, in contrast, are everlasting, but without the sensitive life necessary for happiness. Only the gods combine both attributes, and this conjunction consti-

---

[4] *De Natura Deorum* i. 17. 45. For this in Epicurus, cf. Diogenes Laertius, *op.cit.*, x. 139. The critical position which this axiom occupies is recognized by the Academic, Cotta: *De Natura Deorum* i. 30. 85.

[5] *De Finibus* i. 9. 29-30. [6] *Ibid.* i. 10. 32.

[7] *Ibid.* i. 10. 35. [8] *Ibid.* i. 11. 37-39.

tutes their uniqueness. "Nature, which shaped our conviction that there are gods, also engraved on our minds that they are eternal and happy."[9] This hendiadys governs considerations of the internal composition of the gods; while from their happiness alone, their external influence can be easily deduced. With these devices the Epicurean, Velleius, can divide his exposition into analyses of the divine form and of the divine activity.

Cutting across these theological predicates is the basic Epicurean distinction between nature and art, each denoting an autonomous source for knowledge of the divine form.[10] Here, however, the natural is equated with the spontaneous belief issuing from an internal πρόληψις, while reason is constituted by the inferential movements of the mind, *ratio* used as the Latin translation for Epicurus' ἐπιλογισμός.[11] Again, a preconceptual conviction of the mind reveals itself in a universal consent: "From nature all men of all nations possess the belief that the gods have human shape," and this community in belief dominates both dreams and waking thoughts.[12] Scientific inference moves to the same conclusion, whether the conceptual basis of the deduction be the happiness or the eternality of the gods. Velleius gives two arguments: first, it is fitting that the most exalted nature should be the most beautiful in form. ("Convenire videatur" is the expression, and it introduces into Roman theology the *argumentum ex convenientia* which will figure so strongly in the Middle Ages.)[13] Secondly, since virtue is an element of happiness and reason is indispensable for virtue, the gods must possess that shape in which alone intelligence is found.[14] But the anthropomorphic conclusion must be balanced. If the gods are happy, they must possess a human shape; if they are to be eternal, the correlation must not be absolute. Thus, the divine form does not simply identify as a body, but as a quasi-body; and they do not possess blood, but something like blood.[15] This allows for an entitative interpre-

[9] *De Natura Deorum* i. 17. 45.   [10] *Ibid.* i. 17. 46.
[11] Cf. Pease, ed., *De Natura Deorum*, I, 306. For this same distinction, cf. *De Finibus* i. 9. 30; *Tusculanarum Disputationum* i. 13. 29.
[12] *De Natura Deorum* i. 18. 46.   [13] *Ibid.* i. 18. 47.
[14] *Ibid.* i. 18. 48.   [15] *Ibid.* i. 18. 49.

tation of the divine, while in principle distinguishing them from men and from their universe.

As the divine happiness is perfect, so it is utterly reflexive. The argument of the Stoics, *nihil mundo melius*, has its counterpart in the Epicurean axiom about the gods, *nihil beatius*. Physical science had indicated no need to posit a supernal rational agency in the creation or administration of the universe; theology argues that such a concern would militate essentially against the divine nature. The tranquility, ἀταραξία, of the gods would be less than that humanly attainable if they involved themselves in the ownership or governance of the world of men and things. This would be to make their own pleasure contingent on such variables as the virtue and piety of men or their sins and injustice, as well as to involve them in an endless task of righting wrong and punishing evil. Such gods, rather than the happiest, would be the most grievously burdened of rational beings. But their happiness is an initial given, a constant which determines all subsequent inference. Therefore, a god is one who "does nothing, is involved in no duties, performs no tasks."[16] Their removal from any external commitments left the divine life a permanent calm of soul, a freedom from pain which identified with the purest and eternal pleasures. Positively, the focus of the divine activity is the god himself: "He takes his joy in his own wisdom and his own virtue, and he is certain that he will aways enjoy the greatest, eternal pleasures."[17] His thought is of himself; his happiness is with himself; his contentment is with his own future. Nothing else matters to him. The absence of external concerns possesses its correlative in the internal self-possession in joy.

Two consequences follow from this doctrine. The Epicurean theology allows for a rejection of the gods as actional principles and of the god who comprehensively identifies with the universe, as their physics had already obviated the reduction of human freedom to an epiphenomenon covering an inexorable fate. For the god who is properly called happy contrasts sharply with the overworked god of the Stoics. The very revo-

---

16 *Ibid.* i. 19. 51. 17 *Ibid.*

lutionary movement of the cosmos entails an incredible amount of labor, while repose is at the heart of happiness; the government and disposition of the universe destroyed for these Stoic or popular deities that tranquility which constituted an essential element of their transcendence over the human.[18] On the other hand, if the cosmic motion is not the product of mind, neither can its nature be simply identified with the necessity and determination of the Stoic εἱμαρμένη, "the theory that every event issues as the result of eternal truth and an uninterrupted sequence of causes [*causarumque continuatione fluxisse*]."[19] It was the Epicurean introduction of the swerve into atomic physics which spelled the death of any absolutely determined series of concatenated causes.[20] The sharp separation in principles allows for different orders in movement which do not reduce to one another: the divine and the cosmic, the human and the irrational.

The second thrust of this theology is towards the destruction of fear and superstition. Judgment is not visited upon men by these gods who do not concern themselves with human histories, and divination is fraudulent for the divine does not act upon the irrational processes of nature. Epicurean theology becomes therapeutic and cathartic. In discovering the real causes of human changes and of the movements of the universe, it rids men of an unscientific ascription of value to prophetic rites and releases them from overriding terrors before future punishments.[21] While this purifies the human race from a false worship built upon contract and propitiation, it liberates a true reverence for the gods. The Epicurean contended his was an altruistic *pietas*, one which venerated the gods simply for what they were and which looked for no return either in this life or the next.[22] No concept of barter or bargain here with the divine for material prosperity! It left the wise man free for a life which resembled that of the gods: "He is always happy. His desires are limited. He is fearless before death. He

---

[18] *Ibid*. i. 20. 52.   [19] *Ibid*. i. 20. 55.   [20] *De Fato* 9. 18-20.

[21] *De Natura Deorum* i. 16. 43; 17. 45; 20. 55; 20. 56. *De Finibus* i. 19. 63; 21. 71.

[22] *De Natura Deorum* i. 17. 45; 22. 56.

has no terror because he knows the truth about the immortal gods."[23]

There is certainly no significant difference between such a position, countered the Stoics, and an open, avowed atheism. The latter denied the *esse deos*, while the former deprived them of all rational care and significant activity. A translation takes place as the conclusions of one philosophy are transmuted into the terms of another, and within the organic, interrelated Stoic world-order, reflexive principles become artificial diremptions of the real. Rephrased in the comprehensive principle which identifies with the world, the autonomous and isolated Epicurean gods in being excluded from the universe are excluded from existence itself. In Balbus, this comprehensivity in causal explanation merges with the pragmatic orientation of Roman philosophizing: "It is not evident to me that anything which does not act can be said to exist at all."[24] Whoever grants the existence of the gods must concede them some activity, indeed activity of the highest sort.[25] In problematic fashion, questions of the divine nature are distinguished from those of the providential care of the universe, but the effect of the single principle tells in the one reality which is the ultimate solution of them all.[26]

An equation can be drawn between the divine nature and the world, beginning with either one of the terms. A priori, one can begin with the notion of the gods, one that specifies that in all nature nothing is more exalted. But the world is essentially that *quo nihil excellentius.* "And by this method [*ratione*] one can conclude that the world is god."[27] Or one can argue a posteriori from those things which the world produces, particularly in the uniformity and regularity which it authors in movements and change.[28] In a world permeated with rationality, one could begin either from definition or from effects to the same purpose. Problematically, the initia-

---

[23] *De Finibus* i. 19. 62.

[24] *De Natura Deorum* ii. 16. 44.

[25] *Ibid.* ii. 30. 76.

[26] *Ibid.* ii. 16. 44; 29. 73.

[27] *Ibid.* ii. 17. 45-47.

[28] *Ibid.* ii. 18. 48–21. 56. The Stoics preferred the a posteriori to the a priori argument. Under the influence of a basically problematic method, "facilius cognoscentur ex eis rebus ipsis quas mundus efficit."

tions of the argument might differ, but their conclusions must identify. As god merges entitatively with the universe in movement, so the divine form is not a human one, but "a figure which alone encircles and encloses in itself all other figures." Epicurean ignorance of physics and of geometry prevents their comprehending the global contour of the gods, for it follows necessarily from a theology which merges with physical science: "Their regular motion and steady order could not have been maintained in any other shape."[29] The same arguments establish the divinity of elements within the divine universe, i.e., of the stars, the moon, the sun, and planets:

> This regularity in the stars, their exact punctuality throughout all eternity notwithstanding the enormous divergences within their paths—I can't understand all this without seeing it the product of mind and reason and purpose. Since we observe the same thing among the planets, we must enroll them also in the number of the gods.[30]

An eternally constant order in the changes upon the earth, in the movements of the planets, and in the motions of the stars indicated the existence of an intelligence productive of this regularity—and as such it had served as a basis for the demonstration *deos esse*. Now it found the attribution of spherical, as the necessary condition of this order. Motion serves as a foundation for inquiry into either the existence or the presence or the nature of the gods. Balbus frequently pauses in his considerations to show that one argument substantiates convictions about the other two. Thus, at the completion of his arguments of the divine form, he has concluded to a vast company of divinities, within the deified universe, whose single principle is the craftsman-fire and whose movements conspire to preserve and to protect all things.[31]

The providence which the Stoics predicate of the world was both creator of the dynamic order of the subsumed parts and its abiding, conserving cause. Within the context of the rhetorical, the problems of providence became a vast topic (*mag-*

---

[29] *Ibid*. ii. 18. 47-48.   [30] *Ibid*. ii. 21. 54.   [31] *Ibid*. ii. 23. 60.

nus sane locus est) treated usually by the school in three parts. These parts are not a logistic sequence of arguments, the one building on the other, but a problematic breakdown whose individuality was due to the peculiar data from which each began. These three *partes* or *loci* (Balbus uses either indifferently) are not unlike the Thomistic *viae* in their autonomy and complementarity, though very different in their facts and argumentation. The first simply prolongs the methods previously employed to prove the existence of the gods, extending those arguments to demonstrate that the world is governed by their judgment. The second argues to a comprehensive, sensate nature to which all other things are subject. The third details the Stoic description of the interrelation and mutual involvement of heavenly and terrestrial movements and natures. The first emphasizes methodology (*ab ea ratione quae docet*); the second, the comprehensive principle (*omnes res subjectas esse naturae sentienti*); the third, the entitative sub-structure of all reality. It is only an emphasis, as principle, method, and interpretation figure in all three *partes*.[32]

If the divine activity must be the most distinguished and nothing can be more distinguished than to govern the universe, the world must lie under the providence of the gods.[33] Or if the world is not administered by the gods, it must be governed by something superior to them. But nothing is superior to the gods.[34] Human intelligence itself can only be explained as something which has come from the divine, and to concede divine intelligence is to grant a providence exercised over things of the highest moment.[35] These arguments amplify previous demonstrations of the divine existence and they extend their lines to picture the gods mutually involved in their governance of the universe: "The gods are united together into a society or community, governing the one world as a united republic or a city."[36] Whereas the Epicureans had anthropomorphized the divine in giving them human shape, a form denied to the stellar or cosmic deities by the Stoics, these

[32] *Ibid*. ii. 30. 75.   [33] *Ibid*. ii. 30. 76.   [34] *Ibid*. ii. 30. 77.
[35] *Ibid*. ii. 31. 78-79.   [36] *Ibid*. ii. 31. 78.

latter gave the gods political and social relations like those of men.

The relation which the Stoics established between all things and the universal nature was contrasted with that of the Epicurean physics on two points: nature as a principle and nature as the world. The Epicureans split nature and reason, making the first an irrational force necessarily causative of the movements of bodies. The Stoics' nature participated in intelligence and methodologically indicated the essences and the purposes for which she worked—possessed of a skill that no human art or technique could attain by imitation.[37] The Epicureans divide nature as the world between the void and the atoms and their attributes. The Stoics assimilated the universe to a tree or an animal, uniting a diversity of elements into a single organic whole. Three lines of argument come out of such an assimilation.

If some parts are rational, a fortiori, the whole must be intelligent. The union of these parts points to a single unifying nature; a unity in sympathetic motion includes everything within its ambit: "Those things which travel towards the center of the earth, or which move from the center upwards, or which rotate in circles around the center constitute the one continuous nature of the universe [*ea continentem mundi efficiunt unamque naturam*]."[38] One could tell the presence of intelligence in the marshalling of any army or in the navigation of a fleet: "When do these ever evidence such a degree of skill in nature as does the world itself?"[39] The alternatives which this initial argument posits are: either one must admit that nothing is ruled by an intelligent nature or that the world is so ruled.[40] The second argument runs from effect to cause: how would it be possible that the universe which contains everything not possess such an intelligent nature? Things which produce something from within them must have a more perfect nature than the effects which are produced from them. The rationality of the product indicates the character of the whole.[41] The third is the boldest contention the Stoics ad-

[37] *Ibid*. ii. 32. 81.   [38] *Ibid*. ii. 33. 83.   [39] *Ibid*. ii. 33. 85.
[40] *Ibid*.   [41] *Ibid*. ii. 33. 86.

vanced: the argument from this as the best of possible worlds. "Given the existence of these elements, the best that could be produced from them has been produced."[42] In spite of the probabilities against it, the world has effected life and reason, and the "parts of the universe are so constructed that they could not be better for utility or for beauty."[43] The products of nature are manifestly better than those of art. If the latter could not be produced without intelligence, how could the former? One spontaneously recognizes the effects of intelligence in a statue or a painting, in the course of a ship, the working of a sundial or of a water clock. How can anyone pretend to rational consistency in denying the same or a greater intelligence to a universe which includes both the works of art in question, the craftsmen who made them, and all of nature besides?[44] To deny reason of nature is to think more highly of an Archimedes in making a model of the revolutions of the firmament than of the nature which created and conserves them.[45] The arguments under the first *pars* rose to the motions of the cosmic body politic; in the second, they mount again to a consideration of rational movements of the entire universe. Just as the shepherd in the *Medea* first thinks he sees some lifeless and inanimate object but comes to understand the artificial nature of a ship in the character of its movement, so must philosophic inquiry proceed. The scientific mind might well be puzzled at the first confrontation with the universe, but after he has seen "that its movements are bounded and regular and that all things are controlled by a fixed order and a changeless regularity," the rational nature of the process should indicate the product and the presence of mind.[46] It is the argument from constancy and invariance in motion to the provident god of the cosmos.

It is in the *pars tertia* that the great advantage of the wedding of the rhetorical and problematic appears. The inability of the arguments from change and movement to convince stems not from their inherent weakness, but from the jaded sensibilities of the unreflecting man. Aristotle had maintained

42 *Ibid.* ii. 34. 86.   43 *Ibid.* ii. 34. 87.   44 *Ibid.* ii. 35. 88.
45 *Ibid.*   46 *Ibid.* ii. 35. 89-90.

that if men lived beneath the earth in a world of artifacts and had suddenly emerged into the light of day, the vision of the sky and the experience of the invariant processes of the heavenly bodies would have convinced them immediately "that the gods exist and that these mighty marvels are their handiwork."[47] Familiarity has dulled the impact these should have upon the human mind. They fail to move men because "daily repetition and habit accustom our eyes with the sight, and we feel no wonder or scientific desire to uncover the causes [*rationes*] of those things which we always see."[48] What evokes this wonder is novelty rather than the intrinsic worth of the thing itself.[49] If the philosophical quest is to obtain its term, this sense of wonder must be reawakened; attention must be aroused and re-focused upon that beauty which men have callously taken for granted. The third *pars* rejects subtle argumentation for a phenomenological description of the harmonious movements and beneficent interchanges within the universe.[50]

The description moves from the earth, its atmosphere, the sun, planets, and constellations to the celestial order of the universe.[51] "If any man fails to be impressed by this cooperation of all things, . . . I know for certain that he has simply failed to give them his attentive consideration."[52] From the heavens, the Stoic turns to the earth and its life: vegetation, animals, and a prolonged, final description of the wonder that is man himself—his mind, his speech, his artistic control over nature and his scientific conquest even of the heavens, terminating in astronomy, for in "contemplating the heavenly bodies, the mind arrives at a knowledge of the gods."[53] The thrust of this, by far the longest section of Balbus' tractate, is not so much inferential as it is phenomenological—an effort to detail what his interlocutors already know, but to describe it with such eloquence that its intrinsic marvel appears in a new light. Here speech becomes the *domina rerum*; the *eloquendi vis* is both *praeclara* and *divina*;[54] and the Stoic acknowledges the

---

[47] *Ibid*. ii. 37. 95.
[49] *Ibid*.
[51] *Ibid*. ii. 39. 98–46. 118.
[53] *Ibid*. ii. 47. 120–61. 153.

[48] *Ibid*. ii. 38. 96.
[50] *Ibid*. ii. 39. 98.
[52] *Ibid*. ii. 46. 119.
[54] *Ibid*. ii. 59. 148.

critical role of rhetorical skill in this reawakening of human awe: "When I discuss this, how I wish that I possessed your eloquence, Cotta."[55] Rhetoric provides the instrumentalities not only for the invention and defense of scientific positions, but for the wonder which generates the entire philosophic enterprise and to which it is ultimately resolved.

The world that is both divine and provident constitutes a comprehensive deity into which the Stoic assimilates all others, after rejecting the reflexive gods of the Epicureans as a doctrine of veiled atheism. The actional gods of popular religion are demythologized. They are either departed benefactors whom the community has later vested with divinity or some major force, corporeal or intellectual, which has been abstracted, personified, and divinized. Zeno introduced this latter explanation in his analysis of religious myths as primitive science. The legend of Uranus' mutilation by Saturn, and Saturn's imprisonment by Jove, for example, contained a clever, early understanding of physics: the primordial fire needed no sexual organs to create the universe. Saturn, the Greek Kronos (to be identified with χρόνος) is obviously that time whose bonds lie with the movements of the heavens.[56] One does not repudiate these myths, but attempts to grasp the understanding contained within their rude imagery.[57]

From these actional gods, the assimilative process moves towards the concatenated series of efficient causes which the Stoics called "fate": "an orderly succession of causes in which cause, linked to cause, generates something of itself."[58] It is sequence, without beginning or end, and, for some Stoics, absolutely determinant: "Nothing has happened which was not bound to happen, and likewise nothing is going to happen which will not find in nature every efficient cause of its happening."[59] Nothing is left to indeterminacy or chance, and if a man could know the connections between the causes, he could predict any future event without fail. Only the divine can possess this sort of knowledge, but men come to it through

[55] *Ibid.* ii. 59. 147.
[57] *Ibid.* ii. 28. 70.
[59] *Ibid.*

[56] *Ibid.* ii. 23. 59–24. 63.
[58] *De Divinatione* i. 55. 125.

signs. It is this which underlies all valid forms of divination, because the diviners grasp the symptoms or tokens of the future in present events. Time unrolls not haphazardly, but "the evolution of time is like the unwinding of a cable; it creates nothing new and only unfolds each event in its order."[60]

These efficient causes are themselves contained within the universal nature.[61] Fate is not the ultimate explanation of the universe; nature is. This is finally the "one and the same home for all," and it explains even divination.[62] The problem of the order of fate and that of human freedom was an ongoing discussion even within the Stoa; it involved ethics in its concern for human character and it dominated the logical analyses of future conditionals.[63] The solutions of Quintus do not seem to be those of Chrysippus.[64] But in either case, fate involved an order and this order was an effect of the providential nature.

It is this nature which Zeno, the master of the investigation of truth, had established as "hujus disputationis principium."[65] The divine is above all the comprehensive, underlying nature of the world—fire, as the rational energy which gives reality and definition to everything else, which conserves the patterns of the least and the greatest, and which contains all things in its embrace.[66] Popular deities have given way to natures; natures manifest the external order of beauty and the internal orientations of fate; fate itself is the final order under the rule of the single, divine nature, which stands in relation to them all as creator and providence.[67] This divine nature is ultimate in movement. As vegetable and animal life moves to a goal of full development and completion, so is nature as a whole in process. Though many external forces may impede the perfection of any of the individual natures, "nothing can frustrate the universal nature because this itself comprehends and contains all natures."[68] Thus, just as human thought became a moment in auto-revelation of world-thinking, so does each

---

[60] *Ibid.* i. 56. 127.   [61] *Ibid.* i. 55. 126.   [62] *Ibid.* i. 57. 131.
[63] *De Fato* 1. 1.
[64] Cf. *De Divinatione* i. 55. 125 with *De Fato* 17. 39.
[65] *De Natura Deorum* ii. 21. 57. Cf. *Academica* i. 10. 39.
[66] *De Natura Deorum* ii. 21. 57-58.
[67] *Ibid.* ii. 22. 58.   [68] *Ibid.* ii. 13. 35.

motion become an instantiation of the single movement of the divine nature towards its inexorable completion and perfection.

The Epicureans found the nature of god reflexive, utterly transcending human concerns and physical events; the Stoics posited a comprehensive divinity who merged immanently with the processes of nature and with the history and thoughts of men. The foundations of either position lie deep within the soil of their physical sciences, ethical analyses, and epistemological or dialectical theories. Here the Academy brings its guns to bear. With Velleius, the conflict of Cotta is mortal and his purpose refutation (*refellere*); with the Stoics, it is questioning and his purpose is discovery (*requirere*).[69] For Cotta, Velleius speaks well, coherently and carefully, but his position is basically wrong.[70] Balbus, on the other hand, does not defend his position as well as he might, but his position is more acceptable. Indeed Cotta is anxious to have Balbus regroup and return to sweep the field.[71] One should not, however, confuse the position of Cicero (which forms the final chapter of this section) with that of Cotta. In the *De Natura Deorum* Cicero sits only as a silent party to the conversation and distinguishes himself quite openly from the doctrine of Cotta.[72] In the other two dialogues the position of the Academy is represented by Cicero against the Stoics, while the Epicureans have no representative.

For Cotta, the Epicureans erred about the composition of the gods because of a false physics. There is no evidence for indivisible atoms nor for a void, and the postulation of a swerve is just as gratuitous as the denial of necessity to the disjunctive propositions.[73] If atomic construction were true, the Epicurean gods could not be immortal, for the composed come into existence, and what has become will perish, as the Epicureans themselves argued against the Platonists.[74] To parry this obvious thrust, the Epicureans speak of quasi-bodies and quasi-blood, but the most ordinary language analysis will

[69] *Ibid*. iii. 1. 1.
[70] *Ibid*. i. 21. 58-59; iii. 1. 3.
[71] *Ibid*. iii. 40. 95. Cf. *ibid*. i. 36. 100.
[72] *Ibid*. iii. 40. 95.
[73] *Ibid*. i. 23. 65; 25. 69-70.
[74] *Ibid*. i. 24. 68; 39. 110.

reveal that this is to talk nonsense: neither the proponents nor the adversaries of this doctrine can understand it.[75] Epicurean physics moves from unfounded principles through contradictory positions to absurd doctrines.

Nor is the canonical assessment of man and his thinking any more successful. The Roman belief, that the divine form is human, is due to institutional conditioning not to an internal *prolepsis*, is productive of an impossible dilemma, and is not the universal conviction of all men. Any knowledge of the history of political institutions would have indicated that a human frame was given the gods by the men in power to civilize the masses through the effects of religious practice. Psychologically, one could explain the belief through the irrational drive for an intimacy with the divine by reducing the gods to human dimensions. Whatever its origin, anthropomorphism is fostered by the fine arts and by the natural persuasion of men that the human form must be the most beautiful.[76] This last was just as culturally conditioned a belief as the other dogma of Epicurus that intelligence could only dwell within a human shape.[77] If the gods must have the most beautiful shape, an impossible consequence follows: either they are all alike or there is a degree of beauty among them. If each is identical to the other, they would have no means of distinguishing among themselves; if not identical, the divine is not the most beautiful.[78] Finally, the Epicureans have failed again in their statistical survey. A study of comparative religions indicates that neither the Egyptians nor the Syrians fasten on human form as characteristic of divinity. The former, for example, worship the crocodile, the ibis, and the cat.[79] What Velleius had done was to explain a universal belief in terms of underlying concepts. Cotta counters with a contrary explanation through cultural or psychological conditioning, with a contradiction inherent in the Epicurean position, and with a sweeping denial of the universality of the belief. The failure of the Epicurean lies within the *Canon* itself: the preconception is not a self-justifying concept. It is like any other empty

[75] *Ibid*. i. 25. 71–26. 74.   [76] *Ibid*. i. 27. 77.   [77] *Ibid*. i. 36. 87.
[78] *Ibid*. i. 29. 80.   [79] *Ibid*. i. 30. 81.

imagining—one not founded on the sensation derived from a manifest object. If the only proof for the existence and nature of the gods is that some men possess this idea, "What difference does it make whether we think of a hippocentaur or of a god?"[80] Even granted the concept, the concept does not justify the reality or explain the nature of its referent.[81] There is an ironic twist to the Academic dismissal: Velleius, who denied that god can be demonstrated from motion, hears his principle of internal preconception twice reduced to a *motus animi inanis*.[82]

The Epicureans' error in ethics issues from their analysis of the existence and nature of human happiness. Epicurus proposes to remove the influence of the divine from human history in order to free men from the terrors of superstition. Cotta suggests that "terrors that do not very seriously alarm ordinary people, according to Epicurus haunt the minds of all mortal men."[83] In fact, Cotta contends he has never met anyone more terrified than Epicurus of the things which he protests are not terrible at all, indicating that the terrors of religion are more the product of Epicurean projection than of sociological survey.[84] Secondly, there is a fatal error in the doctrine of happiness. Even if one takes seriously the Epicurean affectation of distaste for the pleasures which merely appeal to the senses and prescinds from the identification of pleasure with happiness, one is left with utter idleness: "Obviously, like spoilt children, Epicurus thinks there is nothing better than idleness [*nihil cessatione melius*]."[85] The gods are given a state that a man would think unbearable.[86] Even virtue is denied them, for virtues lie with some activity, and these deities are totally inactive.[87] By his own standards of pleasure, Epicurus fails, for he has made god so reflexive as to be incapable of any pleasure from another and of any thought except about himself. Cotta asks what a hollow happiness is this which consists of each god occupied eternally in considering how happy he

---

[80] *Ibid*. i. 38. 105-106.   [81] *Ibid*. i. 38. 107.   [82] *Ibid*. i. 38. 105-106.
[83] *Ibid*. i. 31. 86. Cf. *Tusculanarum Disputationum* i. 21. 48.
[84] *De Natura Deorum* i. 31. 86.
[85] *Ibid*. i. 36. 102.   [86] *Ibid*. i. 24. 67.   [87] *Ibid*. i. 40. 110.

is.[88] Inactive happiness is just as absurd as self-justifying concepts and uncaused swerves.

Cotta's arguments against this physics, canonic, and ethics give way to the central charge against Epicurus: he destroys the very foundations of religion.[89] The final test of anything in Roman philosophizing lies with its *actio*, with its effects upon political and social life. If these are false, the antecedent argumentation must be in error. It is the *actio* which indicates the *natura*, not in the problematic sense that activity is structured by and significant of form, but in the practical relevance of life to argument. Life judges philosophizing, and Cotta maintains that Epicurean theology fails this test. If the gods do not concern themselves with men, why should men concern themselves with the gods?[90] The sanction for oaths, the piety of the home, and the ritual practices of the state are destroyed. The altruistic boast of Epicurean religion simply does not wash: there is neither excellence left in their gods nor obligation remaining to man. What is the objective worth of any being so totally caught up in the fascination of his own pleasure, so engrossed in himself that he benefits no one, so egoistically self-centered that his life is eternally idle and useless? On the other hand, piety flows out of justice; and what is the obligation of any human being to such a god?[91] "Epicurus, when he removed from the immortal gods their power to confer aid and favor, uprooted and destroyed all religion from the human soul."[92]

In postulating these gods who care neither for themselves nor for each other, Epicurus was not actually attempting a defense of deities in whom he believed. Posidonius is quite correct in his analysis: Epicurus does not really believe in the gods at all. He could not have been so imperceptive to miss that these gods in human form, with quasi-bodies and quasi-blood, incapable of caring or acting, are impossible. Epicurus saw this and "actually abolishes the gods, although professing to retain them." To avoid public odium, he has defended the existence

[88] *Ibid.* i. 41. 114.
[89] *Ibid.* i. 41. 115.
[90] *Ibid.* i. 41. 115; 44. 123.
[91] *Ibid.* i. 41. 116–42. 117.
[92] *Ibid.* i. 43. 121.

of the gods, but he has given them a nature which makes their existence impossible or irrelevant.[93]

Stoic theology emerged from the philosophy of nature, and it was here that the Academic joined the issues against the equation between the world and the divine. The Stoic errors issue out of a misuse of language, a simple-minded interpretation, and a mistaken principle. The word "melius" from which so many of the rational attributes of the world were drawn is a highly ambiguous term.[94] Using it in the manner of the Stoics, one could argue from the proposition that nothing is better than the world, to further predication of literate, orator, mathematician and musician.[95] These are all better than their contraries, but unless the meaning of the superiority of the universe is nailed down, it offers no ground for further inference. Nothing is better than Rome, but this does not argue to its reasoning mind![96] Zeno, who originated this line of argument, was only a victim of language.[97] Equally demanding analysis was the premise that the part indicates the nature of the whole, for using it in the unexamined fashion of the Stoics could conclude to a world that was harpist and lute player.[98] If there was error in the divinization of the world, it was compounded in the discussions of the stars. In both cases, the Stoics built an a posteriori argument from the regularity and order of the movements. But not everything with a marvelous constancy and invariant repetition is to be deified, i.e., to be interpreted with a divine substructure. If this were true, one would have to divinize the regular currents of the Euripus at Chalcis or in the Straits of Messina, to say nothing of the pathological regularities of the malarial fevers.[99] Equally mistaken is this identification between even animate bodies and gods because any body is incapable of warding off eventual destruction. Either the internal, composite nature indicates origin and disintegration, or the sensitive and appetitive elements show a dependence upon external forces which spells eventual corruption. No living thing (*animal*) is everlasting.[100]

---

[93] *Ibid*. i. 44. 123-124.　　[94] *Ibid*. iii. 8. 21.　　[95] *Ibid*. iii. 9. 23.
[96] *Ibid*. iii. 9. 21.　　[97] *Ibid*. iii. 9. 22-23.　　[98] *Ibid*. iii. 9. 23.
[99] *Ibid*. iii. 9. 23–10. 24.　　[100] *Ibid*. iii. 12. 29–14. 34.

The central fault of the Stoics lies with what they did to nature. They correctly surmised that phenomena called for a rational explanation, but they merged all their principles into one nature, which identified ultimately with fire and with the world. Cotta follows the Epicureans in his distinction between nature and art, but turns them from reflexive to actional principles. Nature does not move by art (*artificiose*) as Zeno would have it, but communicates activity to all things by its own mutations and changes.[101] The great concordance, interconnection, and punctuality of the universe is not attributable to a single divine spirit, but to the forces of nature (*viribus naturae*), and nature herself moves not by divine reason (*divina ratione*), but spontaneously (*sua sponte*).[102] The Academic is proposing a third definition of *natura*, one which is neither comprehensive of all reality nor reduced to atoms indeterminately in motion. Nature becomes an actional principle, one which posits reality other than itself by its own activity and which will allow one region to be distinguished from another through its total dependence upon a particular efficient cause. This induces Cotta to correct the Stoics: "But not all things, Balbus, which possess a definite path and a constancy are to be attributed to a god rather than to nature."[103] This makes the Stoic reduction of popular deities to human benefactors or to natural forces absurd. These are autonomous realms and to attempt such a merger is to leave no distinction between the divine and the human, between the genuine divinities of accepted religious practice and the stars, the earth, the rivers, the heroes, and deified abstractions.[104] The attempt of the Stoics to demythologize popular legends raises their authors to the level of sophisticated physicists and continues the superstitions in the imaginations of the religious.[105] Besides straining credibility, it ends in nonsense: "Your notion of the sea or of the land possessing a rational intelligence is not merely something that I cannot fully understand, but I have not the slightest inkling what it means."[106]

[101] *Ibid*. iii. 11. 28.
[102] *Ibid*.
[103] *Ibid*. iii. 9. 24.
[104] *Ibid*. iii. 16. 40–20. 52.
[105] *Ibid*. iii. 23. 60–24. 62.
[106] *Ibid*. iii. 25. 64.

The Stoics fail equally in their attempts to prove a providence. The possession of intelligence, for example, is more conducive to the destruction of men than to their moral development. Moral evil is far more frequently the product of reason than are right actions, so much so that it would have been better if the gods had not given so terrible a power to men. Wine may occasionally aid the sick, but in general it debilitates them; thus, those who love the ill do not offer them wine. "That which we term 'reason' is disastrous to many and wholesome for but a few . . . . Since we cannot presume that the gods care only for these few, it follows that they are concerned with none at all."[107] The alternative is that the gods did not realize how men would use their powers, which is to argue against the competency of the divine knowledge. The issue is clear: if the gods are wise, they do not care; if they care, they are not wise. Under either hypothesis, the beneficent providence of the Stoics fails.[108]

The history of the evil and of the just comes to the same conclusion. Ennius' *Telamon*, in mourning over the dead Ajax, framed the judgment accurately: "If they were concerned, good men would prosper and the evil would receive evil. But it is not so."[109] The Academic pushes this one step further: if the gods were really involved with human history and with the good of men, they should have made all men good. If this was not possible, they could have at least rewarded the good. But they have done neither.[110] Roman history piles example upon example of the evil who prospered and of the good who suffered.[111] No house or republic would possess an internal structure and order if there were no reward for moral conduct and no judgment visited upon the evil, "so there is no divine providence [*moderatio*] if it makes no distinction between the good and the bad."[112] Whether one argues from the use made of inherent abilities or from the consequences which follow human virtue, the conviction is inescapable: "Either providence does not know its own powers, or

---

[107] *Ibid*. iii. 27. 69-70. [108] *Ibid*. iii. 31. 78. [109] *Ibid*. iii. 32. 79.
[110] *Ibid*. iii. 32. 79-80. [111] *Ibid*. iii. 32. 80-83. [112] *Ibid*. iii. 35. 85.

it does not regard human affairs, or it does not grasp what is the best."[113] The Academic is submitting the Stoic providence to the pragmatic test, to the external *actio* within life which alone can finally determine the validity of theory; and it does not pass the scrutiny. There is no reason within the history of men to postulate a comprehensive, benevolent providence, and the judgment against the Stoic rings almost as harsh as the condemnation of the Epicureans: "You wished to show me the nature of the gods [*quales di essent*], and you have only shown there are none."[114]

This does not leave the Academic atheistic. Quite the contrary, his gods are more orthodox than either the reflexive deities or the comprehensive world. Cotta takes his theology not from the physics of Zeno or the canonic of Epicurus, but from the political philosophy of Rome. These are the actional deities whose worship lies at the foundation of the body politic, the gods of the community established by the ancestors; and no *oratio* could ever move him from this faith. For the source of his belief is not philosophic, but civic; and its conservation lies with tradition and authority, with the forefathers and the *pontifices maximi* who have preceded him. His is the worship of the Roman people divided into *sacra, auspicia*, and prophecy; it is a religion of rites and these rites have worked. They have ennobled the city of Romulus, who established the *auspicia*, and of Numa, who constituted the *sacra*, and have marked her growth to become the most powerful city in the world. Cotta believes in the gods because he believes in the ritual of the gods. Its efficacy and the authority of the body politic should be proof enough for any man.[115] But this belief does not obviate debate. There is a distinction between the opinion which one shares with his fellow man upon good authority and the *ratio* which it is the philosophic task to deliver. The diremption is not the problematic distinction between the fact and the reasoned fact, but between the grounds for opinion—*ratio* and *auctoritas*: "From you, a philosopher,

---

[113] *Ibid*. iii. 39. 92.   [114] *Ibid*. iii. 8. 20.
[115] *Ibid*. iii. 2. 5. Cf. *ibid*. iii. 17. 43.

I ought to obtain the cause [*ratio*] of religion; in our ancestors, on the contrary, I ought to believe even when no reason is given."[116] Scepticism and orthodoxy join in accepting the community's gods *auctoritate maiorum* and in attacking the pretensions of philosophers to establish a scientific theology.[117]

[116] *Ibid.* iii. 2. 6.　　　　[117] *Ibid.* iii. 3. 7.

XII.

The Judgment of Cicero

WITHIN the complexus of the Ciceronian dialogues, a schematism emerges which is both diagrammatic in its structure and encyclopedic in the options which it offers for decision. Distinguishing between locomotion and the motions of the mind, the Epicureans established reflexive deities principally characterized by happiness. Stoics assimilated all movement, change, and variation to the organic motion of the world, arguing from this basis to a comprehensive god who identified with the universe and whose fundamental attributes appeared in a provident care of events and history. The Academic, Cotta, differentiated the spontaneous movements of nature in change from the traditions of the body politic, accepting from the latter those actional gods whose characteristic favor was won by rite and worship. In each of the three, universal consent figures in varying patterns. The Epicurean explained international beliefs through preconcepts of the mind. The Stoic subsumed any agreement under a universal nature whose epigenesis found divergent instantiations in opinions, divinations, theophanies, and the changes within bodies. The Academic accepted a consensus which formed an element within the public philosophy of Rome, and its universality was not a contemporary agreement among nations, but the abiding persuasion within the republic and its history. Motion denoted ambiguously the basis for belief—motions of the mind, changes within the universe, traditions of the body politic. Theological positions issued successively from the defenses of a canonic, the solutions of a physics, and the demands of social ethics.

Within the operational context of the dialogues, each of these doctrines has an *actio* which flows necessarily from its theories and which judges the value of its qualitative predications. (Under the heading of the qualitative issue, it was necessary to consider the divergent manners in which speculation would be transformed into deed because these *actiones* spelled out the real significance of the theoretical answers.) Doctrines on the changes in bodies, the motions of thought, the life of society have their ultimate meaning in the movements of men. In a philosophy whose central concern is relevance and commitment, the intelligibility and the truth of each proposition lie with its consequences upon human life. As each philosophic perspective had its representation within the dialogue and its results within life, so the interchanges of the debates embody a community which both allows for an *actio* of Cicero distinct from each and which exhibits his philosophy as an ongoing process, as a deed. The conversation itself is as much a part of the Ciceronian doctrine as first principles are embedded within Aristotelian conclusions. To remove problematic propositions from their basis in subject matters, principles, and methods, is to obtain individual sentences of no scientific value. Similarly, if one excises a "Ciceronian philosophy" from its location within the discriminations of positions and the activity of arguments, one pieces together divergent statements distorted and impoverished in their divorce from invention and judgment. The sterility of "Aristotle" and the eclecticism of "Cicero" come out of this simple-minded failure to understand a philosophy within the context of its own methodological structures and coordinates.

Cicero underlines the importance and purpose of his method in each of the theological tractates, emphasizing the product of debate as analogous to judicial decision. The Academic is not to be identified with the dogmatic sceptic, with those to whom nothing appeared true. The philosophic mind, confronting the confused intermixture of the specious and the authentic, must renounce the common claim to certitude, but not in favor of an equally doctrinaire agnosticism. The location of the scientific temper is at neither extreme, but in the middle, in the region of the probable.[1] The negativity of the

---

[1] *De Natura Deorum* i. 5. 12.

operationalists lies in their testing of each position advanced; the positive outcome is the discovery of verisimilitude, the invention of probability in argumentations or in conclusions. Essentially, it is a court procedure which attempts through debate to attain the probability possible for the wise, and its final moment is the judgment of the hearers, a judgment which the antithetical method leaves "whole and free."[2] This *judicium audientium* is an *actio* proper to every dialogue, not a suspension of judgment, but a decision reached through the open discussion possible to educated men, a decision about probability.[3] It completes a dialogue as a point terminates a line. Philosophy here is the continuous deed, the interchange of thought and discourse. The decision constitutes both the limit of its continuity and the product of its efforts. The Ciceronian does not differ from the other schools so much in individual doctrines, but in the character ascribed to its convictions: "As other philosophies contend that some things are certain, others uncertain, we are distinct from them in maintaining that some things are probable, others not."[4]

Probability does not characterize things, but statements, just as debate itself is constituted by oral discourse. In Ciceronian dialogue one does not focus immediately upon things or thoughts; he examines statements about either. If there is no statement, there is nothing upon which philosophic inquiry can be brought to bear or from which it can be composed. This correlation between scientific attention and human expression marks Ciceronian selection as semantic and pragmatic. Much like the orientation of contemporary American philosophy, Cicero attempts to establish probabilities about the nature of things or the workings of thought through an examination of warrantable statements and demonstrable activity. So the theological tractates are formulated in terms of discourse and practice. The nature of the gods is to be approached consciously through divergent statements of clashing positions: "I now lay before you the opinions [*sententias*] of the phi-

---

[2] *De Divinatione* ii. 72. 150. Cf. *Tusculanarum Disputationum* v. 4. 10-11; *De Natura Deorum* i. 6. 13-14.

[3] *De Fato* I. I.   [4] *De Officiis* ii. 2. 7.

losophers on the nature of the gods."[5] The entire world is
called to sit in judgment upon this topic and to render a decision because it involves the Roman society itself in profession
and in practice:

> . . . to attend in court, to try the case, and to deliver their
> verdict as to what opinions we are to hold about religion,
> piety, holiness, ritual, honor and loyalty to oaths, temples,
> shrines, solemn sacrifices, and about the very auspices over
> which I myself preside. For all these matters must be as-
> signed [*referenda*] to this question on the immortal gods.[6]

The Ciceronian focus upon *facta et verba* translated itself into
the peculiar relationship among the theological tractates. Comprehensively, *De Natura Deorum* deals with divergent theological questions and establishes the nature of the divine as
comprehensive. The other two do not introduce subjects which
have not yet been assimilated within the master dialogue, but
draw out its implications for the prophecies of the diviner and
for the free deeds of men before fate. As the problems in divinity had issued from Roman social usage and the perspectives were introduced through a consideration of statement,
so the consequences of theology must tell upon the speech of
prophets and upon actions possible to men.[7] The operational
use of statement and deed both contributes to and is determined by the Ciceronian judgment of the views constitutive
of the debates.

Epicurus babbled on the nature of the gods (*Epicurum bal-
butientem de natura deorum*), but his conclusions on divination and fate are correct.[8] In battle with the Old Academy, the
Peripatetics, and the Stoics, the Epicureans and the New
Academy join forces in their refusal to accept intrinsic values
of prophetic rituals.[9] Epicurus is consistent in this denial of
divination, for his indifferent deities are incapable of influ-
encing events and histories beyond their own; but his pivotal
doctrines of the nature of the divine are absurd—gods being

---

[5] *De Natura Deorum* i. 6. 13.
[7] *De Divinatione* ii. 1. 3.
[9] *Ibid*. i. 1. 1–5. 9. Cf. *ibid*. ii. 23. 51.

[6] *Ibid*. i. 6. 14. Cf. *ibid*. i. 2. 3-4.
[8] *Ibid*. i. 3. 5. Cf. *ibid*. ii. 50. 103.

transparent, living between two worlds, and possessed of limbs they cannot use. The qualitative propositions of Epicurus cut two ways: "He destroys the gods by an indirect path [*circumitione quadam deos tollens*] and does not hesitate to destroy divination directly."[10] Similarly, the Epicureans were correct in their denials of a necessitating fate, but the grounds of their convictions were such as to destroy all physical science —the introduction of the atomic indeterminacy and the denial of the necessity of disjunctive propositions.[11] On both divination and fate the Epicureans were right for the wrong reasons, and it was the accomplishment of Carneades to annihilate the pretensions of divination and the dogmas of fate without the postulation of Epicurean theology and physics.[12]

With the Stoics, the judgment was almost the reverse. Cicero regretted that they had rashly equated a defense of divination with an establishment of the divine, thus giving the Epicureans a handle for their humor.[13] Divination cannot be substantiated, while the existence of the gods must be true.[14] There is neither a matter proper to divination, nor formal consistency within the doctrine, nor any external evidence from which to demonstrate it. Whatever these natural or artistic rituals arrogate to themselves would be better handled by scientific study or technical control, individual experiences or political action: "There is no subject for divination, as reason indicates, nor can one discover a topic [*locus*] or a subject-matter [*materia*] for which we can prefer divination."[15] The Stoic teachings on fate and divination do not mesh. If actions are antecedently determined in a necessary sequence, of what use is prophecy? If these are not so determined, how is divination or any sure knowledge of the future possible?[16] Further, how is it possible to postulate fate and then to define divination as the knowledge of those things which happen by chance?[17] So mistaken were the predictions during the previous civil war, that the diviners were more often wrong than

[10] *Ibid.* ii. 17. 40.   [11] *De Fato* 9. 18.
[12] *De Divinatione* ii. 72. 150; *De Fato* 14. 31.
[13] *De Divinatione* ii. 17. 40.   [14] *Ibid.* ii. 17. 41.
[15] *Ibid.* ii. 4. 12.   [16] *Ibid.* ii. 8. 20-21.
[17] *Ibid.* ii. 10. 25-26.

right.[18] The few cases in which these practices worked are more easily explained by chance than by any art of divination.[19]

Within the operational method, however, a new perspective is given divination and fate, a sense in which the latter can be made acceptable and the former is to be fostered. For divination can be redefined in terms of the social uses of the body politic, and fate becomes the general laws of the physical universe. "The augural practices, religious rites and laws, discipline, the authority of the augural college are to be maintained because of the opinion of the masses and because of their great usefulness to the state."[20] Even though no intrinsic validity attaches itself to the claims of soothsaying, "I think that it ought to be fostered for the sake of the state and the religion of the community."[21] As divination is justified politically, so fate can be understood as physics, denoting those natural interconnections which govern the universe and to be distinguished from free choice in the manner in which Carneades does. These interconnections were constituted of efficient causes (*causae efficientes*)—meant quite literally as causes (1) antecedent to their effects in time and (2) determinant or factive of the result. Free choice was not so determined in its causes.[22] Even the god of prophecy could have no knowledge prior to the choice itself: "How much less had he knowledge of future events; for only by knowing the efficient causes of all things was it possible to know the future." Apollo could not foretell the deed of Oedipus for there were no causes in the nature of things making this murder a necessary object of choice.[23] With Carneades, one can allow for a fate in a natural philosophy while maintaining the freedom of man, and within these perspectives fate and divination are acceptable while true religion is purified from superstition.[24]

The Stoics came closer to Cicero in their understanding of the nature of the universe and the nature of the divine. The

[18] *Ibid.* ii. 24. 53.
[19] *Ibid.* ii. 21. 48; *De Fato* 3. 6.
[20] *De Divinatione* ii. 33. 70.
[21] *Ibid.* ii. 12. 28.
[22] *De Fato* 14. 32-33.
[23] *Ibid.* 14. 33.
[24] *Ibid.* 17. 39; *De Divinatione* ii. 72. 148.

interharmonies of the Stoic movement find their counterparts in the Ciceronian physics: "I must grant that there is a certain contact [*contagio*] among the things in nature."[25] These mutual influences have been established by the Stoic biological and physical researches, and they found a doctrine of the natural kinship (*cognatio naturalis*) among all things. Animals grow or decline with the changes in the seasons, while the ebb and flow of the sea are governed by the motion of the moon.[26] Astronomers have recorded the movements of the planets, and the fruits of their investigations show in the invention of an order within the stars which was not previously known.[27] Order within movements, which figured so dominantly in the Stoic theology, carries over into the Ciceronian.[28] The *De Natura Deorum* had indicated Cicero's opinion that "while Velleius thought that Cotta's speech was truer, I thought that Balbus came closer to the appearance [*similitudinem*] of the truth."[29] *De Divinatione* spells out this agreement in more detail: the characteristics of the universe in movement can found a demonstration of the existence of god. "The beauty of the world and the order of the heavenly bodies compel us to acknowledge that there is some excellent and eternal nature, one which deserves the reverence and the homage of the human race."[30] From the constancies and splendor which mark the movements of the physical world, one can argue to the *praestantem aliquam aeternamque naturam.*

The Stoics, the Epicureans, and the New Academy had accepted variations on the theme of universal consent, and even within the battles of the dialogues the common agreement on the *esse deos* emerges. *Controversia* formed a method of testing the pervasive character of this agreement, and out of the experiment comes a Ciceronian version of the same argument. In the dialogues, men got together, representing the major divergent views of the time—and agreed. The dialogues, then, instantiate this consensus, and the argument

[25] *Ibid.* ii. 14. 33.　　[26] *Ibid.* ii. 14. 33-34.　　[27] *Ibid.* ii. 71. 146.
[28] For order in movement in Stoic argumentation to the divine existence, cf. *De Natura Deorum* ii. 5. 15-16; 16. 43; 21. 56; 38. 97.
[29] *Ibid.* iii. 40. 95.　　[30] *Ibid.* ii. 72. 148.

from common belief incorporates the others and becomes the strongest.[31] There is no race so barbarous, no man so dehumanized that the existence of the divine is not professed. This *deorum opinio* may vary greatly in the *natura et vis* it ascribes to the gods, in the qualitative propositions it forms; but all men believe that there is a god. So pervasive a persuasion cannot issue from particular cultural conditionings or social formation. It must be regarded as a law of nature itself.[32] "We know that the gods are by nature; what they are [*quales*], we know by reason."[33]

With the Epicureans, then, Cicero rejects divination and theophanies as devices with which to prove the divine existence, while admitting the argument from universal consent. With the Stoics, he accepts both the movement of the universe and the movement of the mind as solid bases from which to infer the existence of the divine. In the argument from things, one arrives at a nature; in the argument from concept, one is taught by nature. There is a continuity here, running between nature as source and as final term. Further, nature is that which structures law, and it is supreme as the things which men seek in their activities.[34] Nature was either the character of a particular thing, the laws according to which it would operate, or the forces which it contained.[35] This character was not an underlying substructure, as with the Stoics, but the qualitative amalgam constituting the operational nature. What men did intellectually but prior to inference was done *duce natura*, as "led by nature, they say that the gods exist."[36] The phenomenally given would act in a particular

[31] For an example of this demonstration through consensus, cf. *Tusculanarum Disputationum* v.

[32] *Ibid.* i. 13. 30; *De Legibus* i. 8. 24-25.

[33] *Tusculanarum Disputationum* i. 16. 36.

[34] *De Legibus* ii. 1. 2.

[35] For *natura* in these three variations, cf. *De Divinatione* ii. 38. 80; 12. 50; 69. 143. Sometimes *natura* can be used with the genitive as a periphrasis for the thing itself. Cf. *De Natura Deorum* ii. 11. 29; 30. 77; 22. 58; i. 9. 23. For a discussion of the term in Cicero, cf. Pease, ed., *De Natura Deorum*, I, 109-110, 119, 250, 257, 268, 270, 299; II, 579, 614, 642-43, 683-84, 751, 753-54, 772, 990.

[36] *De Natura Deorum* i. 1. 2. For this expression in Cicero, cf. *ibid.* ii. 51.

way, and thus law and regularity could be found in nature.[37]
Many of the formulae for natural law Cicero would share with
the Stoics, but in the transposition these formulae were without the entitative interpretation which would ground them in
constructions which underlay the given. Just as for the Epicureans and the Stoics nature could denote either the principle
of action or the whole ruled by this activity, so for Cicero nature could indicate characteristics of the particular—whether
in attributes, activities, or influences—or the totality; but in
Cicero it is this totality which is the principle.

Men can be grouped with the gods on the basis of nature
as characteristic in kind. When one questions the nature of
men (*cum de natura hominis quaeritur*), he discovers that he
alone of mortals shares knowledge and virtue with the gods.[38]
It is for this reason that nature (taken now as the whole within
which man lives) has lavished so much upon the human race
and that men learn from it by imitation.[39] This makes possible an assimilation: men look up to the stars, see their revolutions and their movements (*conversiones omnesque motus*),
and learn that the human souls resemble his who formed
and fashioned them in the heavens.[40] Just as the movements
within the universe cannot take place without the influence of
the divine, so the motions of the mind by which a man imi-
tates these—as Archimedes in his orrery—could not take place
without a genius which is also divine.[41] This kinship between
the men and gods in reason founds the great totality which
binds them together, the *prima homini cum deo rationis soci-
etas*.[42]

Those who possess reason must also have right reason; since
right reason identifies with law, men are also associated (*con-
sociati*) in a community of law and in a community of correlative rights. Those who share among themselves in such

---

128; *De Finibus* i. 21. 71; ii. 10. 32; 33. 109; iv. 15. 41; v. 24. 69; *Tusculanarum Disputationum* i. 13. 30; iii. 2. 3; *De Legibus* i. 6. 20; *De Officiis* i. 35.
129; ii. 21. 73.

[37] *De Legibus* i. 6. 18; 15. 42; ii. 4. 8, 10.

[38] *Ibid.* i. 8. 24-25.   [39] *Ibid.* i. 8. 25-9. 27.

[40] *Tusculanarum Disputationum* i. 25. 62.

[41] *Ibid.* i. 25. 63.   [42] *De Legibus* i. 7. 23.

communities form a single *civitas*; and it is here that the final intelligibility of the gods and of the universe is reached, allowing both for qualitative predications about the gods and a proper understanding of providence. Both the gods and men obey this "celestial system, the divine mind, and the transcendently powerful god." It is the complexus itself, the order, which is finally divine, and the order is one of social and political relations. Mounting through the possession of reason, the community in laws and rights, an assimilation into the same unity, Cicero defines the societal universe as a comprehensive principle in terms of which all other things are ultimately explained: "This universe [*universus mundus*] must be conceived as a single city [*civitas*] common to both gods and men."[43] The divine, celestial system is that *natura* which is the source of all law prior to human societies and which identifies with this nature as the "force, the nature, the reason, the power, the mind, the will of the immortal gods."[44]

This characterization of theological reality as essentially social and political has many resemblances to that of the Stoics. For the Stoics also the universe is a community, and from them comes the definition, "The world is as it were the common home of the gods and men or the city of both; for they alone have the use of reason and live by law."[45] But in the Stoics, the political reality is only a moment in the understanding of the world in terms of a single underlying energy-principle. In both Cicero and the Stoics, the principle is comprehensive, and this principle identified with the universe. In the Stoics, the universe is a community of gods and men because of an underlying, thinking, single nature by which everything else is finally constituted and structured. In Cicero, the political universe does not reveal a level of reality deeper than itself; it is the system itself that is divine, a social order of justice and law. Men do not ultimately identify with the gods; they imitate them in the constancy and moderation they incorporate

[43] *Ibid.*

[44] *Ibid.* i. 7. 21. For eternal law which rules the universe, cf. *ibid.* ii. 4. 8-10; 7. 15-16.

[45] *De Natura Deorum* ii. 62. 154; *De Divinatione* i. 57. 131; *De Finibus* iii. 19. 64; iv. 3. 7.

into their private lives and in the building of societies and associations for men.[46] The universe is a unity not because of what underlies, but because of the activities by which the separate elements are mutually involved. Technically, Cicero takes from the Stoics a comprehensive principle, but he transmutes it through an existential interpretation which sees intelligibility through the statements and actions of men and which posits reality as the project of men and gods.

Here the full force of the translative question tells. The operational conflict emerges with probabilities which can be drawn in the formulation of a new philosophy—Cicero's own. But these conclusions are not simply transferred from the Stoics or from the Epicureans without the translative process, without a transmutation. Part of this translation consists in removing ontic interpretation and radically recasting the original significances of the propositions adopted. To posit a phenomenal interpretation is not to keep the experiences of the Stoics and to deny an underlying explanation; it is rather to transform the realm of explanation and of meaning. Reality is not an underlying unknown; it is rather the culminating principle of that which is. Reality is fundamentally societal, the product of the discourse of men and gods; and the translative question must refocus any meaningful proposition ultimately in terms of this society. It is this debate in which gods and men function as partners which constitutes the universe, the *universus mundus*, the total cosmic order. The operational method reaches its fulfillment in this translation, for the universe is constituted not by the irrational activity of things, but by the operations of rational beings—men and gods—in terms of which it is finally defined. The cosmic society is constituted as one in the dialogue of gods and men. The existentialist interpretation profoundly alters the original Stoic statement. The Stoics posited original gods to which the cosmic energy ultimately added men. Cicero's world is a community constituted by both gods and men, and there would be no world if there were not the actions and passions of men. The argument between the Stoic and the Ciceronian universe is one of

[46] *Ibid.* iv. 5. 11-12; *De Senectute* 21. 77; *Academica* ii. 41. 127-128.

interpretation here. It is not that one is more complete than the other. State either of them in terms of the other, and there is incompleteness; but stated in itself, there is nothing missing. Cicero is taking from the Stoic interpretation and correcting it in terms of that which is. And what is is the product of human experience and rational discourse.

Religion itself becomes a part of this dialogue between men and gods, part of the societal interchange which solidified the body politic in ceremonial homage of the gods. Religion becomes ritual.[47] Just as philosophy had become deed by dialogue, so religion becomes rite—the moment in which the two great parties of the universe conjoin in activity. These usages form an essential part of the world community and serve in turn the Roman state: "I consider it a part of wisdom to preserve the institutions of our forefathers by retaining their sacred rites and ceremonies."[48] As the Stoics could move from doctrines of society to their explanations within physics, so the Ciceronian dialogues can move from questions of physics to those of constitutions, because the effect of doctrine lies in the realities of politics.[49] The product of the debate is a community of thought, proven in controversy and experimentation, while the process of debate realizes the ongoing community in action and forms part of the great social interchange which is the universe itself.

The movement of the heavens, the motion of the mind, the traditions of the body politic—all of these substantiate the existence of gods, rational and social. These are the divinities attained by the Ciceronian theology, a doctrine whose relevance is in justice and law and whose ultimate principle is the single community of gods and men.

[47] *De Inventione* ii. 22. 66; 53. 161.   [48] *De Divinatione* ii. 72. 148.
[49] *De Republica* i. 13. 19.

PART III

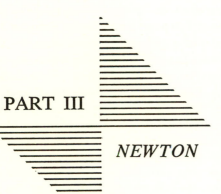

NEWTON

XIII.

Logistic Method

THE JUSTIFICATION of a universal mechanics for Isaac Newton lay in an understanding of the history of science, as its formation issued through the progressive corrections during the continuous battle between the ancients and the moderns.[1] Pappus of Alexandria attested the importance given mechanics in the investigation of natural things, and this evaluation by the *Synagoge* remained even after the moderns had purified physics of inquiries into substantial forms and occult qualities.[2] The errors in ancient philosophy stemmed not only from false principles employed in the explanation of phenomena, but from the problematic diremptions introduced between mathematics and natural philosophy. As Newton read their discussions, geometry constituted a rational mechanics, established by demonstration and distinguished by a perfect accuracy. The manual arts, on the other hand, composed a practical mechanics characterized by imprecisions and so discriminated from the accuracies of the purely mathematical. But exactitude rather differentiates one scientist from another than one body of knowledge from another. The proper relationship between the geometrical and the mechanical is one of inclusion and depend-

---

[1] Isaac Newton, *Philosophiae Naturalis Principia Mathematica* (Editio tertia aucta et emendata; Londini: Apud Guil. et Joh. Innys, Regiae Societatis Typographes, 1726). Reprinted for William Thomson and Hugh Blackburn; Glasgow: James Macleshose, 1871. All quotations from the *Principia* are taken from this edition and have either been translated by the author or checked by him in Motte's translation as revised by Cajori: Newton's *Mathematical Principles of Natural Philosophy and His System of the World*, trans. Andrew Motte, 1729; trans. rev. Florian Cajori (Berkeley: University of California, 1962). This translation will be cited as Cajori.

[2] Pappi Alexandrini *Collectionis Reliquias* viii, ed. Fridericus Hultsch (Berolini: Apud Weidmannos, 1878), III, 1022-29.

ence. Geometry is founded on mechanics. Mechanics constructs the definitional principles; and until the problems of the description of right lines and circles are solved, geometrical problems do not even emerge. Geometry is properly subsumed within mechanics, rather than artificially diversified from it: it is "founded upon mechanical practice, and it is nothing but that part of universal mechanics which accurately proposes and demonstrates the art of measuring."[3] It is not a universal mathematics which is assimilating physics, but a universal mechanics which is incorporating mathematics as a method.[4]

The moderns have advanced physics precisely by this merger of philosophy and mathematics so that the laws of either identify, but these advances have not been without their own defects in methods and principle. A popular procedure to which Newton contrasted his own was that of the "confrontation of contrary suppositions," a manner of arriving indirectly at conclusions through the controversial examination of the divergent manners by which any phenomenon might be explained.[5] Within this enumeration of possibilities, one ultimately concluded to an opinion by ruling out its contraries, "by inferring 'tis thus because not otherwise." This procedure lent itself to endless controversy, and it conflicted on almost every point with what formed "the proper method for inquiring after the properties of things . . . by deriving it from experiments concluding positively and directly."[6] Newton's loathing of controversy is common knowledge, but his letter to Oldenburg of July 11, 1672 explains this aversion not as the spontaneous reaction of temperament, but as the deliberate choice of scientific method: the conflict of possibilities is not the proper method of experimental philosophy.[7] The faults of controversy

---

[3] *Principia* "Auctoris Praefatio ad Lectorem" p. xiii (Cajori, i, xvii).

[4] For a comparison between the Cartesian universal mathematics and the Newtonian universal mechanics, cf. Richard McKeon, "Philosophy and the Development of Scientific Methods," *Journal of the History of Ideas*, xxvii, No. 1 (January-March, 1966), 17-18.

[5] *Isaaci Newtoni Opera quae exstant Omnia*, Commentariis illustrabat Samuel Horsley (Londini: Excudebat Joannes Nichols, 1779-1785), iv, 320. Henceforth cited as *Opera Omnia*. Note that it is precisely the method which Cicero employed which Newton is rejecting.

[6] *Ibid.*   [7] Cf. Cajori, ii, 674.

were often shifted to the defective sources of explanation, for the method has its correlative principles in artificial hypotheses —explanations erected without experimental warrant and whose only justification was in accounting for the phenomena under investigation.[8] These hypotheses effected endless objections and drew the energies of the scientist away from positive and direct derivation of theories from experiments and observation. They undermined all certitude in science, for anyone could at any time set up an alternative set of hypotheses.[9] If Newton had found fault with problematic distinctions and reflexive forms, he rejected with equal vigor operational procedure and actional principles.

Within the universal mechanics, one could distinguish the manual arts, geometry, and mechanics. Geometry studied the magnitudes of bodies constructed by mechanics. The manual arts undertook practical problems in the moving of bodies. Rational mechanics constituted the philosophy of all motions, no matter what forces effected them, and of all forces, no matter what motions they caused. Motion, then, became the subject both of arts and of philosophy, differentiated within the universal mechanics not in terms of divergent ends, but rather in terms of distinct powers, natural or manual, with mathematics assumed into either as the method of measurement and demonstration. Newton's own enterprise was with philosophy rather than arts, and the identities accomplished by the universal mechanics allowed for mathematical principles of this natural philosophy.[10]

Aristotelian scientific μέθοδοι allowed a subsequent ἀνάλυσις of their conclusions into correct relationship between the appropriate terms. Ciceronian *controversia* distinguished within the movement of philosophic method itself the supplementary moments of invention and judgment. Newtonian method was a twofold *derivatio*, a deriving of the principles from the phenomena and a deriving of further phenomena from these

---

[8] J. Edleston (ed.), *The Correspondence of Sir Isaac Newton and Professor Cotes* (Cambridge, England: University Press, 1850), pp. 154-56.

[9] *Opera Omnia*, IV, 314, 321.

[10] *Principia* "Auctoris Praefatio" pp. xiii-xiv.

established principles. The *Principia* translated discovery and criticism into the logistic correlatives of investigation and demonstration. The entire task of mechanics was realized either in the heuristic resolution of the phenomena of movement into the component forces or in the subsequent proof of other phenomena through these principles once they are established:

> But I consider philosophy rather than arts, and write not concerning manual but natural powers . . . and therefore, I offer this work as the mathematical principles of philosophy, for the whole burden [*difficultae*] of philosophy seems to consist in this: from the phenomena of motion, we investigate [*investigemus*] the forces of nature, and from these forces, we demonstrate [*demonstremus*] the remaining phenomena.[11]

These initial indications of method determine the broad outlines of the *Principia* and its system of the world. From the phenomena of the celestial movements, the system of the world derives the forces of gravity which account for the attractions exercised over the planets investigated. From these forces, once obtained, the subsequent sections of the book demonstrate the complicated motions of all the planets, the comets, the moon, and the sea.

Motion, or rather, the phenomena of motions, figure at each end of the total method, and the forces which effect these movements locate both as the objects of investigation and as the principles of demonstration. The method proceeds from the motions to forces, and from forces to posterior motions. The logistic method transforms not only the processes of philosophizing, but also the understanding of movement itself. Motion, for Newton, was not to be problematically distinguished into changes, alterations, increase-decrease, and locomotion; it was to be understood as the recession of bodies from each other or their impulsion towards one another or their coherence in shape and figure. All motions are locomotion, and they will vary among themselves in direction, velocity, and momentum. All physical phenomena can reduce to

11 *Ibid.* p. xiv.

these movements, as the motions themselves are resolved to succession in space; and this reduction makes the accomplishments of the *Principia* not exhaustive of the possibilities of the method, but suggestive of the future projects of the universal mechanics: "I would wish to derive the rest of the phenomena of nature by the same kind of reasoning from mechanical principles."[12]

As the Euclidean commentator, Pappus, had indicated a program in the investigations of physics, so the components of the method could be best translated into the devices which *Elements* XIII had established in the constructions and demonstrations of geometry—analysis and synthesis. Synthesis, for Aristotle, had contrasted with *diairesis* as the proposition allowed for composition of significant expressions or their division. Pappus attributes the contrast of *synthesis* with *analysis* to the traditions of mathematics originating in Euclid, Apollonius of Perga, and Aristeus the elder. Analysis was defined as "an assumption of that which is sought as if it were admitted [and the passage] through its consequences to something admitted [to be] true." Synthesis was the reverse, namely, "an assumption of that which is admitted [and the passage] through its consequences to the finishing or attainment of what is sought." In geometry, analysis meant the moving from a proposition to be proved to the internal elements which could make it possible; synthesis, from elements already established to their consequences in theorems and propositions.[13] Pappus maintained that this special doctrine was confined to linear problems, but Newton found in it distinctions with which to codify his own composition and resolution of forces. The conjunctions effected between natural philosophy and mathematics allowed for the similarities in procedure and in vocabulary.

The method of analysis ought to precede the method of

---

[12] *Ibid.*

[13] Pappi Alexandrini *Collectionis Reliquiae* vii (II, 634-36). *The Thirteen Books of Euclid's Elements*, trans. Thomas L. Heath (New York: Dover, 1956), I, 138-39, 141-42; III, 442-43. For the critical importance of these texts, cf. McKeon, "Philosophy and the Development of Scientific Methods," p. 7.

composition, but analysis changed radically in its mechanical employ. Observation and experimentation dominate its initial phases.[14] The philosophy of nature has become under Newton "experimental philosophy," and it is this contact through perception and experimentation which provides the ground for all subsequent work.[15] It is not warrantable statements nor the processes of thought, but the phenomena of motion itself which offer both the subject-matter of the science and the area from which the principles of the method are deduced. Newtonian selection is "metaphysical," not in the sense that he is doing metaphysics, but that the natural objects are not approached through antecedent critiques of conceptual frameworks or linguistic analysis. So pivotal a place does this contact with the given occupy that Newton insisted to Oldenburg that only two legitimate objections could be leveled at the *Principia*: either that experiments were insufficient to solve the questions raised or that other experiments could be produced which would directly contradict the conclusions obtained.[16] The level of observation and experiment produced for the logistic method a stage comparable to the other particular method, the problematic, a series of facts which demanded explanation, whether these facts were codified in Kepler's three laws of planetary revolution or the progression of projectiles over the curve of a parabola. The initial moment of method lay in the apprehension of the phenomena, and this apprehension was the work of observation and experimentation.

From these, analysis was to draw general conclusions about the character of the causes involved. It was the move "from compounds to ingredients and from motions to the forces pro-

[14] Isaac Newton, *Opticks or a Treatise of Reflections, Refractions, Inflections and Colours of Light* (New York: Dover, 1952), Query 31, p. 404: "As in Mathematicks, so in Natural Philosophy, the Investigation of difficult Things by the Method of Analysis, ought ever to precede the Method of Composition. This Analysis consists in making Experiments and Observations, and in drawing Conclusions from them by Induction, and admitting of no Objections against the Conclusions, but such as are taken from Experiments, or other certain truths."

[15] *Ibid*. Cf. "Letter to Oldenburg, July 11, 1672," *Opera Omnia*, IV, 320-21, and *Principia* iii, "Rules of Reasoning in Philosophy," pp. 387-89.

[16] *Opera Omnia*, IV, 321.

ducing them, and in general from effects to their causes."[17]
Deduction and induction functioned here within the analytic:
one deduced from the phenomena the principles involved and
generalized them through induction. Deduction was the illation from effect to cause, while its correlative induction was
the relating of this cause to other effects in the gradual increase
of the comprehension of the cause.[18] For the analysis proceeded
not only from effect to cause, but "from particular causes to
more general ones, till the argument end in the most general.
This is the method of analysis."[19] The inductive process was
evidential, and it gave to the principles discovered "the highest
evidence that a proposition can have in this philosophy."[20] It
distinguished the principles obtained sharply from the "hypothesis" of alien schools, and Newton defined hypothesis
precisely as "only such a proposition as is not a phenomenon
nor deduced from any phenomena, but assumed or supposed
—without any experimental proof."[21] It was in this sense that
Newton claimed: "I frame no hypotheses; for whatever is not
deduced from the phenomena is to be called a hypothesis, and
hypotheses, whether metaphysical or physical, whether of occult qualities or mechanical, have no place in experimental
philosophy."[22] Deduction obtained particular propositions from
phenomena—propositions such as the laws of motion or the
properties of gravity—while induction generalized these laws
into the axioms of all motions and the foundations of celestial
mechanics.[23] The contrast with Aristotle could not be sharper:
in universal mechanics, deduction must precede induction in
the derivation of scientific explanation, and hypotheses do not
underlie philosophy but destroy it.

[17] *Opticks*, loc.cit.
[18] *Correspondence*, op.cit., pp. 154-55. "These principles are deduced from
phenomena and made general by induction, which is the highest evidence that
a proposition can have in this philosophy. . . . In this philosophy, propositions are deduced from phenomena, and afterward made general by induction." In citing from the correspondence of Newton, use is made of either the
English translation or the modern English rendition as in H. S. Thayer (ed.),
Newton's Philosophy of Nature (New York: Hafner, 1960).
[19] *Opticks*, loc.cit.   [20] *Opera Omnia*, IV, 314.   [21] *Ibid*.
[22] *Principia* iii, "General Scholium," p. 530 (Cajori, II, 545).
[23] *Correspondence*, pp. 154-56.

One could not quarrel with inductive generalization of scientific propositions on the grounds that there was a single method, geometric demonstration, for all science. The logistic method is plural, allowing particular methods adapted to the divergencies within the problematic treated.[24] The argument from induction was the highest method which experimental philosophy allowed in the resolution of observational phenomena into their causes.[25] It was the confirmation and extension of a proposition by experiments, as, for example, Newton could conclude that "the Third Law, so far as it regards percussion and reflections, is proved by a theory exactly agreeing with experience."[26] The entire scholium at the end of the sixth corollary of the laws of motion is an inductive argument, as Newton explained: "I was aiming only to show by those examples the great extent and certainty of the Third Law of Motion."[27] And the heuristic analysis was productive, through deduction from phenomena and inductive generalizations, of the impenetrability, the mobility, the impulsive force of bodies, and the laws of motion and gravitation.[28]

The method of analysis is the illation to principles; that of the composition or synthesis is the demonstration of new phenomena through these established principles. Synthesis took as established the causes discovered in the analytic moments, assumed them as principles, and employed them in the explanation of other phenomena.[29] The method of composition was a return to the area of observation and phenomena, not in order to break it down into component ingredients, but to relate these ingredients, elements, and forces to the understanding of the phenomena in terms of propositions and dem-

---

[24] For the pluralism of the logistic method, cf. Richard McKeon, "Philosophic Semantics and Philosophic Inquiry" (mimeographed, 1966), pp. 3-5.

[25] "In experimental philosophy, propositions gathered [collectae] out of phenomena through induction, contrary hypotheses notwithstanding, ought to be held as true—either accurately or as closely as possible—until other phenomena appear, through which they are rendered more accurate or suffer exceptions." *Principia* iii, "Fourth Rule for Philosophizing," p. 389.

[26] *Ibid.* i, 25 (Cajori, 1, 25).   [27] *Ibid.* i, 27 (Cajori, 1, 28).

[28] Cf. *ibid.* iii, "Third Rule for Philosophizing," pp. 387-88; "General Scholium," p. 530.

[29] *Opticks, loc.cit.*

onstrations. It was the unifying moment, relating into system the principles and their effects, composing the causes with effects in a cohesive sequence which issued in precision and order. Synthesis was a restoration of the whole, just as analysis had been the resolution of this whole into its parts. One could move equally from part to whole or from whole to part in the study of motions, convinced that "the motion of the whole is the sum of the motions of all the parts."[30]

The methodological contrast which Newton drew between the universal mechanics and operational or problematic procedures was extended under his approval in the preface authored by Roger Cotes and prefixed to the second edition of the *Principia*, 1713. It localized these rejected methods with the Peripatetics and the Cartesians, as "Those who have treated of natural philosophy may be reduced to about three classes." Aristotelianism was scored both for its method of tracing effects back "to the peculiar nature of these bodies," and for "doctrine of occult qualities." The Cartesians, on the other hand, are correct in method, but wrong in principle. "By going on from simple things to those which are more compounded they certainly proceed right." But they "assume hypotheses as first principles of their speculation, although they afterward proceed with the greatest accuracy from these principles."[31] The Peripatetics are the purest nominalists, naming things without investigating them; the Cartesians under the influence of their "uncertain conjectures" form philosophy into clever romances.[32] Neither deserves the title of experimental philosophy which, while it obtains the explanation of nature from simple components, "assumes nothing as a principle which is not proved by phenomena."[33] It is in this latter sense that Cotes reiterates Newton's claim to frame no hypotheses and breaks his procedure into the "twofold method, synthetical and analytical":

From some select phenomena they deduce by analysis the forces of Nature and the more simple laws of forces, and

[30] *Principia*, "Definition 2," p. 1. [31] Cajori, I, xx.
[32] *Ibid.*, I, xxii. [33] *Ibid.*, I, xx.

from thence by synthesis show the constitution of the rest. This is that incomparably best way of philosophizing which our renowned author most justly embraced in preference to the rest. . . .[34]

The analytic movement of the true method of philosophy would eventually result in questions of the causes of the causes discovered or the origin of the entire system of the world. And it was here that the theological question arose.[35] Was the final explanation of universal mechanics a mechanical one or was the comprehensivity of the new science to include the problems of divine existence? When Simplicio leveled a similar question in the kinematics of Galileo, Salviati replied that such considerations belonged *a più alte dottrine che le nostre*.[36] Newton, on the other hand, admitted no such division: "And these things concerning God: to discourse of whom from the appearances of things does certainly belong to Natural Philosophy."[37] The universal mechanics, moving from effects to causes, and from causes less general to those which were more general, followed an unbreakable series of cause: "Though every true step made in this philosophy brings us not immediately to the knowledge of the first cause, yet it brings us nearer to it, and on that account is to be highly valued."[38] Newton's own commentary on the *Principia*, found in his correspondence with Richard Bentley, spelled out this orientation in detail: "When I wrote my treatise about our system, I had an eye upon such principles as might work with considering men for the belief of a Deity."[39]

---

[34] *Ibid.*, I, xx-xxi.

[35] *Opticks,* "Query 28," p. 369: "Later Philosophers banish the Consideration of such a Cause out of natural Philosophy, feigning Hypotheses for explaining all things mechanically, and referring other Causes to Metaphysicks: Whereas the main Business of natural Philosophy is to argue from Phaenomena without feigning Hypotheses, and to deduce Causes from Effects, till we come to the very first Cause, which certainly is not mechanical; and not only to unfold the Mechanism of the World, but chiefly to resolve these and such like Questions."

[36] Galileo Galilei, *Dialogues Concerning Two New Sciences*, trans. Henry Crew and Alfonso de Salvio (New York: Dover, n.d.), p. 194.

[37] *Principia* iii, p. 529.   [38] *Opticks,* "Query 28," p. 370.

[39] *Opera Omnia,* iv, 429.

The logistic *derivatio* translates the Aristotelian and Ciceronian questions of inquiry and controversy into its own progressions in analysis and synthesis. The merger of mathematics and physics allows for a transmutation of the Euclidean sequences into the steps by which the universal mechanics is established and proved. As in Euclid, the definitional question begins the tractate and is concerned not with problematic natures or operational identification but with the principles of the subsequent science. The long chains of reasoning must begin someplace, and these beginnings are definitional sources of the process. Newton differs from Euclid in the kind of principle established by definition as in the kind of progress by which it is constituted, but for both the question of beginnings is a question of definition.

Within the analysis of motion Newton is going to engineer, one must distinguish between the real and the apparent, the absolute and the relative, the mathematical and the common. This entitative interpretation posits the real as the substructure of the phenomenal, and the scholium which justifies this assertion assumes the problems associated with the existence of the real. As the definitions provide the principle of both resolution and composition, so the initial scholium employs the principle for the analysis of motions into the apparent and the real. Only this heuristic employment of the principle allows the solution of the question of existence to emerge and with it, a unique subject-matter for the universal mechanics.

Propositional and qualitative issues translate into the general laws or axioms of motion and into the propositions established about the motions of bodies. For once real motion is deduced, it can be the subject of both general and particular theorems and propositions. The Ciceronian problem of translation becomes the "why" of these individual motions as their final consequence; thus the *Principia* proceeds into an explanation of the entire system of the world. Instead of the operational procedure of a final discrimination of perspective and question, the Newtonian mechanics questions: What is the total condition by which any thing can move?

It is this system, both in its complexity of organization and in the elemental forces by which it is constructed, which leads the universal mechanics out of a final explanation through mechanical causes. Force translates into a theological *dominatio*, and God becomes the analytic principle which can alone explain "that harmony in the system which, as I explained above, was the effect of choice rather than chance."[40] Just as the logistic method had changed motions into the locomotion of bodies in space, so it resolved the questions of planetary interrelation into a cause "not blind and fortuitous but very well skilled in mechanics and geometry."[41] The mechanics of the scientist mirrored the mechanics of God. The conclusion to God as Lord of the universe permitted a new understanding of the system itself, new properties of that space and time which had allowed the initial steps in the mechanics. Time was established by the duration of God and space was theologically understood now as his sensorium. Thus this God, who mechanically set up the system and whose own existence constitutes its possibility, becomes the object of mechanical demonstration. The stages by which this natural philosophy moves from principles of motion to the principles of all motions form the burden of the next few pages.

[40] *Ibid.*, IV, 433.   [41] *Ibid.*, IV, 432.

XIV.

Through Definition to Principle

THE ENTERPRISE of Newtonian mechanics might be successfully launched in astronomical inquiries, progressively enlarged through an assimilation of optics, thermodynamics, and hydrostatics, and suggests hopes of an eventual explanation of *caetera naturae phaenomena* only if one discovered a basis comprehensive enough to found so universal a science. The task is not to discover or to erect assumptions correlative to a particular subject-matter, but to derive a total principle correlative to the entirety of physical reality. Physics becomes mechanics in Newton because of his method; the mechanics becomes universal because of its principle. So inclusive a source of motion, the definitional sequence establishes. In Aristotle, the definition responds to the questions of essence. In Cicero, it shifts to an identification of subject prior to a determination of nature. In Newton, as before in Euclid, the definitional sets up the principle of the logistic constructions and deductions. Without this, the method would induce only an infinite regress. Euclid's definitions differ in kind from those of Newton, but for both the problem of definition becomes an issue touching the principles of science. In Euclid, these are laid down as a series of arbitrary definitions, neither in an attempt to describe phenomena nor to assert their composing parts. In Newton, the definitional series builds from the quantitative description of given appearances through increasing complexity to achieve a force completely responsive both to the phenomena and to their underlying reality. The eight definitions progress from the simple quantity of matter to the force which measures not only this quantity but the quantity of every movement and change within the universe.

"The quantity of matter is the measure of the same, arising from its density and size conjoined."[1] Ernst Mach would score this strongly as a pseudo-definition, insisting that "the true definition of mass can be deduced only from the dynamical relations of bodies."[2] The objection stems from a failure to follow the purpose of the eight definitions, a failure which Mach himself suggests when he criticizes the *Principia* for pleonasm and tautology.[3] The initial definition asserts only a phenomenal quantity, obvious and apparent, and asserts it in terms of sensible measurements. Real mass will only become evident from absolute force, but here it is defined through the sort of yardstick measurements which Newton will later reject. In Aristotelian essentialism, definitions bifurcate into the verbal and the real; in Newtonian entitative interpretation, this differentiation translates into the phenomenal and the real, which the logistic procedure begins with the quantities given by the former and terminates in quantities found within the nature of things. Just as the perceived motions of the heavenly bodies are one thing and their real motions another, so the sensible *mensura* of matter or its motion must be differentiated from the real. The phenomenal offers a quantity, and it is with this quantity that the subsequent definitions will build. It is to this quantity that the name "body" (*corpus*) is attached. What denoted a substantial reality in Aristotle and served as the criterion for existence in Cicero becomes in the mechanics of Newton another designation for the quantity of matter, another designation for "mass," and it can be known by, though not identified with, its weight.[4]

The second definition adds velocity to the quantity of matter to achieve a proportion for the quantity of motion. The conjunction of mass and velocity is momentum, and every motion is in turn described as the sum of the motions of its several parts. One can calculate the whole motion by the addi-

---

[1] *Principia*, "Definition 1," p. 1.

[2] Ernst Mach, *The Science of Mechanics: A Critical and Historical Account of Its Development* (6th ed.; LaSalle, Ill.: Open Court, 1960), p. 300.

[3] *Ibid.*, p. 302.

[4] *Principia*, "Definition 1," p. 1.

tion of its quantitative elements or resolve its momentum into the components. Motion in mechanics allows for either process, for just as body has been reduced to mass, so movement itself is another quantity with body as one of its elements.[5]

Force is not introduced until the third definition, and it is here as the power to resist any change in matter or its momentum. What is added in the third definition is not another component of either quantity; inertia differs from the inactivity of the mass only in the manner of its conception. Rather definitions one and two had treated an isolated body and its movement. Now other bodies are added to the picture and these allow for consideration of the third critical term—change. Any measurement of matter without reference to outside influences would obtain mass or momentum; if either is measured with this reference, inertial force is obtained. And since inertial force identifies with the mass, one can derive in these interactions a measurement of the mass other than the sensible computations of the prior definitions. Mass can be measured as resisting change, and the force which engineers change can become the critical standard for the estimation of mass and momentum. The progress of the definitions has been from *materia*, through *motus*, to *mutatio*; and it is this careful dependence which allows the former to be measured by the latter.

Newtonian mechanics engineers here a sharp diremption between change and motion, while drawing a sensible equation between motion and rest. Instead of the Aristotelian distinction of change into change (properly-so-called) and motion, Newtonian mechanics distinguishes rest from motion as two species of state and opposes change equally to either as its alteration. Cutting across this, the entitative interpretation allows for the further discrimination in asserting that "motion and rest, as commonly conceived, are only relatively distinguished; nor are those bodies always truly at rest which are popularly [*vulgo*] accepted as such."[6] One set of devices tells upon another, leaving the differentiation of motion and rest a

[5] *Ibid.*, "Definition 2," p. 1.   [6] *Ibid.*, "Definition 3," p. 2.

fourfold one, but finding each of these a state contrasted to change. This schema also lines up the central problem for the *Principia*: How can one distinguish among these four? "How one can obtain true motions from their causes, effects and apparent differences, and the converse, will be taught at great length in what follows. For it was for this purpose that I wrote what follows."[7]

The *de facto* identity asserted between inertial force and mass turns the definitional establishment of principle into an analysis of the causes of change. One will be able to determine the quantity of motion through change, just as one will obtain the true mass through momentum. Just as mass assimilates with inertial force, so the cause of change is also a force—impressed force. It is *actio*, not the problematic denotation of a relationship, but an activity exercised upon a body during a change in the state of rest or of motion. Action authors the change in movement, and it is this action which broadly identifies with force impressed. Inertia was the force within the patient resisting this change; impressed force is the action as from the agent. Inertia pervades both states, either as resisting change or as maintaining a state of rest or of uniform motion. Impressed force only exists under the influence of another's actions, and the kinds of impressed forces are differentiated according to the divergencies in origin. Force can be impressed *upon* a body *from* percussion (*ex ictu*), from pressure (*ex pressione*), or from centripetal force (*ex vi centripeta*).[8] Of the three, Newton turns to the third for the comprehensive principle which will nail down a universal mechanics. The other two are not adequate. Percussion does not offer a durational continuity needed to understand a universe in continuous acceleration, while pressure provides for an endless series of explanation through prior forces. Neither demands a determination of the direction of motion, while both are open to the endless and the random. Centripetal force can both constitute a universe in order and author every change within it.

Centripetal force is defined as a force by which bodies are

[7] *Ibid.*, "Scholium after definition 8," p. 12.
[8] *Ibid.*, "Definition 4," p. 2.

drawn or impelled in any way towards a point as to a center. The definition is geometrical rather than physical, i.e., it is not a description of natural activity or of pushing or pulling, but a description of force by the terminus of the change.[9] Impressed force is defined by the direction of the change it authors and includes gravity, magnetism, planetary movements, and the orbiting of a stone in a sling. Centripetal force serves both to account for the change in any of these bodies and to delimit it within geometrical proportion. The equation drawn between the mathematical and the mechanical make it possible to join here the tasks of either: "It belongs to the mathematicians to find [*invenire*] the force which may serve exactly to retain a body in a given orbit with a given velocity and *vice versa*."[10] In order to do this, action and force must follow the path already traced out for motion and matter; they must become quantities in the mathematicizing of centripetal force: "The quantity of this centripetal force is of three kinds: absolute, accelerative, and motive."[11] These three quantities correspond to the quantities with which the definitional progression began, making it very difficult to agree with Mach that it is a matter of taste or of external form whether one explains the idea of force in one or several definitions.[12] Rather, it is a question of method.

Absolute force is proportional to the mass of the attracting body, prescinding from any alteration of velocity. Greater absolute force can move heavier bodies.[13] Accelerative force takes up the element omitted; it is proportioned to the velocity authored (acceleration) irrespective of the masses moved. Falling from the same height, the accelerative force of each body is the same.[14] The final definition puts the two quantities together. Just as momentum conjoined velocity and mass, so

---

[9] *Ibid.*, "Definition 8," pp. 5-6.   [10] *Ibid.*, "Definition 5," p. 4.

[11] *Ibid.* Cajori's translation here is misleading: "The quantity of any centripetal force *may be considered* as of three kinds: absolute, accelerative, and motive" (*op.cit.*, I, 4; italics mine). For Newton, it is not a question of differentiating various perspectives which one can obtain of the phenomenal, but rather a statement of quantities which are involved in any centripetal force. It is the difference between an operational and a logistic method.

[12] Mach, *op.cit.*, p. 301.   [13] *Principia*, "Definition 6," p. 4.

[14] *Ibid.*, "Definition 7," p. 4.

motive force combines absolute and accelerative force. As momentum was the sum of its parts, so motive force is the quantitative product of its components: "For just as the quantity of motion arises from the velocity multiplied by the quantity of matter, so the motive force arises from the accelerative force multiplied by the same quantity of matter."[15] One can distinguish the three quantities and refer them to the body in which the change is effected, the space it occupies, or the center from which the force is propagated. But this differentiation is not a discrimination between kinds of physical causality. Force, even motive force, remains a quantity and "this concept is only mathematical—I am not discussing the causes of these forces nor their physical location."[16] Motion includes speed as one of its components; motive force comprehends the totality of accelerative forces: "The sum of the actions of the accelerative force upon each particle of the body is the motive force of the whole."[17] Motive force is the *summa actionis*, the comprehensive principle of the *Principia*, summarizing within itself all the causality needed for a universal mechanics and identified neither with the relational orientations of Aristotle nor with the phenomenal chains of Cicero. No attempt is made to determine whether this movement towards a center is attraction or impulse nor to assess the ontological structure of the entities from which it progresses. The universal mechanics achieves its comprehensivity by "considering these forces not physically but mathematically."[18] The centers towards which the bodies accelerate are mathematical points, and the forces are the quantities which compose this movement and by which momentum and mass are ultimately measured.

These eight definitions and their careful progress are of critical importance in the understanding of Newtonian mechanics. They embody a logistic combination of increasing mathematical complexity until the motive force is achieved, comprehending in its quantity all other measurements of centripetal force, just as this centripetal force will itself comprehend percussion and pressure. In contrast to the problematic

---

[15] *Ibid.*, "Definition 8," p. 5.   [16] *Ibid.*, p. 6.
[17] *Ibid.*, p. 5.   [18] *Ibid.*, p. 6.

movement from things better known to us to things better known by nature, the logistic method has followed an analytic sequence from quantities phenomenally given and sensibly measured to a principle catholic enough to account for the movement of the entire universe and to serve as the criterion by which the apparent is differentiated from the real.

XV.

Absolute Motion

THIS differentiation between the apparent and the real transforms the question of existence. In Aristotelian physics, one could refute any denial of the reality of motion by an appeal to sense perception: "We have sufficient grounds for rejecting all these theories in the single fact that we *see* some things that are sometimes in motion and sometimes at rest."[1] The Ciceronian debate presumed a consensus of all participants about the experience of motion as warrant enough for its validity, a confluence of perspectives and philosophic doctrines. In Newtonian mechanics, neither phenomenal interpretation is adequate, whether one find a structure of intelligibility and meaning within the given or within the clash of theory and opinion. Reality was deeper than experience or agreement could instantiate. If one were to deal with motion philosophically, two levels of reality would have to be distinguished and ground discovered in the phenomenal for the assertion of motion as absolute. This entitative interpretation distinguishes sharply between the absolute and the relative, the true and the apparent, the mathematical and the popular (*vulgares*).[2] These antimonies characterize a bifurcation between the sensibly given and a level which lies beneath, which forms the substructure of the apparent, and of which the sensible is, at best, indication and warrant. Newtonian mechanics does not deny the motions given in immediate experience or in common estimation, but argues that to analyze them on this level is to defile the purity of true scientific knowledge: "Nor do they less contaminate mathematics and philosophy—those who con-

---

[1] *Ph.* viii. 3. 254ª35-37.
[2] *Principia*, "Scholium after definition 8," p. 6.

fuse [*confundant*] the true quantities with their relations and popular measures."[3] There is a plane on which motion and its correlatives in time, space, and place are relative, sensible measurements which depend upon perspective and situation. Newton never denied this relativity; on the contrary, he found that *omnibus notissima.* "The crowd [*vulgus*] conceives these quantities only from a relation to sensible objects."[4] It was the exclusive attribution of these quantities to the merely relative which he denied, and this denial constituted an essential moment in setting up the universal mechanics. For the scholium attached to the definitions allows the scientist to move from the comprehensive principle to the existence of a subject-matter, using the principle (motive force) to establish motion on a deeper, more basic level than mere appearance.

Just as the derivation of principles had been contrasted with the operational projection of hypotheses, so Newton discriminated between the mathematical quantities themselves and their sensible measurements, between the quantities measured (*quantitates mensuratae*) and the quantities which are their sensible measurements (*mensurae sensibiles*).[5] The absolute motion, time, space, and place are the quantities measured, not the measurement itself. True time is duration, a perseverance in existence which is without relation to anything external, thus absolute. It is this fundamental duration which particular motions measure, using the orbit of the moon or the diurnal revolution of the earth as sensible indications of continuity in existence.[6] Sensible motions are employed as the measurement of time, but its duration is beyond motion, cannot be accelerated and retarded, is utterly changeless. "All motions can be accelerated and retarded, but the flow of absolute time [*fluxus temporis absoluti*] cannot be changed. The duration of perseverance of the existence of things is the same, whether the motions are quick or slow or none."[7]

Space is the logistic void, the absolute and true dimensions within which all motions occur, and which is denoted in no way by the bodies or movements within. Space, like time, is mathe-

---

[3] *Ibid.*, p. 11.   [4] *Ibid.*, p. 6.   [5] *Ibid.*, pp. 6-7, 11.
[6] *Ibid.*, p. 6.   [7] *Ibid.*, p. 8.

matical in that it is a qualityless extension. Its continuity can be measured sensibly by the positional relationships among bodies, by determination of dimensional situations among masses and their movements, but its absolute dimensions are the same and unchangeable.[8] Within mathematical space, the true location of a particular body is its absolute place; within relative space, the parts occupied constitute relative place.[9] All things are within time and space, the absolutes which form the coordinates of the universe. Bodies are in time by order of succession in duration; they are in space because they are in place, and they are in place by order of their situation.[10]

Absolute duration and changeless space make possible the definition of absolute, true, mathematical motion as "the translation [*translatio*] of a body from one absolute place into another absolute place," just as relative motion is a "translation from one relative place into another."[11] Both time and space constitute locations, durational and extensional quantities within which motion occurs and by which it is defined and given geometrical determination.[12] As coordinates, they are above motion, changelessly existing from eternity to eternity and from infinity—characteristics which will involve the mechanical assumptions of the *Principia* in immediate theological problems.[13] Within their infinity, the finite occurs as it is within the endless perseverance in existence that the temporal measurements are projected.

Granted these definitions and the mathematical determinations of absolute motion through dimension and duration, the inadequacy of relative measurements becomes apparent. The usual calibration of movement has been through position and situation taken from the fixed stars or from any body considered immobile; by these positions, place was determined; and by relative places, motion was delimited. This procedure is adequate in the normal course of life (*in rebus humanis*) but is philosophically defective in method, knowledge and sub-

---

[8] *Ibid.*, p. 6.   [9] *Ibid.*, p. 7.   [10] *Ibid.*, p. 8.
[11] *Ibid.*, p. 7.   [12] *Ibid.*, p. 8.
[13] *Ibid.*, p. 9. Cf. *ibid.* iii, "General Scholium," pp. 528-29. Cf. *infra*, Chapter XVII.

ject. The philosophic inquiry demands an abstraction from sensible objects: "In philosophical matters, however, one must abstract [*abstrahendum est*] from the senses."[14] Secondly, it is not evident that any phenomenally given frame of reference can serve as a standard or indication of any absolute; and, thirdly, the focus of philosophic investigation should be upon true quantities rather than their common measurements.[15]

If a sensible referent does not afford placement for mathematical and philosophic motion, what will ground any science of mechanics? Absolute motion has been defined through absolute place, but absolute place has been placed beyond any sense perception. How can one assert as existent and as subject-matter of his science that whose very criteria are opaque? It is in answer to this question that the comprehensive nature of motive force becomes clearer. Motive force is not only the final explanation of any change in movement and mass, it is equally the sole source by which absolute motion can be distinguished from relative. Force figures in a double relationship to motion: as cause or as effect. It can either denote the causes by which a motion is generated or it can denote the effect of movement around the axis in rotation. Two features indicate the reality of motion through force as cause: absolute motion is only generated by force impressed upon the body changed, while relative motion can result from an alteration of the environment. Conversely, true movement always suffers some change from a force impressed, though relative to its context it may seem to be at rest. Both features indicate that no necessary correlation exists between apparent movement and true motion. Relative motion may occur with a body actually at rest, while a body in absolute movement may in certain perspectives project an appearance of rest. The effect of true motion is evident when that motion is rotary; it is the force of recession from the axis of circular movement. These receding-forces do not occur in a motion which is purely relative. The example of the vessel of water whirling at the end of an untwisting cord indicates this: the swifter the movement, the higher the water rises on the

---

[14] *Principia*, "Scholium after definition 8," p. 8.
[15] *Ibid.*, p. 11.

sides of the pail. At the height of real movement, the concave formed by the water will be at rest relative to the vessel itself, but the true motion of the water can be estimated by this force of recession from the axis of the motion: "There is only one real circular motion of any one revolving body, corresponding to only one power of endeavoring to recede from its axis of motion, as its proper and adequate effect."[16]

Just as he had combined absolute and accelerative force to obtain motive force, so Newton conjoins both of these—force as cause and force as effect of motion—to investigate and establish true motion. While no positional coordination of bodies and movement by antecedent and subsequent position is adequate for an assertion of absolute motion, one can proceed from the differences within relative motions and "from the forces which are the causes and effects of true motions."[17] It is at this point in his argument that Newton introduces the crucial experiment of the connected globes.[18]

It is an analytic experiment in three stages. Initially, two balls are placed at a certain distance from each other, connected by a cord, and whirled around a common center. The tension in the cord indicates the endeavor to recede from the axis of motion, the tension restraining the balls from flying off tangentially, indicating the existence of true motion—a quantity which can be calculated by the tension on the cord. In the second stage, equal forces are impressed on opposite faces of the revolving globes to increase or to decrease their momentum. By this alteration of forces, one can discover

---

[16] *Ibid.*, p. 9.   [17] *Ibid.*, pp. 9, 11.

[18] In his book, *Newtonian Science* (London: Arnold, 1961), p. 113, Arthur E. Bell brings his highly inaccurate history of science to the writing of the *Principia* and then devotes no more than a paragraph to the initial eight definitions and their scholium. He ignores the experiments and the argument of these pages and concludes that Newton "did not dispose of these problems very satisfactorily. One is left with a belief that his absolute quantities cannot be justified by what he says of them." This "belief" seems to be "left," rather, by ignoring what Newton says of them. Even a much finer piece of commentary, "Analytical View of Sir Isaac Newton's Principia," ignores this establishment of absolute motion totally: Henry Lord Brougham and E. J. Routh, *Analytical View of Newtonian Science* (London: Longman, Brown, Green, and Longmans, 1844), pp. 12-15.

which surfaces the impressed forces should contact in order to augment the momentum to its maximum possibility, "that is, the back faces [*facies posticae*], or those which follow in circular movement."[19] Once these sides and the opposite sides which precede them are known, the *determinatio motus* has been ascertained. The first stage of the experiment terminated in a knowledge of the fact that there was this quantity, this absolute motion; the second stage, in the understanding of its determination. Neither of these steps is dependent upon relative positions or the displacement of bodies, "and thus one might discover [*inveniri possat*] both the quantity and the determination of this circular motion, even in an immense vacuum, where there was nothing external or sensible with which the globes could be compared."[20] From the tension on the cord, Newton derives an absolute motion; from the modification of this motion by impressed forces, he obtains its absolute determination. The third stage relates this absolute motion to the universe. If bodies are discovered within the cosmos relatively at rest among themselves, but in relative motion to the globes, one could conclude that their rest was absolute rest, measured by the absolute movement discovered in the revolving globes.[21]

Because of the history of physics which followed, it should be noted what Newton is not claiming. He is not obliterating the relativity of sensible motion, measured by position and displacement. He is not obtaining rectilinear movement as absolute; to claim that he is doing so is to miss the point of the experiment with the globes. Just as impressed force became centripetal force in the definition for need of a principle, so the concentration here is upon rotational motion. From the forces which it effects, one ascertains its presence; only then is force as cause used, not to determine whether this is true motion—that has already been proven—but by variance among true forces to nail down its direction. Only then are all other movements, such as rectilinear motion, given an absolute motion by which they may be judged. The relativity of careening automobiles, of trains leaving their stations, or of falling ele-

[19] *Principia*, "Scholium after definition 8," p. 8.
[20] *Ibid.*, p. 11.   [21] *Ibid.*, p. 12.

vators would constitute only another instance in Newtonian mechanics that positional correlations do not guarantee absolute movement. Much less is he resting his position of absolute motion on an hypothesized stagnant ether; in the demonstration of absolute motion the term "ether" does not occur. In precise contradiction to a measurement by bodies or by ether, Newtonian mechanics denies that absolute motion can be discovered by comparison with any external frame of reference because "the parts of that immovable space in which these motions are performed do by no means come under the observation of our senses."[22]

No positional reference indicates absolute motion, but this is not to conclude that absolute motion is without experimental sanction. One discovers this motion through the measurements of force, motive force. Thus in a logistic mechanics, motive force achieves a comprehensivity denied nature in the physics of Aristotle or the indeterminant atoms of Epicurus; motive force is, in the terms of the schoolmen, the logistic correlative of a principle which would be both a *ratio essendi* and a *ratio cognoscendi*—a comprehensive cause of being and of knowledge, one which alone accounts for real motion and is that by which real motion can be discovered, an assimilative principle which includes within itself both the source of proof and the source of discovery. Motive force makes any determination of motion independent of all circumadjacent bodies and positional coordinates, for it is the tension on the cord and not the displacement of the globes which demonstrates the existence of an absolute motion.

These revolving globes are absolutely imperative for the Newtonian assertion of a subject-matter for universal mechanics, absolute motion. It equally allows the differentiation between relative and absolute to extend to place, space, and time. If there is absolute motion, the places in which this *translatio* occurs are absolute places. That whole of which these places are parts is absolute space. The duration of this unchanging and unchangeable space, the duration also of the absolute mo-

[22] *Ibid.*, p. 11.

tion (both measured by sensible motions), indicate an absolute time. The assertion of existence terminates in absolute motion, place, space, and time. These underlying quantities do not constitute another world, no more than the Platonic ontological interpretation posits two distinct worlds. One lives in a single world and it is not a question of going to another, to a "really real world." The real world is not something more abstract or something inductively separate, but the real admits of distinctions. The importance of motive force is that it enables mechanics to identify the deepest realities within this world; the whirling globes allow the philosopher to point to real motion, absolute place, and absolute time, to designate that aspect of the real which is not dependent upon perspective and reference, to discover within the many relative and sensible motions those which he can denote as absolute and true.

This establishment of absolute motion also constitutes the basic problem of the universal mechanics. The purpose of the entire *Principia* is lodged here: "How we are to obtain the true motions from their causes, effects, and apparent differences, and the converse, shall be taught at great length in what follows. For it was for this purpose that I composed what follows."[23]

23 *Ibid.*, p. 12.

XVI.

Motion in Statement and System

IN THE initial moments of his geometry, Euclid defines those elements which will enter into the problems, theorems, and porisms or into the figures to be constructed, the propositions to be demonstrated, and the possibilities to be explored. The subsequent postulates bring the defined elements into propositions of existences, not by examining deeper levels within the phenomenally given, but by indicating operations which can be performed or processes which can be authored through which these lines, points, circles, angles, and parallels can be given reality. The existential in Euclid becomes a problem of establishing the reality of what has been antecedently defined and made, contrasting sharply with the existential demonstrations in the Newtonian assertions of absolute motion. Euclid follows his postulates with "common notions"—ideas generally accepted among mathematicians through which the original elements are generalized into universal statements about all quantities. Through the commentaries of Proclus, these common notions became "axioms" and entered Western mathematics as the "axioms of Euclidean geometry."[1] In Newton, the transformation went one step further: "Common notions" are dropped, and mechanical propositions are introduced with three "axioms or laws of motion."[2]

The propositional question of Aristotle or the qualitative issue in Cicero becomes in Newton the statements which can be made about motion, once it has been proven absolute, true, and mathematical. The three axioms are the most general of

---

[1] *Euclid's Elements, op.cit.*, I, 221-22. For the distinction among problems, theorems, and porisms, cf. Pappus, *op.cit.*, vii (II, 648-60).

[2] *Principia*, p. 13.

these statements which can have motion as a subject, and thus the question of fact is translated by the universal mechanics into synthetic statements about its subject-matter. The conviction that mathematics is a subdivision of mechanics makes these the mathematical principles of natural philosophy, while the initial laws are Euclidean-like notions, first truths about movement upon which all subsequent propositions must be based—"laws" in that they are the facts by which the universe itself is governed, general laws of the universe.

When Mach writes that the first two laws are already contained in the definitions of force, he fails to follow this development in Newton's mechanics: from principle, to existence, to propositions about the motion now discovered in a common experience.[3] Until these demonstrations were completed, no laws of motion were possible; propositions are subsequent to a determination of a subject-matter. Centripetal force allowed for this elaboration of a real and defined motion, not merely of what might be the case, but true propositions of what is the case. The axioms and the subsequent two books of theorems propose a progressive delimitation of movement first through laws which are of universal realization and then through propositions proper to different kinds of movement; both terminate in the third book through the demonstration of the entire universe. The comprehensive principle, motive force, governs this progression from universal laws to the universe of these laws, from general statements about all motion to general statements about every motion, to a universe of motion. The correlation between force and motion polarizes the three books and, thus, necessarily constitutes the axioms of the entire tractate.

Rest and motion are collapsed into variant states, and in the absence of impressed force these states remain unchanged.[4] Positively, the change of motion (*mutationem motus*) is proportioned to and in the direction of impressed force.[5] Finally, the third law shifts the *actio-passio* causal relationship of problematic inquiry to an *actio-reactio* interchange of logistic phys-

[3] Mach, *op.cit.*, p. 302.   [4] *Principia*, "Law 1," p. 13.
[5] *Ibid.*, "Law 2," pp. 13-14.

ics: to every action, the activity of force impressed, there is a corresponding reaction. In mechanics, causality is always mutual and any expended force elicits a correspondent force in the effect. Force is both the cause and effect of itself, as well as the comprehensive account of any change. The result of the three axioms is to confirm the inclusive character of motive force.[6]

The corollaries indicate how to make a shift from the general laws to particular propositions to a universe of motion—by the composition and resolution of motions and forces. This is a question of method, but method now adapted to the peculiar task of dealing logistically with a comprehensive principle and with motion whose inertia, change, and reaction are so general as to constitute its three axioms. How is one to obtain further statements, prove successive theorems or demonstrate the necessity of general descriptions of movement already authored by Galileo and Kepler? How is force to figure in statement and in system? The formulation of propositions is not through a process of application of the axioms of motion, but through the *derivatio* which marks Newtonian method. When any particular problem is considered, such as that of the phases of the moon, solutions are obtained not by bringing antecedent structures to bear, but by discovering within the phenomena the relevant laws, those operative in the determination of the movements. One must move from the analytic or the heuristic moment of the method in the investigation of these laws, to the synthetic expression of these laws in propositions. This is possible because of the composition of movements and of systems.

The first corollary reduces any motion to the composition of forces which generated it; time is a constant and the resultant direction describes the diagonal of the parallelogram of these forces. Inertial force will preserve a movement, but it will not explain it. Motion can be adequately treated only through a resolution back to the forces causative of its generation, causative of its origin; and this will form an enormously

[6] *Ibid.*, "Law 3," p. 14.

important point in subsequent discussion of the God of motion. Impressed forces bear upon the origin of movements, and from the motion already in progress the antecedent causes can be judged. Cause then precedes effect, just as change precedes a state of motion.[7] These composite forces, according to the second corollary, are themselves not to be explained through anything else. Motion can be reduced back to change, and change can be explained through forces. But force is only explained in terms of itself. A single force can be resolved into further, oblique forces which compose it; or these oblique forces can be composed into a single resultant force. But the composition and resolution is of forces to forces. Nothing is more fundamental and basic. Motion, on the other hand, can be resolved to originating forces or composed of forces; but forces resolve to or compose into other forces. This allows for the double movement in the Newtonian method, adumbrated in the preface to the *Principia* but now nailed down to principle and interpretation: composition and resolution.[8] This conjunction of the coordinates of Newtonian principle and method stands at the critical moment of the entire mechanical enterprise:

> The use of this corollary extends far and wide, and by the extent of its diffusion, it demonstrates [*evincit*] its truth. For upon what has been said depends all of mechanics howsoever demonstrated by its authors. For from these [assertions] are easily derived [*derivatur*] the forces of machines, which are usually composed of wheels, pullies, levers, cords and weights, ascending directly or indirectly, and other mechanical powers [*caeterisque potentiis mechanicis*] as also the forces of the tendons in moving the bones of animals.[9]

The method allows mechanics to isolate systems within the universe by resolving various vector quantities into a single quantity of the system and to locate the quantity at a common center of gravity. Thus, it is with the third and fourth corollary that mechanics moves from the possibility of statement to

---

[7] *Principia*, pp. 14-15.   [8] *Ibid.*, p. 15.   [9] *Ibid.*, p. 17.

the possibility of system. Just as the comprehensive principle allowed for a universality to the science, so the composition and resolution in the method could section off various elements within the universe and combine them into a single system. Constancy could be predicated of the momentum of such a structure of interacting bodies, and their combined momentum is summarized (*colligitur*) through the simple addition and subtraction of the quantities involved.[10] The subsequent corollary places the sum of these processes at a point within the entire system. A series of interacting bodies—since body itself is a quantity—can be resolved into a mass point answering for the entire system. This resolution comes out of the method, not a method of acting *as if* the system were a mass point, but a method of mathematically resolving the quantities to a final sum. This location of forces allows the structure to be treated as a whole, as a single system in relation to other such systems similarly resolved. It allows for a universe of such systems, and the last two corollaries deal with bodies in this new unity, in the system which Newtonian mechanics indicated as a "given space of included bodies (*corporum dato spacio inclusorum*)." Just as mass unites, the entire system can have inertia unaffected by the interaction of its component bodies; or it can be acted upon by other such systems with uniformly accelerated forces, and the entire system will remain relatively unaffected. In either case, the system remains, and the system is the component bodies whose various quantities have been methodologically reduced to one —to a unity in quantity.[11]

The logistic method can thus establish statements and systems within the universe and move synthetically through these systems until it obtains the system of the entire world. The title of the concluding book of the *Principia* is "De Mundi Systemate," "Concerning the System of the World."[12] The

[10] *Ibid.*, pp. 17-18.

[11] *Ibid.*, pp. 19-21. The subsequent scholium attempts to confirm these corollaries inductively by indicating that they found the rest of mechanics and that they are repeatedly tested and proved by experimentation. Cf. *Opera Omnia*, IV, 155.

[12] *Principia*, p. 386.

first two books investigated motions analytically, first without consideration of resisting media and then with the addition of the medium. Just as motive force assimilated absolute and accelerative force, so the third book summarized in an example the principles, laws, and propositions previously derived. These serve as components, elements whose final effect is the constitution of the structure of the world (*constitutionem systematis mundani*).[13] In its concern with the entire system, the universal mechanics shifts to the translative question of Cicero. It is a question of consequences heuristically derived and of the synthetic use of principles. For the "principia mathematica" are precisely the laws and theorems—the propositions —of the first two books; and the third book opens: "In the preceding books, I have treated the principles of philosophy, not philosophical principles, but only mathematical—namely, those out of which philosophic disputations can arise." These are the "laws and conditions of motions and forces."[14] The system of the universe is the consequence of these established propositions; and without such a consequential demonstration, the propositions themselves would seem *sterilia*.[15]

Mathematical regularities indicated initially that the universe is such a system, substructured by laws of universal application. The force by which a circumscribing body is drawn off its inertial course is that of the inverse square of the distance, whether one is demonstrating the orbits of the moons of Jupiter, Saturn, and Earth, or the ellipses of the planets themselves around the sun. Further, there is a universal centripetal attraction which makes motive force the principle of the universe, a principle which translates now into gravity: "The force which keeps the celestial bodies in their orbits has hitherto been called centripetal force. It is established now that it is the same as gravity, and therefore we shall call it gravity in the future."[16] Gravity draws the masses within the influence of the sun into a unity, attracting them into regular orbits in a space which is "perfectly void of air

---

[13] *Ibid.*   [14] *Ibid.*   [15] *Ibid.*
[16] *Ibid.* iii, "Scholium after proposition 5, theorem 5," p. 399.

and exhalation."[17] The solar system, like any sub-system of bodies, has a center of gravity, giving a quantitative unity to the whole, "a center of the world."[18] It is about this center that the great masses and their regular movements revolve. In the universal mechanics, the world is a quantitative structure in which every momentum can be demonstrated, whether from the masses of the sun and other planets, the figure of the earth, or investigated in the precession of the equinoxes, the irregularities of the moon, the fluctuations of the tides; even the seemingly random movements of the comets are analyzed into calculable orbits. Motive force, or in its astronomical translation, gravity, accounts for all acceleration, from the descent of a stone to the orbit of a planet; and through gravity, universal mechanics demonstrates "all the motions of the celestial bodies and of our sea."[19]

This system of the world gives the total condition within the quantities of motion which allows for something to move in the manner in which it does. The universe explains the movement of each part, just as a universal motive force explains the universe. The entire solar system becomes a single demonstrated unity—a whole of synthetically demonstrated movements. But it is precisely here that the theological question arises: How is so intricately contrived or thoroughly elaborated a structure possible? Universal mechanics moves through force from axioms to statements to system; but what force accounts for the system itself?

[17] *Ibid.*, "Proposition 10, theorem 10," p. 407.
[18] *Ibid.*, "Proposition 12, theorem 12," p. 408.
[19] *Ibid.*, "General Scholium," p. 530: "It is enough that gravity really exists, and that it acts according to the laws exposed by us, and that it suffices to explain all the movements of the heavenly bodies and of our sea."

XVII.

The God of Natural Philosophy

CONCOMITANT with the history of natural philosophy runs the issue of theological inference, and the resolution of this question bifurcates also between the ancients and the moderns. The Greek and Phoenician atomists constructed a philosophy whose first principles were the void, the atoms within the void, and the gravity of the atoms; but they opened physics to theological speculation in "tacitly attributing Gravity to some other Cause than dense Matter."[1] Later physicists shut off this inquiry, problematically relegating any consideration of divine causality to metaphysics, and isolating natural philosophy through the artificial projections of mechanical explanation, "feigning Hypotheses for explaining all things mechanically."[2] In the history of Newton, the atomists become theists while the believing French have erected a godless natural philosophy, one which is false both in problem and in principle: in principle, for the philosopher is to move from effects to causes, not to hypotheses, "till we come to the very first Cause, which is certainly not mechanical;" in problem, for the problematic found within the compass of natural inquiry demands a resolution that goes deeper than mechanical determinations.[3] As Aristotelian physics moves from nature to a non-natural cause, so the universal mechanics proceeds from quantities of mass and momentum to a reality whose attributes consisted of neither.

The mechanical philosophy carried its investigation to a system of bodies in orbit around the sun. The diremption between change and state allows for a distinction between the generation and the perseverance of such a structure. The forces

[1] *Opticks*, "Query 28," p. 369.   [2] *Ibid*.   [3] *Ibid*.

of gravitation and inertia can explain the former, but they are themselves antecedently determined by the positions and velocities of the masses within the system.[4] Mechanical laws cannot explain the origin of the assemblage, though they can describe its continuous operation. The quantitative interrelations of a system are contingent upon this prior establishment of its functional units, and the pattern of the universe indicates that these have been established by intelligence and volition.

Astronomical systems demonstrate a non-mechanical origin. Within the solar system six primary planets rotate about the sun in concentric movements which are the same in figure and almost the same in plane. Around three of these, ten moons circle in concentric movements which are the same in figure and almost the same in plane. "And all these regular motions do not have an origin [*originem*] from mechanical causes." Add to this complexity the eccentric movements of the comets, passing through the orbits of the planets with velocity geared to cause a minimum of interference. "This most splendid structure [*compages*] of the sun, the planets, and the comets could not have arisen [*oriri*] except through the deliberation and the dominion [*dominio*] of a being intelligent and powerful." The solar system evinces the intelligence and the power of its maker, as do the fixed stars, if each forms another solar system. Unless these systems had been positioned at immense distances from each other, their gravitational attraction would have fused them into a single mass.[5] Mechanics has demonstrated a complicated series of interconnections dependent upon the masses, the momenta, and positions of the component bodies, but it can no more explain these quantities by further mechanical resolution than it can hypothesize masses which justify the wisdom manifest in the entire composition.

The alternative explanation through "blind metaphysical necessity" is equally bankrupt. For the system is a unity of extraordinary diversities, and "blind metaphysical necessity, which is always and everywhere the same, authors no variety

[4] *Principia*, "General Scholium," p. 527.
[5] *Ibid.*

194

in things."[6] To achieve a structure which will perdure requires the careful balancing of quantitative proportions, an intellect which can calculate these qualities and a power which can dispose them in an optimum relationship. Any comprehensive principle which would identify with the world, such as blind necessity, would be the product, not the author of the structures, and a world soul would be contingent upon the several parts for its own movement. Granted the systems of the universe, the philosopher must search for a non-mechanical, but intelligent cause.

Universal mechanics needs to resolve not only the construction of the world system as a whole, but also the composition of each of its quantitative units. If space were finite and the matter evenly scattered throughout the void, the gravitational attraction would merge the variant bodies into one great spherical mass. A finite space would need a divine power which would sustain its parts.[7] But the infinite space of Newtonian physics equally demands this power in the composition of its individual masses:

> But how the matter should divide itself into two sorts, and that part of it which is fit to compose a shining body should fall down into one mass and make a sun and the rest which is fit to compose an opaque body should coalesce, not into one great body, like the shining matter, but into many little ones; or if the sun at first were an opaque body like the planets or the planets lucid bodies like the sun, how he alone should be changed into a shining body whilst they continue opaque, or they be changed into opaque ones whilst he remains unchanged, I do not think explicable by mere natural causes, but am forced to ascribe it to the counsel and contrivance of a voluntary agent.[8]

The divergent combination of the elements in a structure necessary for its harmonious cooperation in movement can only be resolved to intelligence. The Aristotelian fourfold division of the causes of motion is transformed in the logistic

---

[6] Ibid., p. 529.   [7] Opera Omnia, IV, 430, 441.   [8] Ibid., p. 430.

mechanics into mechanical forces contingent upon mass and momenta, metaphysical necessity, and intelligence. Chance and fortune merge with necessity, and the critical distinction becomes the presence or absence of guiding intelligence in making.

Just as the composition of the solar bodies indicates this intelligence, so do their disposition within the system, their positions and transverse velocities. The sun is placed in the center "to warm and enlighten the rest."[9] Had the larger planets not been placed at a greater distance from the sun, their gravitating powers would have disturbed the entire system.[10] The diurnal revolutions of the planets require a force impressed from some source other than gravitational attraction. Gravity gives the planets a motion directly towards the sun, and thus the transverse velocity of each of these masses must be carefully calculated to balance out this downward pull into a regular orbit.[11] The regular motion of each planet is a function of its mass, its position from the sun, its tangential velocity, and the correlative determination of every other unit within the system.[12] "I answer that the motions which the planets now have could not spring from any natural cause alone, but were impressed by an intelligent agent."[13] For the originating cause must grasp the proportions of internal composition necessary for each body as well as the resultant gravitational attraction that such a mass would author, the positional relationships between the planets and their sun and between the moons and their planets, the precise velocity to be impressed which would combine with gravitational impulses to preserve a concentric orbit: "And to compare and adjust all these things together, in so great a variety of bodies, argues that cause to be, not blind and fortuitous, but very well skilled in mechanics and geometry."[14]

Within the single system of the earth, biological and physical phenomena pose an identical problem. The bodies of animals show the presence of art. "Was the Eye contrived with-

[9] Ibid.
[10] Ibid., p. 432.
[11] Ibid., pp. 436-37.
[12] Ibid., pp. 434-37.
[13] Ibid., p. 431.
[14] Ibid., p. 432.

out Skill in Opticks, and the Ear without Knowledge of Sound?" asks one of the last Queries in the *Opticks*.[15] The motions of animals as well as the eclipses of planets break down to a cause intelligent and powerful. The uniformity within the planetary system indicates choice; the study of nature shows that nothing is done in vain and that the world itself is characterized by order and beauty.[16] The design of each thing, its composition within a smaller system, shows the effect of a synthetic intellect coordinating the ultimate mass particles "to make up that harmony in the system which, as I explained above, was the effect of choice rather than chance."[17]

It is in this way that mechanics leads to a God of motion, but in a manner which contrasts sharply with that of Aristotle or Cicero. Motion is neither the actualization of potency as such nor whatever philosophers call motion. It is the translation of mass from one absolute place to another; it is locomotion. All the kinds of transition are variant phenomenal manifestations of this movement, while "changes of corporeal Things are to be placed only in the various Separations and new Associations and Motions of these permanent Particles."[18] These motions can be resolved into forces of generation or composed into a system of harmonious movements, and to explain either the congruous structures or the minutest components is necessary if motion itself is to be resolved to its cause. The resolution of bodies and movements to masses and momenta does not obviate the need for a non-mechanical, intelligent force. On the contrary, it specifies that the constructing agent be skilled in mechanics, geometry, optics, and sound. God does not enter mechanics as he does Aristotelian physics or Ciceronian controversy. He is not the moving or final cause of endless movement nor is he that which men reach when they discuss motion. He stands at the origin of the system, specifying the quantities which will compose the structures and placing them in the correct, mathematical relationship which will insure the perdurance of their compositions. This is the God who is discovered analytically in the

[15] *Opticks*, "Query 28," pp. 369-70.   [16] *Ibid.*
[17] *Opera Omnia*, IV, p. 433.   [18] *Opticks*, "Query 31," p. 400.

Principia. For the investigations of the universal mechanics include not only the resolution to quantities which continue the interactions of organized movements, but also the mechanic or agent who set up the entire system. The analysis discovers both the forces or functional units operative within the universe and the cause antecedent to its effect in time. This later dimension brings the resolution to its final moment, a theological inquiry subsumed within the philosophy of nature.

For God does not enter mechanics as a principle alien to its investigation. He enters as force. Just as force (*vis*) had translated into gravity (*gravitas*) in astronomy, in mechanical theism it translates into domination (*dominatio*). For the word *Deus* (God) indicates a relation; just as sensible time or place, *Deus* is a relative word whose correlative is *servi* (servants or slaves). Newton followed Pocock in deriving *deus* from the Arabic *du*, "which signifies Lord [*Dominus*]." This explains its widespread use: to signify princes or Moses in sacred scripture or the souls of dead princes in pagan antiquity. This latter was most incorrect because of a lack of any dominion whatsoever. The One who governs all things is also titled *Deus*, but because of his supreme dominion, he is called *Dominus Deus*, "Lord God." There are many who have been titled gods; only one is justly called, "Lord God." And the converse is true: not every lord is God. Just as *aseitas* was the essence of the divine for Duns Scotus, so the essence of deity for Newton is *dominatio*. "Deity is the domination of God, not over a body belonging to him—as think those for whom God is the soul of the world—but over servants." Force enabled one to distinguish relative motion from absolute motion; dominion distinguishes gods from the Lord God. Even a being which was absolutely perfect but without *dominatio* would not be God. This is one reason why neither space nor time is God: neither exercises a divine force over bodies. Thus we do not say, "my Eternal," or "my Infinite." Both the endless duration and the infinite space is *perfectum*, but neither of them signifies a possession of dominion. The comprehensivity of force reaches its fullest exposition in the nature of

God as force, but distinguished from quantitative or astro-nomical force as a spiritual domination.[19]

For Aquinas, the divine attributes followed demonstra-tively because God was *Ipsum Esse Subsistens*. For Newton, the divine properties flow from his domination. "It is the dom-ination of a spiritual being which constitutes a God: a true, supreme, or imaginary dominion makes a true, supreme, or imaginary God." From his true dominion follows the divine life, his intelligence, and his power, as from the complexus of his perfection issues his supremacy and perfection. His omnip-otence lies in ruling all things and his omniscience, in know-ing all things. He is eternal and infinite, and it is here that mechanics relates the *dominatio entis spiritualis* to the abso-lutes of space and time, a relation which gives both of these locations of absolute motion a new understanding.[20]

This resolution of the systematic, functional units to the *dominatio* of God is not the problematic demonstration of God as the middle term (moving or final cause) for the con-junction between eternal and motion. The investigation is not unlike the discovery of absolute motion. Just as there is a detection of real motion through the forces which it effects or which affect it, so there is a detection of the divine through the domination which alone can account for the movement of the universe. The world is a coordinate unity which manifests the presence of the divine domination in the quantities which compose it, in the positions and velocities of the masses as in the constitution of the whole. The universal mechanics ana-lyzes these composites back to the original force which au-thored the entire structure and its parts. And this force is God. The subsequent demonstration of space as the sensorium of God is a derivation of God by the discovery that the natural philosopher has been in discourse about his presence from the beginning, as absolute motion indicated an absolute space as the initial condition of its own reality.

The comprehensive force which permeates the universe, which by its own existing constitutes the coordinates of time

[19] *Principia*, "General Scholium," p. 528.
[20] *Ibid*.

and space, does not identify with the world. It is simply false to accuse Newton of pantheism. Only if the divine domination identified with the phenomena, only if his interpretation were existential rather than entitative, would this be an accurate proposition. The distinction of levels within reality allows God to underlie the universe without merging with it, as it allowed absolute time to underlie its sensible indications without identifying with them.

God is eternal in that he lasts from the eternal to the eternal (*durat ab aeterno*) and he is infinite in that he is present from the infinite to the infinite (*adest ab infinito in infinitum*). God is not eternity as he is not duration; he is eternal. God is not infinity as he is not space; he is infinite. This is an indicated necessity by the cross-determinations of space and time. Every particle of space exists always (*semper*) and every moment of time exists everywhere (*ubique*). But the God of the universe is the maker of all things (*omnium rerum fabricator*) as well as their lord; as such he exists always and everywhere. This existence is constitutive of space and time: "He lasts always and is present everywhere, and by existing always and everywhere he constitutes duration and space."[21] This constituting of space and time shifts the demonstration of God from one who began the system to one who makes the system possible by constituting the coordinates within which all movement occurs. It is a transition from the God of a single past act, that of creation, to the God of abiding presence. The attributes of space and time had been severely criticized by Bishop Berkeley in his *Principles of Human Knowledge* as containing a "dangerous dilemma": "Either that real space is God or else that there is something besides God which is eternal, uncreated, infinite, indivisible, immutable. Both of which may be justly thought pernicious and absurd notions."[22] Newton's answer lies in his *General Scholium*, appended to the second

[21] *Ibid.* Newton can move from force to presence because of his denial of *actio in distans.* Cf. Cajori, II, 636-37.

[22] George Berkeley, "Principles of Human Knowledge," *The Works of George Berkeley, Bishop of Cloyne,* ed. A. A. Luce and T. E. Jessop (Edinburgh: Nelson, 1948-1957), No. 117, p. 94.

edition of the *Principia*. The infinity of space and the eternality of duration is a derived characteristic, constituted by the
One whose existence is not derived. They are coordinates
which his existence sets up; neither is divine. There are successive parts to time and situational parts to space, but not to
God. He himself is indivisible—the same always and everywhere. It is his power which sustains time and space, and
thus, God is present as substance (*per substantiam*) because
"power [*virtus*] is not able to subsist without substance."[23]
Far from believing in *actio in distans*, Newton urges the contrary to substantiate the claim of the omnipresent God: space
and time are resolved to the divine power, and the power itself
to the presence of God himself.

This allows for a synthetic view of time and space. At the
beginning of the universal mechanics, they had been found
necessities if motion was to be absolute. They had been discovered analytically. The theological culmination of physics
permits a comparison. "Is not the sensory of Animals that
place to which the sensitive substance is present, and into
which the sensible Species of Things are carried through the
Nerves and Brain, that there they may be perceived by their
immediate presence to that Substance."[24] The sensory, in
Newtonian psychology, is a particular place, the place where
a thing is known or sensed. It is neither the absolute place
of the moving object nor the organ by which it is initially
grasped; it is that place in which it and the substance which
knows it are immediately present to one another. God, unlike
any knowing creature, is immediately present to each thing
in its absolute place, and to all creatures in absolute space.
Infinite space, then, is the sensorium of God, "who in Infinite
Space, as it were in his Sensory, sees the things themselves
intimately and thoroughly perceives them and comprehends
them wholly by their immediate presence to himself."[25] Leibnitz failed to make this distinction between the organ of sense
and the sensorium, and thus wrote mistakenly to the Princess

---

[23] *Principia*, "General Scholium," p. 528.
[24] *Opticks*, "Query 28," p. 370.   [25] *Ibid.*

of Wales: "Sir Isaac Newton says, that Space is an Organ, which God makes use of to perceive Things by."[26] But this is precisely what Sir Isaac did not say. The *Opticks* discriminate among the object sensed, the image of this object, the organ of sense, and the sensorium. All four are operative in human perception, because only the image is immediately present to the man knowing—and present immediately in the sensorium, having been brought there by the organs of sense: "Of which things are Images only carried through the Organ of Sense into our little Sensoriums, are there seen and beheld by that which in us perceives and thinks."[27] But God is present not to the images, but in space to the things themselves. Thus he does not know their images nor make use of an organ of transmission. He knows all things directly, and space is most profoundly the divine sensorium, the place in which his knowing occurs.[28]

Space as sensorium makes it possible for Newton to move one step further than Leibnitz. God, being present in all things as in "his boundless uniform Sensorium," can engineer whatever motions he will and "thereby to form and reform the Parts of the Universe."[29] The *Fabricator omnium* not only began the system, but conserves it or repairs it. Leibnitz scores this as "God Almighty wants to wind up his Watch from Time to Time."[30] Newtonian mechanics argued that "there is not always the same quantity of Motion in the World,"[31] that by reason of the resistance of fluids, the attrition of parts, and an elasticity in solids, "motion is much more apt to be lost than got, and is always upon the Decay."[32] But this urges the necessity of such activity-principles as the cause of gravity, the cause of formation, and the cohesion of bodies.[33] Newton did not identify the causes of these principles with God; in

[26] G. H. Alexander (ed.), *The Leibniz-Clarke Correspondence* (Manchester: University Press, 1956), p. 3. For a commentary on this interchange, cf. Alexandre Koyré, *From the Closed World To the Infinite Universe* (New York: Harper, 1958), pp. 235ff.

[27] *Opticks*, "Query 28," p. 370.   [28] Cf. Koyré, *op.cit.*, pp. 237ff.

[29] *Opticks*, "Query 31," p. 403.   [30] Alexander (ed.), *op.cit.*, p. 5.

[31] *Opticks*, "Query 31," p. 397.   [32] *Ibid.*, p. 398.

[33] *Ibid.*, pp. 399, 401.

fact, he specifically refused to do so: "Hitherto, I have not been able to discover the causes of those properties of gravity from phenomena, and I frame no hypotheses."[34] Like the ancient atomic theories praised in the *Opticks*, universal mechanics leaves open the cause of gravity just as it left the system of the world open to a re-formation by God. In the subsequent controversy with Leibnitz, Clarke suggested that only this openness of structure allowed for the free activity of God and for the possibilities of divine revelation, providence, and concursus, further contending that Leibnitz' self-sufficient universe excluded the action of God and posited a world whose laws were necessity.[35]

God is above all quantitative measurements; indeed he effects those coordinates which make measurements possible. Containing all things, he identifies with none and is affected by none, while no mass or movement suffers any change or resistance because of his omnipresence. By the same necessity with which he exists, he exists always and everywhere, "but in a manner not at all human, in a manner not at all corporeal, in a manner totally unknown to us."[36] Just as time and space were qualityless; so the divine spirituality is denoted by an absence of mass, movement, change, and bodily figure. Newton distinguishes between the idea of his attributes and the knowledge of his substance: his existence and attributes are manifested in the phenomena of a world in movement; but men perceive and understand not the real substance of anything bodily, let alone the real substance of God. Masses are known by their figures, colors, sounds and surfaces, smells and savors; God is known only by the system he has authored.[37]

Newtonian mechanics involves God in either movement of its method: either in the resolution of the system of the world back to its original forces, the domination of God, or in the composite propositions that all space and time becomes the location of his presence, space as the sensorium of God. In

---

[34] *Principia*, "General Scholium," p. 530.
[35] Cf. Koyré, *op.cit.*, pp. 237ff.
[36] *Principia*, "General Scholium," p. 529.
[37] *Ibid.*

either movement, the divine domination is the comprehensive principle of theological inquiry. For "we admire him because of his perfections, but we adore and worship him because of his dominion."[38]

[38] *Ibid.*

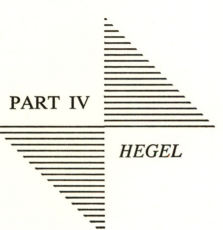

PART IV

HEGEL

XVIII.

Dialectical Method

THE FOCI of divergent philosophies are formed by the dominant intellectual tendency of an age to converge its inquiries either upon the structures of things or the processes of thought or the expressions of men in language and action. The "selection" of the philosophic community dictates both the primary area of discussion or investigation and the fundamental source of categories and principles. This selection is itself indicated by the subsequent doctrine elaborated on world-order. Aristotelian science came to bear directly upon the nature of things, and the god of movement entered in the constitution of a cosmos either for physics or for first philosophy. Κόσμος translated into the Latin *mundus*, and in the pragmatic or semantic selection of Cicero, world-order converted into political inter-relations, a republic of men and gods, mutually involved in the practical deeds of the body politic and in the philosophic interchanges of discourse. Newtonian mechanics recaptured the focus of Aristotle only in so far as it sought the subject-matter of its discipline, the simples of its arguments, and the principles of its conclusions within the extramental operations of things. In the *Principia, mundus* became *mundi systema*, the mechanical system of the universe of which the god of motion was both origin through his dominance and the final definitor of space and time through his existence. After the Kantian revolution, men sought the justification of science and the criteria for assertions in the processes of thought, and the consequent Hegelian dialectic formed an order which was neither primarily the physical universe nor the city of gods and men. Systems are above all systems of knowledge. The

Hegelian task is the elevation of *Wissen* to *Wissenschaft*, and the only form in which *Wissenschaft* can exist is *das wissenschaftliche System*.[1] The primary order to be obtained is one of thought, a project symptomatic of a philosophy which, while it will score the Kantian insistence upon antecedent critique, will itself erect as the first steps of science a phenomenology of consciousness, merge logic and metaphysics, and obtain existence through the actuality of pure thought.[2] In such a system, philosophy can develop finally from the mere love of knowledge to actual knowledge, and both the inner necessity of cognition and the progressive development of German theoretic science evince the pattern of this evolution. This twofold necessity can be substantiated only by the actual accomplishment of the system, for the order of knowledge not only unites divergent elements into a whole but reflexively justifies its own program within philosophy and its history.[3]

System mirrors the organic interrelations of truth itself. Truth is concrete, is a whole of which any concept or judgment is a balanced part. To remove parts is to author abstractions, and to leave them abstract is to commit them to falsity. "Truth is only possible as a universe or a totality of thought," and it is this universe which identifies as the system.[4] Like the

---

[1] Georg Wilhelm Friedrich Hegel, *Phänomenologie des Geistes*, Vol. v of *Sämtliche Werke*, ed. Johannes Hofmeister (Hamburg: Verlag von Felix Meiner, 1952), p. 12. Hereafter cited as PG. The English translation of the "Preface" is that of Walter Kaufmann, *Hegel: Texts and Commentary* (Garden City, N.Y.: Doubleday, 1966). Hereafter cited as PGK. The English translation of the rest of PG is that of Sir James Baillie, *The Phenomenology of Mind* (London: Allen and Unwin, 1964). Hereafter cited as PGB. A translation from the German by the author is indicated by an (m) after the citation of the German text. Whenever the German text is cited, the English translation is indicated in parentheses, thus: (PGK 12).

[2] G.W.F. Hegel, *Wissenschaft der Logik*, ed. Georg Lasson (2 vols.; Leipzig: Verlag von Felix Meiner, 1948), I, 6-8, 46-47, 52. Hereafter cited as WL. The English translation is that of W. H. Johnson and L. G. Struthers in Hegel's *Science of Logic* (2 vols.; London: Allen and Unwin, 1961). Hereafter cited as WLJS. (WLJS, I, 36-37, 74-75, 80.)

[3] PG, p. 12 (PGK, p. 12).

[4] G.W.F. Hegel, *Enzyklopädie der Philosophischen Wissenschaften im Grundrisse*, ed. Friedhelm Nicolin and Otto Pöggeler (Hamburg: Verlag von Felix Meiner, 1959), No. 14, pp. 47-48. The work is divided into *Logik*, *Naturphilosophie*, and *Philosophie des Geistes*. Hereafter cited as EL, EN,

truth which it realizes, the system must possess its own unifying processes and developmental movement. Here the propos-
als for system turn to the questions of method. For method
identifies with system as the concrete form of truth. Method
becomes of the same critical importance as the truth itself:

> Method at first may appear as the mere manner and fashion
> of cognition, and indeed such is its nature. But manner and
> fashion as method are not only a modality of Being, deter-
> mined in and for itself, but are posited as modality of cog-
> nition as determined by the Notion, and form in so far as
> form is the soul of all objectivity and every content other-
> wise determined has its truth in form alone.[5]

The question of method turns on the relation between the
form and the content of knowledge. If the latter is made external to method, no ultimate assimilation is possible between the
movement of thought and the processes of things; if, on the
other hand, the form is not arbitrarily chosen and contingently
superimposed upon the content, method becomes "the absolute
foundation and ultimate truth."[6] The alternative positions
taken through the history of philosophical method not only
exhaust the internal possibilities, but trace a successive, dialectical development of philosophic procedure which reaches its
consummation in Absolute Idealism. The different methods
structure different philosophic systems, and their differences,
far from being a foundation for scepticism, indicate the dynamic unity possessed by the "one philosophy at different
degrees of maturity."[7] The identical evolution of cognition
which expresses itself in the history of philosophy is also exhibited in the system of philosophy itself.[8]

This history of philosophic method, then, does not become
a successive refutation and rejection of previous absurdities;
such a posture would be predicated on an abstract opposition
between the true and the false and a failure "to comprehend

---

and EPG. The English translation of the *Logik* used is that of William Wallace, *The Logic of Hegel* (Oxford: Clarendon, 1904). Hereafter cited as
ELW. (ELW, p. 24.)

[5] WLJS, ii, 467-68.   [6] *Ibid.*, ii, 478.   [7] ELW, pp. 22-23.
[8] EL, No. 13, pp. 46-47 (ELW, pp. 21-23).

the difference of the philosophic systems in terms of the progressive development of the truth."[9] The movement is organic,
not suicidal. One form in which a plant may exist is in bud,
but this gives way to the blossom, and the blossom in turn is
replaced by the fruit. "Those forms do not only differ, they
also displace each other because they are incompatible. Their
fluid nature, however, makes them, at the same time, moments
of an organic unity."[10] In the unity of the development of the
whole, these moments not only do not conflict with one another, but are equally necessary and constitute the life of the
plant. In the same manner the opposition of philosophic systems and their proper methods is an antagonism only if the
movement of the developing philosophy is arrested. The understanding of their deficiencies is not to annihilate them, but
to indicate that their truth lies beyond them in an assimilation
into a more universal method.[11] Indeed the procedure proper
to the philosophic only emerges in this fashion, as pure self-
recognition is deepened rather than destroyed, in absolute
otherness—a maxim which stands as the ground and basis of
scientific knowledge in general.[12] The progressive contradiction of alien philosophic methods merely draws out their internal insufficiency and their orientation towards growth and
completion. Refutation, correctly practiced through this internal contradiction, is the inner development of the refuted position and its fulfillment in a further assimilation.[13] Contradiction is not justification for scepticism, but indication of the
progressive nature of scientific method.

The refusal of all scientific method and the reliance upon
the substantial immediacy of intuition, though revived by
Jacobi, represents a pre-philosophic, early stage in the growth
of consciousness.[14] Truth here is not grasped, comprehended
conceptually, but felt and intuited. The Intuitionalist rejects
the concept as the element of the existence of truth, positing
feelings and ecstasy through this exclusion of reflection and

[9] PGK, p. 8.
[10] *Ibid.*
[11] PG, p. 10 (PGK, p. 8).
[12] PG, pp. 24-25 (PGK, p. 40).
[13] PG, pp. 23-24 (PGK, p. 38).
[14] PG, pp. 12-13 (PGK, p. 14).

demonstration.[15] This "substantial knowledge without Concept" is the pre-philosophic dominance of a purely actional principle, one which claims to immerse the thinker in the sacred and profound, but in reality subjects the subject-matter to the contingencies of its enthusiasms and to the dominance of personal arbitrariness. The pretentious claims of intuition to a knowledge higher than science hide its primitive condition, "the unmethod [*die Unmethode*] of intimation and enthusiasm."[16] This imperialism of intuition, whose function is not insight but edification, is not a development of the post-Anselmian philosophic spirit, but a throwback to the pre-scientific. Were it to prevail it would accomplish the destruction of humanity as a community in truth and consciousness. For it is the nature of this humanity to struggle for agreement and discourse with others, while "the anti-human, the animalic consists in remaining at the level of feeling and being able to communicate only through feelings."[17] The Intuitionalists subject the deepest realities of human consciousness to the most arbitrary and contingent aspect of man, destroying not only the interchange through which philosophy proceeds but any alternative scientific method as well. It is the "crude rejection of all Method."[18]

The superiority of the pre-Kantian metaphysics lay in its assertion that truth could alone be apprehended through thought, in its position that harmony lay between things and thinking.[19] Its defect was one of method, a logistic method. In

---

[15] G.W.F. Hegel, *Vorlesungen über die Bewisse vom Dasein Gottes. Werke* (Vollständige Ausgabe durch einen Verein von Freunden des Verewigten: Marheineke, Schulze, Oans, Henning, Hotho, Michelet, Förster; Berlin: Verlag von Duncker und Humbolt, 1840), XII, 359-61. Hereafter cited as VB. The English translation is from E. B. Speirs and J. Burdon Sanderson in Hegel's *Lectures on the Philosophy of Religion Together With a Work on the Proofs of the Existence of God* (London: Kegan Paul, 1895), III. Hereafter cited as VBS. Any other reference to these *Lectures on the Philosophy of Religion* is cited as FR. (VBS, p. 156).

[16] PGK, p. 74. Cf. VB, pp. 387-88 (VBS, pp. 182-83).

[17] PGK, pp. 104-106.   [18] WLJS, I, 64.

[19] WLJS, I, 55: "The older Metaphysics had in this respect a loftier conception of Thought than that which has become current in more modern times. For the older Metaphysics laid down as fundamental that that which

order to obtain system, philosophers from Spinoza to Leibnitz to Wolff modeled philosophic method upon the mathematical.[20] The paradigm was Euclidean geometry. Its manifest advantages told through its demand for insight into structures of meaning and for comprehension of causal relations.[21] But the mathematical apprehension of the truth of a theorem is defective both in the diremption drawn between the movement of things and the movement of thoughts and also in the arbitrary, actional character of its principle. The movement of a mathematical demonstration is external to the figure demonstrated: the triangle does not take itself apart or construct other figures from which it is to be demonstrated. The logistic method does not obtain the becoming or internal movement of the essence, but only the becoming of the existence, i.e., the subjective knowledge of the truth of theorems. Philosophical knowledge unites both of these movements, while the logistic method attains its knowledge not through the internal genesis of its object, but through an activity which remains external to the object.[22] As external to its object, the logistic method cannot take its principle of construction from the self-differentiations of the concept of the theorem, but from an arbitrary command given with a view to a prospective result. The source of mathematical procedure is as external to its concept as its method is to its result.[23] The application of mathematics to physics through mechanics has the improvement of treating movement instead of abstract magnitude, but the shift in object destroys whatever necessity mathematics possessed, applying formulae garnered from experience to assumptions about existents. The method is empirical, rather than mathematical,

---

by thinking is known of and in things, that alone is what is really true in them; that what is really true is not things taken in their immediacy, but only things when they have been taken up into the Form of Thought, as conceptions."

[20] WL, I, 35 (WLJS, I, 64).

[21] PG, p. 35 (PGK, pp. 60-62). Cf. VB, pp. 370-75 (VBS, pp. 166-69).

[22] PG, pp. 35-36 (PGK, pp. 62-64).

[23] PG, pp. 35-37 (PGK, pp. 64-66). In contrast to a method whose unicity mirrors the unicity of the concept, both mathematical and historical proofs are plural. "It is said that some twenty proofs of the Pythagorean problem have been discovered." VBS, p. 212.

and contains only the empty semblance of demonstrations.[24] In this dialectical history of method, Newton is not placed with Spinoza and Leibnitz, but with the British Empiricists, treating concepts like sensuous things and responsible for the methodological separation of physics from true scientific method.[25] Neither the logistic method nor its empirical usages can furnish an ideal for philosophic procedure.

The Kantian revolution lay in the rediscovery of the triplicity of the rhythm of knowledge.[26] Without internal motion and still uncomprehended, the schema of a threefold division begins to appear: in the tables of the categories, the third category emerges from the connection of the second with the first; reason is seen as triadic in its governing ideas, and the critiques themselves divide into three. "Kant has thus made an historic statement of the moments of the whole, and has correctly determined and distinguished them: it is a good introduction to Philosophy."[27] The abstract form of this triplicity had been set up by the Neoplatonists but without finding it the necessity of mind itself. To have demonstrated "the form of the method as a whole as a triplicity" constitutes the infinite merit of Kant's philosophy.[28] Fichte seized upon this triad and raised it to an absolute importance.[29] But the central defect in their procedure lay in making the triplicity a non-dialectical schema, a set of determinations formally exhaustive of the possibilities from which predicates can be derived and applied to any form. The fixity of the lifeless matrix turns the discovered triplicity into operational uses, the method which Hegel calls "construction," and marks critical philosophy as formalistic:

Formalists have seized even upon triplicity, and have held fast to its skeleton; and this form has been rendered tedious

[24] PG, p. 38 (PGK, p. 66).

[25] G.W.F. Hegel, *Lectures on the History of Philosophy*, trans. E. S. Haldane (London: Kegan Paul, 1892), III, 323-24. Hereafter cited as HP.

[26] HP, III, 477; PG, p. 42 (PGK, p. 74).

[27] HP, III, 478.

[28] WLJS, II, 479. For the trinity within neoplatonic thought, cf. HP, II, 440-50.

[29] PG, p. 42 (PGK, p. 74).

and of ill-repute by the shallow misuse and the barrenness of modern so-called philosophic *construction*, which consists simply in attaching the formal framework without concept and immanent determination to all sorts of matter and employing it for external arrangement. But its inner value cannot be diminished by this vapid misuse, and it must still be deemed a great matter that the outward form of rational procedure has been discovered, albeit not understood.[30]

The very nature of formalism lies in the exhaustive classification of the living reality through the application of determinations from a schema; it is the "method of labeling everything in heaven and earth, all natural and spiritual forms," destroying the living organism of the universe through this pigeonholing.[31] The product of such a method is like the tabulation of a skeleton with small pieces of paper stuck all over it or like "the rows of closed, labeled jars in a spicer's stall."[32] The living reality is killed in order to understand it. Through this operational reflection upon the Absolute, the living essence escapes the grasp of philosophy and thought is left with unresolved dualisms and diversities.[33] Kant had shown that dialectical contradiction is not an arbitrary movement, but the necessary procedure of reason. But because of this antinomic character of thinking, the critical philosophy separated the knowledge of appearances from the grasp of actualities and predicated cognition of understanding alone. Kant's refusal to put contradiction into things, "that tenderness towards things which will not permit any contradiction to be attached to them," authored the split worlds of Transcendental Idealism—phenomena and things-in-themselves. Even Fichte's denial of the noumenal did not bring about synthesis, for one is left with the double deductions of theory and practice.[34]

Schelling attempted to overcome these operational diremptions through an intuited Absolute in which all distinctions were merged into an undifferentiated unity. It was an attempt to synthesize the discriminations of the operational method

[30] WLJS, II, 479. Cf. PG, pp. 42-43 (PGK, p. 78).
[31] PGK, p. 78.   [32] *Ibid.*   [33] *Ibid.*
[34] VBS, p. 252; HP, III, 499; WL, I, 38 (WLJS, I, 67).

214

through the introduction of a simple principle. The distinctions of the schema are ultimately merged into the monochromatic simplicity of absolute identity. Philosophy attains an Absolute as principle, the A = A, and imagines that its own actuality has been achieved in this "night in which all cows are black."[35] Within Schelling's principle, an abstract generality has been erected to solve the Fichtean dualisms, but this empty identity misses both the particularization of content and the cultivation of those forms through which actuality is obtained and grasped. In the loss of all concreteness and determinations, the principle explains nothing and supplements a lifeless method with a lifeless source.[36] The formalists remain incomplete because there is no internal movement to their principle and no organic relations between their method and the developments of life. What is needed is a principle which will synthesize the manifold of Fichte's deductions without the identity of Schelling's Absolute and a method whose own motion does not superimpose the foreign upon the object of its study.[37]

As the rhythm of the true dictated the need for system, so it indicates the method and principle of philosophy. "Everything depends upon this, that we comprehend and express the true not as substance, but just as much as subject."[38] Like the Aristotelian nature, the true is subject and author of its own movement, and the identification of this source specifies the commensurate and reflexive nature of the Hegelian principle. Further, the movement of the principle specifies the movement of the method; and the internal motion of any actuality—organism or concept—is dialectical. This movement is not something the subject does; it is something the subject is.[39] Reflec-

---

[35] HP, III, 529-30, 542.   [36] PGK, p. 26.
[37] PG, p. 16 (PGK, p. 24).   [38] PGK, p. 28.
[39] WLJS, I, 36-37: "This movement of Mind, which in its simplicity gives itself its determinateness and hence self-equality, and which thus is the immanent development of the Notion—this movement is the Absolute Method of knowledge, and at the same time the immanent soul of the Content of knowledge." Ibid., I, 65: "It is clear that no expositions can be regarded as scientific which do not follow the course of this Method, and which are not conformable to its simple rhythm, for that is the course of the thing itself."

tion is not upon the concept; it is within the concept both for development and definition. It is this union of content and method that characterizes the philosophic method: "It is the nature of the content and that alone which lives and stirs in philosophic cognition, while it is this very reflection of the content which itself originates and determines the nature of philosophy."[40] Thus philosophic progress is obtained not by elaboration of problems and working out their solutions as in Aristotelian inquiry nor by the antinomic discrimination of perspectives as in the Ciceronian dialogues nor by the resolution of wholes into their parts as in Newtonian mechanics, but by following through the self-movement of the object of study as it passes through the forms or moments of its self-differentiation and recovery. To grasp any subject-matter truly is to grasp it as movement, and to follow it through its motion is the dialectical method of philosophy. This is the only true, universal method: "I know that it is the only true Method. This is evident from the fact that the Method is noways different from its object and content; for it is the content in itself, *the Dialectic which it has in itself*, that moves it on."[41] The *Phenomenology of Spirit* furnished an example of this method working through consciousness to science, but the exposition of the method in itself is the work of logic since "method is the consciousness of the form taken by the inner spontaneous movement of the Logic."[42]

In the history of thought, dialectic has been associated with a negativity; this is correct, though the negativity has often been misunderstood. Diogenes Laertius is cited for the origin of the three major divisions of philosophy. Natural philosophy is attributed to Thales, moral philosophy to Socrates, and dialectic to Plato. The elder Eleatic school, however, had employed its dialectic against motion; Plato had brought it to bear against contemporary ideas and concepts, pure categories and thought-determinations; later scepticism has used its dialectic against the data of experience, maxims of practical living, and the concept of science itself. The conclusion of the dialectic was contradiction, opposite determinations were dem-

[40] *Ibid.*, I, 36.   [41] *Ibid.*, I, 65.   [42] *Ibid.*, I, 64.

onstrated of the same object, and the invalidity of the prior assertion was established through the contradiction of predicates. The dialectic could be objective if the object itself was held to be self-contradictory, as in the Eleatic discussions of motion; it was subjective if cognition was at war with itself, as in scepticism and in Kantian criticism. Within the middle ages, dialectic was an art, an external and negative skill brought to bear upon any subject-matter in order to disturb and unsettle.[43] The Kantian antinomies relieved dialectic from this form of deception or arbitrariness, and found it not merely a movement of the mind, but a necessary movement of the mind. The antinomies discovered contradiction at the very heart of reason, but Kant failed to exploit this discovery in a synthesis of objective and subjective dialectic. He distinguished thing from thought and confined dialectic to the latter. The major contribution of Absolute Idealism was to recognize dialectic as the law both of things and of thoughts—even of propositions— which allowed the movement of the mind to coincide with the reality of things.[44] This recognition permitted philosophic method to advance beyond the fixed diremptions of Transcendental Idealism, "a complete philosophy of Understanding which renounces Reason."[45] When contradiction is understood as the law of life, reason—in contradiction with itself—becomes the only means of grasping what is the case. The internal contradiction becomes the necessary source of the movement of both.

The movement itself is a composite of moments which both chart its progress and spell out the internal determinations of its result. Fichte had indicated the steps of his own triad as "thesis," "antithesis," and "synthesis," and Schelling had followed suit. Hegel did not, and his choice suggests a deliberate attempt to break away from the "lifeless schemata" of his predecessors with a flexibility of vocabulary indicative of "the fluid nature" of the reality which he studied.[46] A double negative

[43] WL, II, 491-93 (WLJS, II, 473-74); EL, No. 81, pp. 102-103 (EDW, p. 149).
[44] WL, I, 38-40 (WLJS, I, 67-68).   [45] HP, III, 476.
[46] PGK, p. 8.

moment follows within the movement of any being; but these determinations are not predicated of the content like a label, but issue out of the life of the content itself. The content or concept develops, becomes what it was not, and then reintegrates this "other" back into itself. It moves from a prior simplicity (antecedent to the new development) into its other, and then realizes this other as a determination and definition of its own nature. The other is the moment of self-positing, of self-determination through self-negation. One becomes something different, something other, and then comprehends this other as a determination of the self. The passage is from immediacy through a stage of negation of this immediacy in mediation to a merger in mediated immediacy. The concept or content passes from being in-itself (*An sich*) to that which is different or in contradiction for-itself (*Für sich*) to subsume (*aufheben*) this difference as that which is in-and-for-itself (*An-und-für-sich*).[47] Each of these moments needs attention.

Any method must have a beginning form. This is not the principle which authors the movement, but the initial phase out of which it moves. Because it is the beginning, its form is simple and its content is immediate, both of which merge into an abstract universality. It is not an entity of sensuous intuition or imagination, but of thought, for sense data present a manifold, while only thought-determinations can be simple, universal, and undifferentiated. Method, as rational process, does not originate without a rational beginning, and only thought-determinations are rational. These determinations, in their earliest stages, are simple and universal, while complexity indicates developments and elaborations. Any concept in its undifferentiated simplicity can constitute a beginning, but the first universality or the most abstract phase of simplicity in itself is Being, simple abstract self-reference, simple Being in-itself (*An sich*). "Method, as the consciousness of the concept," grasps even from the first that this universality is only a moment, that the virtualities of the concept must be posited, that

[47] PG, pp. 19-24 (PGK, pp. 28-38). For the dialectical method and its relationship to Hegelian ontological procedure, cf. Emerich Coreth, *Das Dialektische Sein in Hegels Logik* (Wien: Verlag Heder, 1952).

what is contained only in-itself must emerge as the other of this simplicity.[48]

The second moment is essentially this development, but a development through the negation of the first. It is the stage of difference, determination, and judgment, but not as externally imposed upon the initial stage as dialectic is not a matter of external superimposition. The Hegelian "interpretation" contrasts very sharply with the Platonic dialectic at this point. Socrates will admit that opposite things come from opposite things, but he specifically denies that one opposite as such issues out of another: "We maintain that the opposites themselves would absolutely refuse to tolerate coming into being from one another."[49] Plato's ontological interpretation would allow him to separate *to enantion pragma* from *auto to enantion,* the former being in some imperfect and variant fashion a transcription of the latter within the continuous transmutations of space. For Plato, one form does not generate another; for Hegel, that is precisely what is done. The embryo is human in itself, but not for itself. It is only in generating what is other than the embryonic moment, the educated reason, that actuality is obtained. For Plato, the dialectic is subjective, working upon its subject-matter; for Hegel, it is the soul of the matter itself: "It is rather the matter's very soul putting forth its branches and fruit organically."[50] Hegelian dialectic is not ontological in its interpretation, but entitative: the concept develops itself out of itself through a process which is truly immanent in the engendering of its oppositions and determinations. This interpretation lodges the movement of the dialectic at the substructure of all reality, just as the principle united subject and object and the method lay with the movement through diversities into assimilation. The three together characterize what absolute idealism claimed as the "absolute method": "The absolute method does not hold the

[48] WLJS, II, 469-72.

[49] *Phaedo* 103ᵉ, Edith Hamilton and Huntington Cairns (eds.), *The Collected Dialogues of Plato,* trans. Hugh Tredennick (New York: Pantheon, 1963), p. 84.

[50] G.W.F. Hegel, *The Philosophy of Right,* trans. T. M. Knox (Oxford: Clarendon, 1962), pp. 34-35.

position of external reflection; it draws the determinate element directly from its object itself, since it is the object's immanent principle and soul."[51]

This second moment allows for a dialectical transmutation
of the two forms of the Newtonian method—analysis and
synthesis. The bifurcation of the simple beginning is an analytic moment insofar as the new determination is discovered
immanently within the immediate; it is synthetic, as this determination shows itself to be other than the immediate, its contradiction in fact, and related to its beginning by "this relation
of various."[52] This second moment is the moment of judgment,
of propositions and of two-term assertions. "This equally synthetic and analytic moment of the Judgment, by which the
original universal determines itself out of itself to be its own
Other, may rightly be called the *dialectical* moment."[53] This
second term which arises is the first negative, the negation
of the immediate; but as the negative of a specific immediate,
it contains and preserves this first. "To hold fast the positive
in its negative, and the content of the presupposition in the
result, is the most important part of rational cognition."[54] The
first term is in the second, while the second is the truth of the
first, and the unity of both is expressed in a proposition. The
immediate is the subject, and the mediate is the predicate.
Philosophies which attempt to express truth in propositional,
rather than systematic, form remain on this level; but the
proposition fails to indicate the actual, synthetic movement of
the subject. The judgment is always one-sided, and, insofar,
false. Such philosophies become dogmatisms, characterized by
the opinion that "the true consists in a proposition that is a
fixed result or that is known immediately."[55] Any conceptual
determination involves its negation: extreme anarchy generates extreme despotism; pride goes before a fall; extreme pleas-

---

[51] WLJS, II, 472. VBS, p. 163: "Real knowledge, inasmuch as it does not
remain outside the object, but in point of fact occupies itself with it, must be
immanent in the object, the proper movement of its nature, only expressed
in the form of thought and taken up into consciousness."

[52] WLJS, II, 473. For an application of analytic-synthetic to syllogism, cf.
ibid., II, 478.

[53] *Ibid.*, II, 473.   [54] *Ibid.*, II, 476.   [55] PGK, p. 60.

ure becomes painful. Implicit in any notion is its contradiction.[56] This negativity is the soul, the internal moving principle of the dialectic. So the second negative, the negation of
the mediate as other, follows as the third moment of the dialectic. It is the transcendence of contradiction through assimilation. The moment of alienation is not annihilated, as it will
be with the Marxian actional principle, but *aufgehoben*. The
ambiguity of the terminology indicates the double meaning of
the third moment. The mediated term is both preserved as a
determination of the subject, but ceases as contradiction. Both
the initial abstract beginning and its negation become internal
determinations of the concrete result. Just as they are moments
through which the concept passes in its own development, so
they remain as forms through which its intelligibility is
achieved and by which it is understood.[57] Insofar as intuition
would fix upon the simplicity of the first or insofar as understanding would stabilize the differentiations and distinctions of
the second, they falsify them. The assimilation into the third,
into the concrete, is not through the return to undifferentiated
simplicity as in Schelling, but through the reflexivity of a principle which returns to itself through its own contradiction.
The transcendence achieved carries the internal dialectic—its
own contradiction—within itself; and so the self-positing and
assimilation continues, endlessly spelling out the internal constitution and the implication of any concept.[58] Concepts become self-movements in Absolute Idealism, and the pattern of
their movement identifies with the dialectic method. The
method of the system coincides with the structure of the motion, and in both fixity gives way to fluidity in thought and
things.[59]

The immanent dialectic indicates a radical shift in the problems of motion. Movement is no longer the Newtonian locomotion of bodies in the mathematical dimensions of space and
time. Motion lies, rather, at the heart of the concept itself,

---

[56] EL, No. 81, pp. 102-103 (ELW, pp. 150-51).
[57] WL, I, 93-95 (WLJS, I, 119-20).
[58] WL, II, 497-500 (WLJS, II, 478-80).
[59] PG, pp. 45, 47 (PGK, pp. 82, 86).

while the range of movement is through any actuality and supreme characteristic of spirit. Nor is motion the projection of Ciceronian dialogue, that which men call movement. Cicero's praise of Socrates has to be understood as indicating the need for human opinion to be elevated to the heavens before it can come into the homes of men; and this elevation of movement lies in that identity in which motion, thought, things, and discourse are one.[60] Nor can one adopt the Aristotelian analysis of motion as the actuality of a being in potency insofar as it is potency. Motion is far more the actuality of the potential qua actual; it indicates actuality rather than potentiality. It is not so much differentiated into variants and made the subject of a particular science as it is the constituting life of each science and the form of the single philosophic method. In the dialectical idealism of Hegel, motion and becoming identify in the supreme assimilation which is spirit and actuality.

Just as motion coincides with the method by which it is studied, so the subsequent affirmation of divine existence shifts. The theological question constitutes the highest problem of philosophy, for religion, art, and philosophy have the same object, but differ only in the form by which it is grasped. In art, the Absolute is grasped in the sense object; in religion, the Absolute is present in a figurative representative; philosophy "is the highest manner of comprehending the Absolute Idea, because its manner is the highest—the Notion."[61] Despite the reservation of critical philosophy, human thought— either as common sense or as Absolute Idealism—cannot give over its attempt to demonstrate the divine existence and nature.[62] It is the first concern of philosophy:

That which is in general at the present moment the first concern of philosophy, namely to place God once again abso-

[60] This dialectical transformation of Ciceronian pragmatism appears in Hegel's Latin dissertation, *Dissertatio de Orbitis Planetarum*. For the text in translation, see Walter Kaufmann, *Hegel: A Reinterpretation* (Garden City, N.Y.: Doubleday, 1966), p. 52. Hereafter cited as KH.
[61] WLJS, II, 566. Cf. VB, p. 361 (VBS, p. 157).
[62] VB, pp. 428-31 (VBS, pp. 229-32).

lutely right in front at the head of philosophy as the sole ground of everything, as the only *principium essendi* and *cognoscendi*, after he has been placed long enough alongside other finite things or entirely at the end as a postulate that issues from an absolute finitude.[63]

This is the initial statement of the abiding Hegelian attempt to renovate the proofs for the existence of God, demonstrations of the pre-Kantian metaphysics subsequently destroyed in the Kantian discriminations between faith and understanding.[64] It would be the characteristic of philosophies of Understanding to rest with these abstract divisions and of dialectical philosophy to push beyond their contradiction into a synthesis.[65] The true nature of the proofs for the existence of God is only the reflective consciousness of the proper movement of the object considered in itself and of the motion of reason. The objective movement of the data and the subjective movement of the mind identify in the single elevation of the spirit to God.[66] Demonstration, in Aristotle, was a species of logical discourse in which an assertion was resolved in terms of its proper cause, the cause of science identified reflexively with the cause of the fact demonstrated. In Cicero, positions are proved through the discrimination of positions and their consequent clash in debate. In Newton, demonstration lies with the resolution of movements back to the forces which composed them or the comprehensive force which set them up. In Hegel, proof (*Beweis*) is the unfolding of the content of its object, and

[63] G.W.F. Hegel, "How Common Sense Takes Philosophy, shown through an analysis of the works of Herr Krug," KH, p. 60.

[64] VB, pp. 359-61 (VBS, pp. 155-56).

[65] VB, pp. 364-66 (VBS, pp. 160-61).

[66] VBS, pp. 188-89: "This connection, which is thus present to consciousness must not be a subjective movement of thought outside of reality, but must follow this latter, and must simply unfold its meaning and necessity. *Knowledge is just this unfolding of the objective movement of the content, of the inner necessity which essentially belongs to it, and it is true knowledge since it is in unity with the object.* For us this object must be the elevation of our spirit to God, and is thus what we have referred to as the necessity of absolute truth in the form of that final result into which everything returns in the Spirit." (Italics added.)

thus the initial question of the dialectic comes to bear upon the movement of the concept.[67] What was the question of existence in Aristotelian inquiry becomes in Absolute Idealism the question of the subject of motion.

There is a multiplicity of metaphysical proofs of the existence of God, but the variety has been reduced to three, both by the evolution of the question in the history of philosophy and by the inner connection of the demonstration with the development of spirit.[68] One must simply deny the Thomistic assertion that one can know only that God is and not what God is;[69] each of the three demonstrations gives different characteristics or determinations of God, each successively deepens the internal determinations which constitute the divine essence until they terminate with God as spirit.[70] The first two begin with a finite content, either the contingency of the world or the purposiveness within nature; the last takes the infinite content as its beginning and moves to the being of the divine.[71]

As the question of existence transmutes to that of the subject of movement, so the question of definition shifts to the question of the initial determination of the divine in the cosmological proof—the demonstration from contingency. The qualitative question becomes the question of predicates exhibited by God in nature—the teleological proof. God as utterly reflexive principle even of his own being is the final development of the dialectic—the ontological proof. Each of these is a stage of the single proof, an elevation of the mind from the self-denying motion of the finite to the eternal, self-moving motion which is the result, the content, and the presupposition of the whole:

> We do not have to prove this elevation from the outside; it proves itself in itself, and this means nothing else than it is by its very nature necessary. We have only to look at its own process, and we have there, since it is necessary in itself,

---

[67] VB, pp. 369-70 (VBS, p. 165).   [68] VB, pp. 413-16 (VBS, pp. 212-15).
[69] VB, pp. 395-99, 405ff. (VBS, pp. 192-93, 203).

[70] VB, pp. 416-17. To know God as creator is not adequate to the Christian standpoint; he must be known as spirit. Cf. *ibid.*, pp. 380-81 (VBS, pp. 216, 176).

[71] VB, p. 416 (VBS, p. 215).

the necessity, insight into the nature of which has to be vouched for by proof.[72]

The dialectic transmutes the nature of motion and structure of argument, and it also changes the two foundations which underlay the argument from motion: the motion of the mind and the movement of things. In Aristotle, they did not identify, and the movement of things indicated the unmoved mover. The Epicureans reached god through the archetypes in the mind, the Stoics through the changes in things, the Academic through the traditions of the state, and Cicero through the movement of discourse and debate. Newton took an Epicurean physics and a Stoic argument to build a mechanical demonstration of a non-mechanical force. Hegelian method has characteristically identified the movement of thought and the motion of things, and it assimilates into a single demonstration the diverse proofs through which method passes. One set of proofs infers "from Being to the thought of God," while its opposite "proceeds from the thought of God, from truth in itself, to the Being of this truth."[73] The two extremes are being and thought, extremes brought into synthesis through proof, and either providing an initial step. In a manner somewhat reminiscent of Anselm, Idealism will use both, distinguishing the first into contingent and natural being, and comprehending all three into a single demonstration. Either way of demonstration, from being to thought or from thought to being, is one-sided; neither is indifferent to the other, for both enter into that movement which is the divine reality itself: Infinite Necessity, World Soul, Absolute Spirit.

[72] VBS, p. 164.   [73] Ibid., p. 221.

XIX.

The True as Movement

As THE conjectural question either initiated or grounded Aristotelian inquiry and Ciceronian debate, dialectical science must open with the questions about the beginning of its own movement, about the beginnings of philosophy. The search for a beginning does not immediately identify with the principle. This latter is the objective beginning of all things or an epistemological criterion of all knowledge, while the former can be considered as "something subjective in the sense of some contingent way of introducing the exposition."[1] The dogmatists concern themselves exclusively in the demonstrations of a single, absolute basis of all things, with some content from which the universe of determinate beings proceeds, while the sceptics concentrate upon the canons of understanding and proof with which to meet these uncritical philosophies.[2] Both fail to accomplish in their logistic or operational schemes that assimilation of subjective activity with objective process in a union of "method with content and form with principle."[3] Without this merger, the subjective beginning or the objective principle remains arbitrary or dualistic.[4] The answer to the quest for the beginning of science must emerge from the concept of science itself.

The *Phenomenology of Spirit* began with empirical or sensuous consciousness and moved dialectically to the concept of science, to the concept of pure knowledge identified with its object. Only this phenomenology furnishes the terms with which the question can be framed about the beginning of science. Consciousness constituted the presupposition of the

[1] WL, I, 51 (WLJS, I, 79). [2] WLJS, I, 79.
[3] *Ibid.*, I, 79-80. [4] WL, I, 61-62 (WLJS, I, 88).

ascent, and science its result. The result becomes the presupposition of logic—the idea of pure knowledge, the idea of science. The known has been incorporated into the knowing through a transcendence of the duality between knowledge and its other. Now this simplicity of result, this unity which "has transcended all reference to an Other and to mediation," is grasped as "undifferentiated and as such, ceases to be knowledge; nothing is there but simple immediacy."[5] The concept of pure science, abstracted from an other which is known, becomes simple immediacy—the simple immediacy which is properly expressed as pure being. Thus science, in negating its own nature as knowledge, offers its own beginning as being. The question embodies its own answer; the problem mediates its own resolution.

Being as the absolute beginning of philosophic inquiry contrasts sharply with hypothesis. "Hypothesis," which denoted the subject-matter of a science for Aristotelian inquiry, the issue proper to the rhetorician and not the philosopher in Ciceronian debate, and an explanation unwarranted by experiential evidence in Newtonian mechanics, now is differentiated as a beginning from the absolute. Does philosophy begin with the absolute or with a hypothetical truth, i.e., with an arbitrary beginning demonstrated later to be part of the absolute truth which results? The hypothetical is characteristic of geometric construction in knowledge and of conditional propositions or syllogisms in subjective logic; it has no place in philosophy as such. The philosophic beginning neither is nor seems to be arbitrary or conditionally accepted, contingent upon the experimental verification or ideological acceptability of its conclusions. The beginning is an absolute, determined by the nature of the subject and the content. Pure science must begin with being, as that immediacy into which knowledge returns. As pure being, the beginning is immediate; as the issue of science, it is mediated.[6] The logical evolution of this concept terminates in its absolute foundation, in its principle, for "the result is the principle." The final truth and ultimate source

---

[5] WLJS, I, 81.   [6] WL, I, 56-57 (WLJS, I, 84).

of the beginning is the Absolute Spirit which determines itself even to be. "What is essential for Science is not so much that a pure immediate is the beginning, but that it itself in its totality forms a cycle returning upon itself, wherein the first is also last, and the last first."[7]

The "determinateness" of being lies in its indeterminateness: "In its indeterminate immediacy it is similar to itself alone and also not dissimilar from any other." Any concrete determination of being would rob it of its simple immediacy, of that identity which characterizes it as beginning. The dialectic movement issues directly from this void, this utter indeterminacy, for nothing can be grasped or intuited within abstract being. Being becomes the negation of all determination. Being becomes nothing. Nothing equally lacks any internal determination. Determine either being or nothing, and one obtains something or a positive lack. "In fact, Being, indeterminate immediacy, is Nothing, neither more nor less."[8] If being and nothing are the same, the truth of either lies in neither alone. Being is nothing, but it is equally being. Nothing is being, but it is equally nothing. Nor does their truth lie in annihilation of distinction: Being is the contradictory of abstract nothing, and vice versa. The truth of either lies in the passage of one into the other. Their truth lies in movement: "Their truth is therefore this movement [Bewegung], this immediate disappearance of the one into the other, in a word, Becoming [Werden]." Movement identifies with conceptual adequacy because movement identifies with dialectical becoming. Within movement, both being and non-being are distinct as moments within a transition which dissolves and transcends this distinction into a profound assimilation.[9] Just as within the mechanical tradition, motion tends to identify with locomotion; so in the dialectical, it has inclined to denote generation, radical becoming. Becoming is the first concrete unity within philosophic reflection, a unity of being and nothing.

The history of philosophy embodies the same dialectic as

[7] WLJS, I, 83.   [8] Ibid., I, 94.   [9] Ibid., I, 95.

the passage of thought. Abstract being was the object of Eleatic affirmations: "Being alone is, and Nothing is not." The Oriental world, particularly Buddhism, asserted the contradictory: Nothing or the Void is posited as principle. In Heraclitus, the synthesis of both was obtained through the metaphysics of change, of becoming as that flux in which being and nothing merge. "All things flow" equates with becoming, in this history of science, and becoming brings into one the abstractions of the Italians and the Orientals. Both the history of philosophy and the passage of concepts terminate in the initial truth of the beginning.[10] The concrete, the true, is movement. "The recognition of the fact that Being and non-being are abstractions devoid of truth, that the first truth is to be found in Becoming, forms a great advance."[11] The essential failure of Spinoza lay in the reassertion of the Eleatic diremption between being and nothing and the positing of being alone as principle. The essence of pantheism is to see the actual only as being or as substance.[12] Heraclitus' grasp is of the true as subject of movement: "Everything depends on this, that we comprehend and express the true not as a substance, but just as much as subject."[13] Becoming provides not only a unity for being and nothing, but "the basis and element of all that follows." All philosophic concepts, everything which proceeds within the system of philosophy, is an example of this dynamic unity of contradictions in movement. It occurs in every fact and every thought, permeates all actuality, and constitutes the truth of any abstraction.[14]

The movement that is becoming justifies and embodies the dialectical method. Being generates its contradiction, nothing, and this contradiction is both overcome and transmuted into becoming. The distinction between being and nothing is both made and dissolved within movement; the true grasp of either is only in becoming, which is both actuality and subsistence: "Becoming is the subsistence [*Bestehen*] of Being as much as of No-being; in other words, their subsistence simply is their

10 WL, i, 67, 74 (WLJS, i, 95, 101).   11 HP, i, 283.
12 WL, i, 67-68 (WLJS, i, 95-96).   13 PGK, p. 28.
14 WLJS, i, 97.

being in One; it is just this their subsistence which equally transcends their distinction."[15] With this unity of becoming, being and nothing are inseparable moments; with neither of these isolated, the dynamic aspect of the true is established. Motion, becoming, constitutes that truth, initiates the dialectical generation of concepts, and begins any illation towards a god at the heart of this movement.

The doctrine of the true as subject or of the concept as movement, sharply distinguishes Hegelian natural theology from the causal search of Aristotle, the adequate explanation of Cicero, or the resolution of movement into forces of Newton. Within the dialectic, the differentiation between cause and effect is neither the stable, objective relationship of problematic theory nor the variant justifications offered to support a position within debate nor quantitative measurements of action and reaction. Cause is the power of substance, but a power which only exists in its effects, in accidents. Just as the dialectic differentiates and merges substance and accidents, so cause and effect are first distinguished by understanding as original and as non-original, as necessity and what it posits. The cause is, then, seen as exhausted in its effect, for "Cause contains nothing which is not in its Effect."[16] Then, cause is grasped as equally the effect of the effect, for all causality is mutual or reciprocal. This latter aspect prevents the ascent to the absolute from being a causal inquiry, for it would make the Absolute as much the effect of the finite as the finite the effect of the Absolute. A metaphysics which posited substance as supreme actuality would have to work through causality. A dialectic which understands the true as more profoundly subject will trace finite reality back to its infinity rather than effect back to its cause. In Aristotle, the inquiry was for moving and final cause; in Cicero, the debate located the gods materially within processes and actions of men; in Newton, the mechanics traced a system back to its aboriginal force; in Hegel, the dialectic will discover that the finite is out of the infinite, that nature is formally constituted by world-soul,

---

[15] *Ibid.*, I, 105.   [16] *Ibid.*, II, 191-93.

and that the universal spirit efficiently determines himself. For subject identifies the real as dialectical becoming. To be subject is to be actual only as movement, either the simple negativity of bifurcation or the complex negation in transcendence.[17] The subject of science is not only the focus of scientific inquiry—as it would be in the Thomistic philosophic vocabulary—but, much more importantly, the movement that constitutes both the content and the method of object, concept, and science. The subject as movement allows the dialectic simultaneously to correct propositional speech through system, activate any thought through its generation, and evolve any content into its truth. More specifically, it enables Absolute Idealism to enter into the three classical proofs for the existence of God, to remedy their forms, and to assimilate them to the three stages of the development of the spirit.

[17] PG, pp. 17-19 (PGK, pp. 28-30).

XX.

The Contingent as Motion

IN THE initial moments of speculative reflection, the true was found identified with movement; the subject was coincident with dialectical becoming. "This universal principle is better characterized as Becoming, the truth of Being; since everything is and is not." Heraclitean philosophy introduced this synthesis of being and nothing as a dynamic unity, and "its principle is essential, and it is to be found in the beginning of my Logic."[1] This enables idealism to oppose the common belief that the proofs for the existence of God conclude only to his existence, that no matter what the starting point, the conclusion reads the same: God is. It is far more important to define the nature of God, especially since the predicate "contains mere dry Being."[2] Speculatively understood, the diverse demonstrations result in different determinations of the divine nature, moving in their unity to the grasp of philosophic reason. The assertion of becoming is followed by the predication of meaning, corresponding dialectically to the passage from the conjectural to the definitional question.[3]

The world stands as the starting-point (*der Ausgangspunkt*), but it is not the world as cosmic unity, political society, or mechanical system. *Die Welt* is an aggregate of empirical objects, a collection of material and visible things. It constitutes a whole, but the systematic whole which nature is. "The term world as thus understood expresses the aggregate merely and suggests that it is based simply on the existing mass of things."[4] The chief trait of these things is limited being or

---

[1] HP, I, 283. [2] VBS, p. 203.
[3] VB, pp. 416-17 (VBS, p. 216).
[4] VBS, p. 228. Cf. EL, No. 50, p. 74 (ELW, pp. 102-103).

finitude or contingency. "This is the kind of starting-point from which the spirit raises itself to God."[5] The spirit spontaneously judges that these things are untrue, that true Being is beyond them, that the world of finitudes is not the last word on actuality. The spirit moves through this world in an elevation of the mind to "the Infinite, Eternal, and Unchangeable." This elevation constitutes the general basis of all religions, and the failure of the principle of immediate knowledge does not lie in positing this movement but in not raising it to the level of science.[6] Those who reject natural theology or theological demonstrations do not pass beyond this elevation as a fact. As fact, it coincides with the universal consent of all mankind, as "the inner revelation of God in the human spirit or reason." Here the argument of the Stoics is attributed to Cicero.[7]

Although Absolute Idealism does not deny this interior divine revelation, it finds the argument from universal consent historical in method and doubtful in conclusion.[8] This historical approach lies external to its content; keeping the appearance of treating an object or event, it deals actually with the opinions of others and with the external circumstances of the deed. The appeal *ex consensu gentium* is dubious both because its empirical and historical foundations are weak and because its intrinsic argument is not binding. It is simply not possible to get historical evidence regarding all nations; further, tribes have been discovered which know no god, while others adore divinities to whom their adversaries would never credit divinity. Hegel has merged the arguments of the Stoics with the position of Cicero, and against them he levels the critique of the third academy. But the dialectical elimination of the proof from universal human authority is not to issue in an agnostic conclusion. Even if the historical argument were valid, it would not tell: in a matter of such supreme importance, a man has the right to demand his own witness and not to take his conclusion from the opinions of others.

[5] VBS, p. 228. Cf. EL, No. 50, pp. 74-75 (ELW, pp. 102-103).
[6] VBS, p. 229.   [7] *Ibid.*, pp. 197, 229.
[8] VB, pp. 397-98 (VBS, p. 194).

Every man has the obligation to follow only the witness of immanent spirit, and even in religion the one absolutely valid method of proof is the witness of the Spirit, not miracles, stories, arguments, etc. In this, more than in the academic destruction of the argument, Absolute Idealism parts company from the conclusion of Cicero's debates, and turns to the consideration of the immanent elevation of the thinking spirit.[9] The dialectical demonstration becomes nothing else than "the explicitation of the separate moments of this elevation, and the indication of their necessity."[10]

The cosmological argument, or the argument from contingency, ran through pre-Kantian metaphysics. The illation is from the contingent universe to the absolutely necessary:

> The contingent does not stand upon itself, but has for its presupposition in general that which is necessary in itself— for its essence, ground or cause. But the world is contingent: the single things are contingent and it, as whole, is the aggregate of the same. Therefore, the world has as its presupposition that which is necessary in itself.[11]

The heart of this pre-critical inference runs: "Because what is material is contingent, there exists an absolutely necessary Essence."[12]

Against this demonstration both immediate intuition and critical understanding are brought to bear, both fixing thought at a pre-speculative stage. In his *Letters on the Doctrine of Spinoza*, Jacobi assaulted any demonstration of the divine as an intrinsic negation of its own conclusion. His interpretation of demonstration was as logistic deduction: "to deduce anything from its more immediate causes, or to look at its immediate conditions as a series." The contradiction in such a method was absolute: "To comprehend the Unconditioned, therefore, means to make it into something conditioned or to make it an effect."[13] The Idealist incorporated this criticism, while purifying it of its denial of all proof and method. Jacobi

[9] VB, pp. 400-404 (VBS, pp. 197-201).
[10] VBS, p. 231. [11] VB, p. 463 (m). [12] VBS, p. 281.
[13] *Ibid.*, p. 282.

failed to understand the diremption which obtains in the logistic method between the objective movement of the thing and the subjective movement of the mind. What pre-Kantian metaphysics was establishing was not the objective dependence of the divine, but the subjective dependence of human knowledge of the divine upon contingent realities. The proof was correct in content, in the inner-relations between the contingent and the necessary, but it was wrong in form: "Because the contingent exists, therefore the absolutely-necessary exists."[14] The content of the conclusion makes it quite clear that the inference is not to an absolutely-necessary which depends upon the contingent world; in the prior metaphysics, the content was supposed to remedy the defect in form. Philosophic method profits from Jacobi's attacks insofar as they underscore the need to pass from a logistic to a dialectic form, the method in which the motion of the science identifies with the movement of its object.

Critical philosophy reproved this demonstration both for content and for form, both for conclusion and for method. So devastating have the Kantian criticisms been found that "these arguments have been abandoned and that they are no longer mentioned in any scientific treatise on the subject." They have been consigned to popular edification or elevating rhetoric.[15] The *Critique of Pure Reason* reformulates the proof somewhat: If anything exists, then some absolutely necessary essence must exist. But I exist. Therefore, some absolutely necessary essence exists.[16]

The conclusion is inadequate to express the divine essence, contended Kant. To obtain the divine, method must part company with the empirical and argue the question: What kind of attributes must the absolutely necessary essence possess in order to be absolutely necessary? The answer can only be resolved through the ontological proof: "The most necessary being is the most real," is the convertible proposition, "The most real is the most necessary being." To argue from the reality or actuality of the concept to its necessary existence is the heart

---

[14] *Ibid.*   [15] VB, p. 438 (VBS, p. 240).

[16] VBS, pp. 237-38.

of the ontological proof.[17] Hegel finds Kant's argument inaccurate in three ways: First, the absolutely necessary being can
identify—and historically has often identified—with the divine;
its insufficiency for the Christian conception urges a further
dialectical progression of the content, not to its inaccuracy at
this moment of method. Secondly, the ontological argument is
not the tissue of fallacies, "a whole nest of dialectic assumptions which nevertheless, transcendental criticism is able to lay
bare and destroy."[18] The ontological argument justifies itself
within speculative dialectic at the highest moment of the evolution of spirit, as will be demonstrated. Thirdly, Kant is simply
wrong in asserting that to deduce the first concept from the
second is equivalent to deducing the second from the first. Even
in Euclidean methodology, the convertibility of a proposition
does not indicate the convertibility of the argument by which
it is substantiated. In the cosmological proof, the being of the
absolutely necessary has already been established; further inference to the most real is an illation to content, not to being,
and provides no foundation—even within its original logistic
scheme—for the conversion of arguments. Kant has indicated
the need for further dialectical development of the content, but
he has failed to understand the telling force of a methodology
different from his own.[19]

Kant found the intrinsic argumentation of the proof from
contingency defective in each of the coordinates of discourse:
in method, it argued from effect to cause in an area where
causality is not realized; in interpretation, it failed to distinguish the world of experience from the world of thought; in
principle, necessity was removed from condition. In response,
Hegel corrects the method, reinterprets the relationship between thought and its object, and posits condition reflexively
within the necessary. One does not argue from the contingent
to the necessary as from effect to cause; the proper grasp of
the contingent (as will be seen) is to pass dialectically into the
necessary, for the truth of the contingent is the necessary. The

---

[17] *Ibid.*, p. 243: "Kant carries the degradation of reason as far as those
do who limit all truth to immediate knowledge."
[18] *Ibid.*, p. 240.   [19] VB, pp. 442-46 (VBS, pp. 244-48).

very fact that an infinite series cannot be found within the world of sense indicates that the reason, which necessarily denies such a series, can go beneath sense into the noumenal existence of things-in-themselves. The unconditioned absolute necessity has not destroyed all conditions, but "contains its conditions within itself."[20] In the problem of reflexive principle, Kant has come upon "the essential moment on which the whole question turns: the necessary must have its beginning [*Anfang*] in itself." The *Critique* will allow that existence in general has a necessary element in it, but that no single thing can be understood as necessary in itself, that one can never empirically reach a first cause, so that to assert one is to posit the necessary without proving it—a massive *petitio principii*. Hegel reformulates the question dialectically:

> The sole question is as to how we can begin to show that anything starts from itself, or rather how we can combine the two ideas that the Infinite starts from an Other, and yet in doing this starts equally from itself.[21]

To answer this question, the nature of the contingent must be grasped, the formal defect of the pre-Kantian demonstration remedied, and the illation from the contingent to the necessary seen as the dialectical truth of the contingent. This constitutes the dialectical reformation of the cosmological proof.[22]

The cosmological proof has historically begun with the contingency of material things and reached god as necessary being. There are a multiplicity of ways in which material things could have been defined, and, as each proof gives a different determination of the divine essence, the conclusion would have been somewhat different. The illation could have been from things defined as existing to reach god as pure being (the most abstract of all definitions), or from finite things to the infinite god, or from real being to ideal being, or from immediate being to god as ground of being, or from the part to the whole, or from external and selfless to god as force beneath, or from things as effects to god as cause. Each of these would have proffered a

---

[20] VBS, pp. 247-50.   [21] *Ibid.*, p. 252.
[22] VB, pp. 434-36 (VBS, pp. 236-37).

licit starting-point and founded a valid proof. They represent various historic demonstrations called into play through the history of philosophy, each of which has issued in a description which did not exhaust the divine nature, the series of which ran through the categories of logic in being, infinite, ideal, essence, ground, whole, force, and cause. Why begin with contingency? Because it is the most concrete of all of these logical determinations. Each of these beginnings and its conclusion represent a movement of the finite determinateness of the concept into its infinitude, into its truth: "Each stage through which it passes involves the elevation of a category of finitude, and thus it likewise involves from its starting point onwards a metaphysical conception of god, and . . . a proof of his being."[23] Within logic, one of these developments succeeds another, representing the evolution of the concept until it attains an externalization in nature. The cosmological proof is essentially the proof from the thought-determinations of logic, a metaphysical theology, which traces out the internal development of the concept as it passed through the finite into a more determinate infinity. It focuses through the contingency-necessity relation because "the category of the relation between contingency and necessity is that in which all the relations of the finitude and the infinitude of Being are resumed and comprised."[24] Contingency is the most concrete determination of the finitude of being; absolute necessity is the most concrete determination of infinitude. How so? For contingency indicates the essential truth of the finite in suggesting its true existence as accidental, whose real character is to pass away. Through contingency, the dialectical movement towards the truth of the finite is already indicated.[25]

To say that material things are contingent is not to say that

---

[23] VBS, pp. 233-35.   [24] *Ibid.*, p. 236.

[25] *Ibid.*, pp. 308-309: "It is the contingent itself in which, as was said, the finitude, the limitation of the world has been indicated in order that it may itself directly point to its solution. . . . The analysis of the contingent directly shows that the moments of this mediation are Being in general, or material existence, and the negation of this, whereby it is degraded to the state of something which has a semblance of Being, something which is virtually a nullity."

they are, but that their reality is of possibilities which are. They exist, but they could just as well not exist, with no denial of their nature. The contingent is the possible which is, whether this possible be the isolated thing or the *externally* necessary concatenation of cause and effect.[26] The latter is the conformity to law among material things, but they are as contingent as their elements and as their circumstances. Their necessity is thus relative, while the necessity which they implicate is absolute but beyond them. For the sign of the contingent is to be posited by another, and these laws are posited by the causes which compose and author them.[27] The contingent and the possible differ only by addition: the possible is that which does not contradict itself, i.e., is merely identical with itself; the contingent has in addition a definite existence. Thus existence is not reflexively identical with the contingent; in itself, it neither is nor is-not.[28]

The fault of the pre-Kantian metaphysics lay not in a failure to apprehend the content of the contingent, but in failure to comprehend that content as transition, as dialectically self-negating. The essential, formal defect of the non-dialectical demonstration was to posit the finite as something fixed, true in itself, something affirmative with a meaning and existence all its own. The subsequent search was for a cause through external necessity to the absolutely necessary. In content, this was correct; in form, it was self-defeating. Through the introduction of the dialectic, Absolute Idealism responds to "the protests which have been advanced against this method of proof."[29] The defect stood basic to the logistic method, an inability to identify the movement of the demonstration with the motion of the object itself. The dialectical method is the "immanent and objective form" of its content, and thus the conclusion of the illation is nothing but the transition of the object itself.[30] The deductive syllogisms of pre-Kantian metaphysics froze the finite, making its premises permanent and stable. In this, the

---

[26] VB, pp. 463-64 (VBS, pp. 266-67).
[27] VB, pp. 464-65 (VBS, pp. 267-68).
[28] VB, pp. 470-71 (VBS, p. 275).
[29] VBS, pp. 281-82.   [30] WLJS, II, 471.

content flatly contradicted the form, for the meaning of the contingent is transition and self-negation; its meaning is dialectical.

The contingent is the finite in being. It exists, but it exists as a determinate character distinct from its being. Non-being enters into its meaning as much as being.[31] The content of the contingent is a transition between two moments, affirmation and denial: existence as a determinate form of being, and the antithetical moment of its finitude, mortality. "Thought, if it is to form a conception of the contingent, cannot allow these moments to be separated."[32] The contingent contains both in itself; more speculatively, it is the transition between them. The contingent is a contradiction in itself: "Contingency, on the other hand, is Being which is absolutely unlike itself, which contradicts itself."[33] Understanding would resolve such a contradiction into a nothing, but nothing and contradiction cannot be speculatively identified. Nothing is absolutely empty, devoid of content, is in no sense contradiction; while contradiction is concrete, has a content, and points to the dialectical meaning of its concept.[34] The understanding fails to see the positive moment of the contradiction, and resolves the antinomies into the void.

Speculative reason finds the moments of the contingent as material existence and its negation, being and a virtual nullity. Both exist in dynamic relationship to its other. Each is necessary in the movement that is the contingent, and the dialectic is not fixed at this antithesis. It moves to the denial of the negation, a denial of the non-independent being of the contingent. Material existence generates its own virtual non-existence, and this is in turn transcended by the independent existence of the absolutely necessary. The understanding of the contingent involves a contradiction between the content and its existence—its existence is not its own; its existence is not its existence. And this contradiction is only resolved in the existence of that whose concept and actuality identify. The movement of the dialectic is through that contradiction which any difference or

---

[31] VB, pp. 479-80 (VBS, pp. 284-85). [32] VBS, p. 306.
[33] *Ibid.*, p. 288. [34] VB, p. 499 (VBS, p. 307).

nonreflexivity involves, into its resolution in a reflexive principle.[35] So understood, the contingent becomes itself the movement to the absolute: "The contingent is by its very nature that which resolves itself, disintegrates itself, it is this transition in itself."[36] Secondly, the self-resolution of the contingent is not into nothing, but "is rather within the resolution, that affirmation which we call absolute necessity."[37] Because the contingent is its own denial, the process which is its definition contains its result as immanent. Through its own denial, the contingent reverts back to its truth; just as through nothing, being reverted back to its truth in becoming. Through the dialectic, the impelling power of the contingent and the cosmological demonstration identify in the "movement of the thing or true fact."[38] The logistic method would have resolved the definition of the contingent into its parts and left it fixed. The dialectical method grasps the contingent as contradiction, thus as movement, thus as issuing from the truth of the absolutely necessary.

In Aristotle, the movement was the actualization of the potential in things; in Cicero, motion was identified in discourse or in political traditions; in Newton, it was the locomotion of mass-point within a system. In Hegel, motion is the life of every concept and the soul of every proof. Within the Thomistic framework, only one of the five ways of demonstration was from motion, properly-so-called; within the Hegelian system, every valid demonstration is a proof from motion, for motion is the truth of the content. Through movement, one can reform the cosmological proof to read: "The Being of the contingent is not its own Being, but merely the Being of an Other—of its own Other, the Absolutely-necessary."[39] The contingent was chosen above any of the other

[35] VB, pp. 497-98 (VBS, pp. 306-308).

[36] VBS, p. 310. *Ibid.*, p. 285: "If therefore we begin with the contingent, we must not set out from it as if it were something which is to remain fixed. . . . On the contrary, it is to be posited with its completely determinate character, which implies that non-Being may quite as well be attributed to it, and that it consequently enters into the result as something which passes away. *Not because the contingent is, but, on the contrary, because it is non-Being, merely phenomenal, because its Being is not true reality, the absolute necessity is.*" (Italics added.)

[37] *Ibid.*, p. 310.   [38] *Ibid.*   [39] *Ibid.*, p. 289.

logical categories because it indicated its nature as transition more concretely than any of the others.[40] The resolution of any such transition, whose movement is authored by internal contradiction, is speculatively obtained only through a reflexive principle which unites the antithetical determinations without identifying them.

Absolute necessity becomes such a principle. Like the contingent, the absolutely necessary is a way of possessing being. In the contingent, being and content did not identify; in the absolutely necessary, they do. Being is not mediated through another, but is immediate. Absolute necessity is a self-mediated unity in virtue of this denial of mediation.[41] "In this manner Absolute Necessity is the Reflection or Form of the Absolute; unity of Being and Essence, simple immediacy."[42] Absolute necessity is the truth into which contingency, possibility, formal and real necessity pass, while it is "only because it is, and has otherwise neither condition nor Ground."[43] "Absolute Necessity is not the Necessary, and still less a Necessary: it is Necessity—Being simply as Reflection."[44] As motion itself, this necessity posits contingency as its other, and then recaptures it as itself; contingency is only a moment of the absolutely necessary.[45] The dialectic can be stopped here, and historically has been stopped in those religions which are dominated by the concept of fate or by those philosophies which attain God only as substance. Absolute necessity does not yet reach the divine as subject, i.e., as self-positing in externality, nor as spirit, utter self-determination. It is God as Substance in "the philosophical systems of substantiality."[46] But there is still need for the further reflexivity of subject as spirit.

What has been obtained by the cosmological proof is infinite substance in the determinations of necessity. Being was the permanent subject of the proof, and the transition identified with the predicate of contingent passing over into the predi-

---

[40] VB, pp. 484-86 (VBS, pp. 290-92).
[41] VB, p. 505 (VBS, p. 315).   [42] WLJS, ii, 185.
[43] Ibid., ii, 184-85.   [44] Ibid., ii, 187.
[45] WL, ii, 183 (WLJS, ii, 185).   [46] VBS, p. 320.

cate of absolute necessity.[47] But the contingent is simply finite being, while absolute necessity is infinite being. For the finite always exists in reference to another, which is its negation, while the infinite always exists in reference to itself, even through another which it assimilates. "The infinite is considered as absolute in itself, since it is expressedly determined as negation of the finite."[48] And this negation is not obtained through the simple denial of finitude, but as the return of the infinite upon itself as the truth of finitude. As self-relation, it would be mere abstract or indeterminate being; but it is posited as negating a negation, thus as determinate being, for in containing negation it contains determination as assimilated. The image of the false infinitude is the straight line, which is actually always finite; the image of the true infinity is the circle, turned back upon itself, the line which has reached itself and which has neither beginning nor end.[49] It is this infinity which absolute necessity is, total reflexivity between concept and actuality, between essence and being.

But this determination of the divine essence is not exhaustive nor does this demonstration from the truth of the contingent terminate the dialectic. There is need to move over to nature and its soul.

[47] VB, p. 451 (VBS, p. 253). [48] WLJS, I, 150.
[49] WL, I, 138-39 (WLJS, I, 162).

XXI.

Nature as Motion

THE COSMOLOGICAL argument takes a priority among the proofs for the divine existence in that, through it, the infinite is affirmed and defined as absolutely necessary essence. Through the category of contingency-necessity other logical characteristics were subsumed and concretized, while that reflexivity which identifies with infinity was found to be the truth of the finite.[1] The establishment of the infinite constitutes the heart of the Idealist enterprise: "The proposition that the finite is of ideal nature constitutes Idealism. In Philosophy, Idealism consists of nothing else than the recognition that the finite has no veritable being."[2] Only the infinite resolves the contradiction of the actuality of the finite, and this was realized in the resolution of the actuality of the contingent into the absolutely necessary. God was obtained as the infinite substance, whose concept identified reflexively with his actuality, and within whose determinations were included all the moments of the logical idea short of exteriorization in matter.[3]

Any proof consists of three factors: the starting point, the result, and the mediation. In the universal method of the dialectic, the mediation is through the movement of the concept as it posits its contradiction and then transcends this antithesis through the negation of negation. The differentiation of proofs lies with the distinctions within starting-points and the conse-

---

[1] VB, p. 546 (VBS, p. 347).   [2] WLJS, I, 168.

[3] VB, pp. 433-34 (VBS, p. 235). "Finite Being does not continue to be an Other; there is no gulf between the Infinite and the finite. The finite is something which cancels itself, loses itself in something higher, so that its truth is the Infinite, what has being in-and-for-itself. Finite, contingent Being is something which implicitly negates itself, but this negation which it undergoes is just the Affirmative, a transition to affirmation, and this affirmation is the absolutely necessary Essence." VBS, p. 348.

quent divergence they author within their results.[4] Such is the shift obtained in moving from being as world to being as nature; it is a shift in starting-point. Nature is richer in content than world, for, though it also coincides with the manifold or contingent beings, finite being is here as conformed to an end.[5] "The higher determination accordingly is, that conformity to an end is present in Being."[6] Nature is the whole which "world" denoted, but now systematized, through ordination to end; the whole becomes "a systematic Whole, a system of arrangements and gradations, and particularly of laws."[7] Kant was in error in asserting that this teleological proof of the divine existence predated the cosmological; it first appears with Xenophon's Socrates, understanding his imprisonment in that his fellow citizens think it good.[8] Just as Aristotle explained eternal motion physically through moving cause and metaphysically through final cause, so the dialectic reaches the divine first through the correlative of efficient causality in necessity and then through the final causality which bespeaks rationality.[9] God as necessity is power; as rationality, he is wisdom— Absolute Idealism realizing within the true that union between ability and wisdom which the Ciceronian histories posited within the genius who began civilization. In both philosophies the union of power and intelligence authors a *cosmos*.[10] Nature becomes in Absolute Idealism, not the internal principle of problematic movement, but the "harmonious working of external things, of things which exist in a relation of indifference to each other . . . of a unity in virtue of which there is an absolute conformity amongst them."[11]

[4] VB, p. 519 (VBS, p. 329). [5] VB, p. 536 (VBS, p. 348).
[6] VBS, p. 329. [7] *Ibid.*, p. 228.
[8] VB, p. 518 (VBS, p. 328).
[9] EL, No. 204, pp. 177-78 (ELW, p. 344).
[10] VB, pp. 518-19 (VBS, p. 329). "The real advance accordingly is from this finite mode of life to absolute, universal conformity to an end, to the thought that this world is a κόσμος." VBS, p. 350. "Here it happens again that this definition: God is the one universal active force of life, the soul which produces, posits, organises a κόσμος, is a conception which does not suffice to express the conception of God. It is essentially involved in the conception of God that He is Spirit." VBS, p. 351. For the Ciceronian cosmos, see *supra*, Part II.
[11] VBS, p. 330.

The pre-Kantian metaphysics argued from this evidence of teleology within nature to the existence of a divine cause, urging that this ordination to an end could not arise spontaneously. The activity of each depends upon interrelations and finalities which it neither authors nor explains, and the collection of these activities composes a unity which comes to the whole from without.[12] The essential illation of the proof reads: "Because there are arrangements, ends of a like kind, there is a wisdom which disposes and orders everything."[13] Against this transition or inference are brought to bear the claims of immediate faith, the contentions of critical philosophy, the hypotheses of mechanical explanation, and the contempt of common opinion for any providence found in the workings of nature. Out of these negations Absolute Idealism will obtain an imperative for a dialectical method of mediation, an assimilation of matter into form, an understanding of the hierarchy within nature, and a distinction of teleology through form and content.

Jacobi's central attack is repeated: To demonstrate God is to condition the Unconditioned, and his denial indicates need for a dialectic method to correct the form of the pre-Kantian argument. These logistic deductions had separated the form of the proof from the form of the proved, allowing the defective movement of knowledge to be corrected by the content of the conclusion. The mediation of dependence in human knowledge did not touch the content, God; the subjective movement of inference did not mirror the objective life of the concept. There was need to redress this defect in form, to merge the movements of the Unconditioned in knowledge and in nature, so that the transition that is organic nature becomes the inference that is scientific knowledge.[14]

Besides the basic critical objection to scientific knowledge of the noumenal, the conclusion of the teleological proof is found inadequate, at least without the ontological argument. Kant felt the proof deserving of highest respect, but concluding per se only to a forming cause, to an arranging or manipu-

12 VB, pp. 519-20 (VBS, p. 331).   13 VBS, p. 351.
14 VB, pp. 522-24 (VBS, pp. 333-34).

lating force which worked upon a pre-existent substrate to produce an ordered universe. Teleology could denote the forming demiurge of the *Timaeus*, but not the creating God of *Genesis*.[15] Form in the operational usage of Transcendental Idealism had become arrangements and order superimposed upon the surd of the given manifold, the matter with which knowledge is composed. God's activity in teleology would cover the form, but not the matter—a limitation which would mark his movement as intrinsically finite. Kant's error identifies in the analysis of Hegel with the typical error of a philosophy rooted in understanding: The dichotomy between matter and form is fixed and stable, rather than fluid. This frozen distinction is ultimately inadmissible, for the formless matter of Kantian criticism "is a nonentity, a pure abstraction of the Understanding, which we may certainly construct, but which ought not be given out to be anything true."[16] The matter, initially opposed to form, moves dialectically to merge with form as its truth. "This identity of formlessness, this continuous unity of matter is itself one of the specific qualities of form."[17] Matter does not exist apart from form; "on the contrary, they are both the same."[18] To come to God as forming influence, then, is to come to the explanation of both matter and form, of the world of nature. While it is true that this concept of the divine as world-soul or form is not adequate, its insufficiency merely urges the further dialectical development of its concept, not the rejection of this moment.[19]

The truth of the concept equally repudiates mechanical chance as explanation for the organic interrelations of nature. The mechanists reversed the order of truth, making the inorganic independent, immediate, and unconditioned, while the organic—men, animals, vegetation—approach this primordial actuality from the outside, as dependent, mediated, and condi-

---

[15] VB, pp. 520-22 (VBS, pp. 331-32).

[16] VBS, p. 332. For the general conception of matter in Absolute Idealism, cf. A. R. Caponigri, "Matter in the Idealist Tradition," *The Concept of Matter*, ed. Ernan McMullin (Notre Dame: University of Notre Dame, 1963), pp. 412ff.

[17] VBS, p. 332. [18] VB, pp. 519-20 (VBS, p. 332).

[19] VB, pp. 522-23 (VBS, p. 334).

tioned. The inorganic does not depend upon the organic, but men depend upon animals, animals upon plants—and all, upon the inorganic.[20] What is more, evolutionary stages can be determined in which the organic through additions combines into the organic through the chance conjunction of parts into larger, more dependent wholes. In this logistic account of nature, the harmonious interactions of beings appear as the result of accident, while the inharmonious disappeared as unable to sustain itself in existence. Nature becomes the blind force of necessity.[21] This Empedoclean account of evolution—which Hegel attributes to Aristotle!—fails to grasp the inner dependence of finality. The essential nature of the inorganic is as matter and means; matter to build into temporally posterior organisms, and means, for their sustentation.[22] To fail to grasp the inorganic as matter and means is to miss their true definition or essential nature. Both philosophy and the common opinion of men hold that man is related to the rest of nature as an end, that the organic makes use of the inorganic. This argues to the essential concept of the inorganic as related to the organic, related as dependent for its meaning as means. The immediacy of the inorganic becomes the immediacy of the contingent—the immediacy of something posited by its other and to which it is related as its subsuming truth. This relationship is developed in the science of nature itself, for just as logic corresponded to the demonstration of the divine from contingency, so the science of nature infers from the harmonious correlations of its subject-matter the presence or truth of the divine world-soul.

The common contempt into which the teleological argument has fallen issues less from the telling force of Kantian or mechanical criticisms than from the faulty starting-point. In the cosmological proof, Absolute Idealism had distinguished the form of the mediation from the content of the result in order to purify the argument by correcting the method. Now the distinction between form and content is brought to bear not only upon the mediation, but upon the starting-point. If one

[20] VB, pp. 527-29 (VBS, p. 339).   [21] VB, pp. 529-30 (VBS, p. 340).
[22] VB, p. 530 (VBS, p. 340).

takes the form of the relationship between the organic and the inorganic—as Absolute Idealism will—one considers only the fundamental finitude of dependence and harmony. If one takes up the content of the conformity to end—as the Stoics or Newtonian mechanics did—the proof is burdened with demonstrating in infinite particularity the "wise arrangement of Nature."[23] Such a demonstration, which refuses to work out of the concept, must posit external nature to preserve the life of insects or prove design between animal life and the processes of event. Moreover, the abiding problematic of evil must be treated: ruins of great human enterprises cover the earth and in both nature and morals substantial values are habitually frustrated. While this may provide ground for rising to a higher, ultimate good in which all these values are subsumed and realized, still this universal good cannot be found immediately within the finite. To argue from the universal good to the divine is to beg the question: "This universal end is not discoverable in experience, and thus the general character of the transition is altered, for the transition means that we start from something given, that we reason syllogistically from what we find in experience."[24] One would have to substantiate every particular or meet every objection against the proposition that universal good is found within nature—an impossible task: "We would just have to reckon up the amount of evil and the amount of good which does not attain realization in order to discover which preponderates."[25] It was precisely this impossibility which moved Kant to the moral postulate of the existence of God, but for Absolute Idealism postulation is not enough. It is mere subjective certainty, a belief or a hope, but without guarantee or speculative establishment of its actuality.[26]

The starting-point, now purified, embodies the conformity to end of beings within nature. The finitude of these beings lies in the disjunction between the end and means or between the activity and the materials it must use, just as the finitude of the contingent lay in the disjunction between concept and actuality. In the necessary, possibility and actuality identify in

[23] VBS, p. 343.   [24] *Ibid.*, p. 345.   [25] *Ibid.*
[26] VB, pp. 534-35 (VBS, p. 346).

249

the concept; and the truth of the contingent is found in this infinity. In teleology, infinity is attained through a similar reflexivity: means and matter identify with end. This is that infinite activity of the end: "The end accomplishes itself, realizes itself through its own activity, and thus comes into harmony with itself in the process of realizing itself."[27] Within the finite relationship, with means separated from materials, activity becomes a technical mode of action—distinguished from the immanent movement of the infinite as problematic inquiry had distinguished reflexively the causalities of art and nature. But here, the dialectic method adds assimilation of art into nature, for the truth of the technical is found finally in a living coincidence between end and means. Finite, technical activity is ultimately untrue, for "the end is true only when what uses the means, and the means, as well as the reality, are identical with the end."[28] Aristotle had allowed nature to author the four kinds of causality within a natural operation. Hegel found in such authorship an infinity and dialectically set up this infinity as the truth of art, chance, and fortune. Like Aristotle, Hegel uses reflexive principles, but the difference of the dialectical method allows for an assimilative movement between them.

Teleological activity is found both finite and infinite in organic life. The organs are the means of life and also the material in which life realizes itself. The soul is life as the subject of this ceaseless activity and as the end which "posits itself, realizes itself, and thus the product is the same as the thing that produces."[29] Activity issues from the feeling of need and terminates in a satisfaction which is itself the initiation of a new need. Within the single living subject, "each organ maintains the other, and in this way maintains itself. This activity constitutes an end, a soul, which is present in every point of the organism."[30] Within every living organism, teleological activity exists in its true, its infinite, form. But the subject is just as pervasively finite, incomplete. The living being possesses material of activity as abstracted from the inorganic:

[27] VBS, p. 335.   [28] Ibid.   [29] Ibid., p. 336.   [30] Ibid.

"Finitude shows itself in this, that while the organs draw their nourishment from themselves, they employ material for this taken from the outside."[31] The finite is essentially dependent upon that which it is not, as the moment of finitude is the confrontation by the unassimilated other, a moment of diremption produced by the understanding. Here the disjunction is between the organic and the inorganic: "Everything organic is related to inorganic Nature, which has a definite independent existence."[32] This relates the organic to the inorganic in dependence and tension: man depends upon air, water, light, heat in order to live and upon less organic being in order to sustain this life. The internal activity, which constitutes the reflexivity of organic life, finds both material and means in the external. Further, these means for the organic are not posited by the organic. A harmony is found between the inorganic and the living, but the harmony is not found within the organism itself. A unity is found which neither of them authors, a unity which merges both the preservation and the realization of life. "The question is simply this: How does inorganic Nature pass over into organic Nature, and how is it possible for it to serve as a means for what is organic?"[33]

The essential, formal defect of the pre-Kantian teleological proof was similar to the fault noted under the cosmological discussion: it took the finite as absolute. The pre-Kantians permitted this finite disjunction between ends and means to stand as if it were something fixed, something true from which one could argue to a divine intellect causing the finite relationship as actual being. This is precisely what Absolute Idealism denies, refusing to predicate more than ideal being of that which lives in diremption and finitude. There is but one absolute, an absolute which constitutes the actuality of the finite. Thus in dialectical movement through the concept, "the ground or principle from which we start disappears in what is characterized as the true principle."[34] This makes the illation more than subjective demonstration, a negative-affirmative movement which identifies with the motion of the concept or start-

[31] *Ibid.*, p. 337.   [32] *Ibid.*   [33] *Ibid.*, p. 339.   [34] *Ibid.*, p. 334.

ing-point itself. The denial of autonomous reality to the finite —whether in form or contingency or organic life—is *ipso facto* the affirmation of the infinite, whether as necessity or soul.

The dialectical movement lies at the heart of the finite organic. The organism possesses life in and through itself, its end is coincident with its matter and means. Yet "this life, these ends as they actually are, and as existing in their immediate finite form, do not represent what is true."[35] The contradiction lies in the dependence upon the inorganic, in the separation of means and material. The harmony between the living subject and the non-living nature equates with neither and merges both as moments. The truth of the organic and the inorganic is neither one nor the other; it is their unity and inseparability, the infinite subject or absolute determination by which they are a unity.[36] The unity is dynamically productive of both moments, a living action in which the finite organism passes over into its truth as infinite life. This "correspondence between the Notion as representing the organic and reality as representing the inorganic simply expresses the essence of life itself."[37] The negation of finite life becomes the affirmation of infinite life, of universal life, of soul; and the world becomes "a harmonious whole, an organic life which is determined in accordance with ends. It was this which the ancients held to be νοῦς, and, taken in a more extended signification, this life was also called the world-soul, the λόγος."[38]

Thus the denial of the organic as end is the assertion of a greater living unity. Its life is not its life, but the living relationship with that which it is not, and its unity is not its unity, but a dynamic unity with that which it is not. Its own denial involves its truth, and the finite organic identifies with the movement of dependence and self-denial, of incompleteness and of a harmony within which it possesses its actuality. The soul is not apart from the body; it is rather the living element within the organic, the life-force which penetrates and unites the body. When the truth of the finite organic is grasped, "it is seen to be one principle, one organic life of the universe, one

[35] *Ibid.*, p. 351.
[37] VBS, p. 342.
[36] VB, p. 530 (VBS, p. 342).
[38] *Ibid.*, pp. 342-43.

living system. All that is, simply constitutes the organs of one subject."[39] The planets become members of a single system, not of the Newtonian mechanical system, but of the immortal λόγος, which is the soul of the universe. The world itself becomes "a κόσμος, a system in which everything has an essential relation to everything else, and nothing is isolated." The elements of the cosmos identify materially with those of the world, but now each is necessarily related to each other; the whole is ordered in regularities and in place; each part subsists through the whole, and enters into the active production of the whole.[40] The Aristotelian cosmic order or Ciceronian political reality or the Newtonian world system has now become an eternal, living being—one which Plato rightly called an immortal ζῷον, though he failed to advance further than the category of life.[41] Within the system, all existents are organs through which the one universal active life posits, organizes and conserves a κόσμος, and God—as this life-force—is the "one life movement, the νοῦς of one life movement, the soul, the Universal Soul."[42]

The contingent showed that its being was not its own; the organic showed that its life was not its own. But neither the necessary nor the universal world-soul exhausts the definition of the divine. The first has shown God as reflexively identified with his own actuality; the second has shown God as reflexively identified with his own means, materials, and end. The first was a static reflexivity; the second dynamic. The third will synthesize them in the divine as dynamically productive of his own being, in God as spirit.

---

[39] Ibid., p. 343.
[40] Ibid., p. 350.
[41] VB, p. 531 (VBS, p. 343).
[42] VBS, p. 351.

XXII.

God as Motion

THE SELF-NEGATING movement of the finite has affirmed the infinite. The pre-Hegelian argument had run from the being of the contingent and of the ordered to the divinely necessary and rational; the illation in the dialectic was precisely the opposite: "The truth, however, is that the absolute is just because the finite is self-contradictory opposition—just because it *is not*."[1] Logic achieved the infinite as the absolutely necessary; Science of Nature obtained the infinite as universal life. Philosophy of Spirit could begin from a radically different starting-point, not from limited being but from infinite concept. Again the devices of form and content are used: not to distinguish mediation from result nor to discriminate teleology of organic and inorganic from teleology in natures, organisms, and human events. Form and content differentiate degrees of finitude and infinitude. The cosmological and physicotheological arguments began with finite contents—beings distinct from their actuality or their means. The ontological argument can take the results of their transition, the infinite content. When one asks whether this content determines its own being, the content is finite in form, existing merely according to "the finite existence in our idea of Him."[2] The concept of God as infinite begins the ontological inference, but this beginning exists in finite subjectivity; the entire purpose of the demonstration is to remove this purely subjective existence so that the infinite in content is grasped as infinite in form as well. This movement from the utter finitude of the logical categories to the utter infinitude of the spirit constitutes a single dialectical motion, a single dialectical proof. The demonstra-

<hr>

[1] WLJS, II, 70.   [2] VBS, p. 352.

tion of God identifies with the nature of God, which is one.[3] As the previous proofs went from being to the thought of God, so this proof "goes from the thought of God, from truth itself, to the Being of this truth."[4] Either movement by itself is one-sided; together they constitute a circular unity, a single demonstration.[5] When the circularity of the demonstration is achieved and the one-sidedness of each is negated, the one proof itself becomes infinite, inclusive of all and exclusive of nothing, infinite in form and content, realizing in this infinity the true concept of God.[6]

The ontological proof was the third to appear in world history, first grasped in its basic idea by "one of the great scholastic philosophers, Anselm, Archbishop of Canterbury, that profound philosophical thinker."[7] The ancients were incapable of the idea because world-spirit had to achieve subjectivity within philosophy through the antithesis of concept and being before the transition from subjectivity to objectivity could constitute a philosophic transition.[8] In the ontological proof the initial concept is taken as purely subjective and is delimited by its other in form, object, or reality.[9] Until the universal concept and being "became established in this pure abstraction as these infinite extremes," no synthetic unity between them was possible. Until Anselm, God appeared as existing, and predicates of universal character were attributed to him—necessary, living, etc. With Anselm, a new order was possible: "Being becomes predicate, and the absolute Idea is first of all established as the subject, but the subject of thought."[10] One begins from the idea of God—infinite in content, subjective (finite) in form—and the question which governs the entire ontological demonstration can be posed: "We have the idea of God, but He is not merely an idea, He is. How are we to make this transition?"[11]

Hegel's Anselm begins with a description of the concept of God: God is the most perfect (*das Vollkommenste*), beyond

[3] VB, p. 417 (VBS, p. 215).   [4] VBS, p. 221.
[5] VB, pp. 424-26 (VBS, pp. 224-25).   [6] VB, pp. 546-47 (VBS, p. 360).
[7] VBS, p. 353.   [8] VB, p. 541 (VBS, p. 353).
[9] VB, p. 546-47 (VBS, p. 361).   [10] HP, iii, 63.
[11] VBS, p. 353.

which nothing can be thought (*über welches hinaus nichts gedacht werden kann*). Now if God were merely an idea (*blosse Vorstellung*), then he would not be the most perfect. This condition would contradict the description of his concept; for if God were merely subjective there would be something higher that could be thought, namely that which possesses being (*das Sein*). Thus this beyond-which-nothing-can-be-thought cannot exist in the understanding alone; it is essential to the concept that it be.[12] "Thus it is made clear that Being is in a superficial way subsumed under the universal of reality, that to this extent Being does not enter into opposition with the Notion."[13] Basically, the Anselmian demonstration is an attempt to overcome the finite-in-form, realizing that any idea conceived as subjectivity is defective, imperfect, finite and thus self-denying. Any idea of God which did not overcome this dichotomy by its own force would be a negation of God, for the concept as subjective is the concept as can-be, as possibility. To conceive God as possibility is to be false from the very starting-point. God as possibility could exist only as contingent. Thus the concept of the divine excludes mere possibility. God is defined as infinite actuality, and infinite actuality must include its own being.[14] The finite is precisely that in which concept and being do not identify. In God, the ultimate antithesis between subjectivity and objectivity is effaced in the infinity of concept and form.[15] The infinite consists dynamically in transcending this antimony.[16] Both faith and immediate knowledge concur on this interior unity between the concept of God and being, and agree that this inseparableness is found only in God.[17]

Content and form allow Absolute Idealism a judgment of

---

[12] VB, pp. 547-48 (VBS, p. 361).   [13] HP, iii, 64.

[14] VBS, p. 362: "In the case of the finite, existence does not correspond to the Notion. On the other hand, in the case of the Infinite, which is determined within itself, the reality must correspond to the Notion; this is the Idea, the unity of subject and object."

[15] VB, pp. 544-45 (VBS, p. 357).

[16] VB, pp. 548-49 (VBS, p. 363); cf. HP, iii, 64.

[17] VB, pp. 544-45 (VBS, pp. 357-58).

the adequacy of Anselm's argument in a manner similar to the continual distinction in play between result and mediation. The content of his proof is correct, but the transition is not demonstrated; the illation is faulty in form.[18] Anselm fails to show methodologically how the subjective understanding abrogates itself, the essential point to the proof; and this defect in form lies with the formal process of scholastic reasoning.[19] Anselm attempted to unify concept and being in a third, in the definition of God as the infinite, and so to make the two (concept and being) into one through their union with a third. Two deficiencies are indicated: The concept of infinity or "the highest" is introduced as a hypothesis, and "because Anselm has it before him only in the form of understanding, the opposites are identical and conformable to unity in a third determination only—the Highest—which, in as far as it is regulative, is outside of them."[20] Hypothesis is in contrast with absolute, as something presupposed without antecedent philosophic mediation: "This unity of Notion and Being is hypothetical, and its defect consists just in the fact of its being hypothetical."[21] Anselm presupposed from faith and common opinion the definition of God as infinite; Hegel has demonstrated this infinity through contingency and teleology. Anselm took his presupposition from the non-philosophic, representing the "ordinary idea of God, and this idea thus presupposed . . . is definitely laid down beforehand, and made to represent the so-called Notion of God."[22] Both the externality of the definition and its hypothetical form mark the defective nature of the Anselmian form: "It is the following circumstance which makes the proof unsatisfactory. That most perfect and most real existence is in fact a presupposition measured by which Being-for-itself and the Notion-for-itself are one-sided."[23]

Anselm's own thought was predicated upon a union between faith and understanding: *fides quaerens intellectum*, an intrin-

---

[18] HP, iii, 64; VB, p. 544 (VBS, p. 357).
[19] HP, iii, 64.　　[20] *Ibid.*　　　　　　　　[21] VBS, p. 357.
[22] *Ibid.*, p. 216.　　[23] *Ibid.*, p. 363.

sically correct relation which Absolute Idealism attempted to reestablish after the diremptions of Jacobi and Kant.[24] As philosophy moved from the middle ages into further growth, Anselm's arguments were developed in "a broader and more rational" manner through Descartes, Spinoza, Leibnitz, Mendelssohn, and Wolff, but without the needed correction in form.[25] None goes beyond hypothesis:

> If it is said that we believe it, that we know it immediately, then the unity of the idea and Being is expressed in the form of the presupposition just exactly as it is in Anselm's argument, and we have not got one bit further. This is the presupposition we everywhere meet with in Spinoza too. He defines the Absolute Cause, Substance, as that which cannot be thought of as not existing, the conception of which involves existence; that is, the idea of God is directly bound up with Being.[26]

Whether one takes the grasp of the divine substance from faith, as Anselm, or from initial definition, as Spinoza, the reality of the union is only hypothetical. The dialectical method will found this content by showing that infinity is the truth of any finite being and that infinity posits its own being. Aristotelian method begins from hypothesis; Ciceronian controversy sections off hypothesis for rhetoric; Newtonian mechanics allows no hypothesis as final explanation of causal chains; Absolute Idealism will purify correct conclusions from their methodological failures by an absolute as opposed to a hypothetical beginning.

Kant's criticism bore down on the ontological argument with stunning effectiveness. The ill-repute of the Anselmian argument can be laid to his attacks, and the general repudiation of natural theology stems from his reduction of the cosmological and teleological demonstrations to the ontological.[27] Transcendental Idealism, through its operational, antinomic

---

[24] HP, III, 67. For this relationship between faith and reason through the history of the ontological argument, cf. Lamm, *op.cit.*
[25] VBS, pp. 354, 358, 361-62.   [26] *Ibid.*, p. 358.
[27] VB, pp. 540-41 (VBS, p. 353).

method, discriminated sharply between being and the reality of a concept. Being adds nothing to the intrinsic intelligibility of a concept; the essential predicates of a hundred thalers are identical whether one possesses them in idea or in reality. Being is not among the essential notes of any concept, and, thereby, it cannot issue from them. It must come to the concept "from the outside, from elsewhere. Being is not involved in the Notion."[28] Gaunilon had formed the same objection during Anselm's lifetime: "The fact of my forming an idea of anything does not therefore imply that the thing exists."[29] The thought of the highest perfection is no different whether it actually exists or not; within the essential predicates of the subject, actual existence is not contained.[30] Kant's ontological interpretation distinguishes levels which cannot be merged without error, and his operational method reinforces these distinctions by antinomically indicating the necessity of further discriminations in perspectives and in sciences. Hegel's entitative interpretation insists upon the continuity of the substructure of all reality, being or concept, and the dialectical method allows one concept to generate another in the endless movement which is the final determination of world, nature, and spirit.

Kant's method made him constitutionally incapable of understanding a concept. "To speak of every wretched form of existence as a notion is to go on quite the wrong lines."[31] One hundred thalers is not a concept nor is any abstract sense-idea, such as color, nor is any determination of the Understanding which happens to be in the mind. The concept as concept is in-and-for-itself; this is the concept which identifies with God, the infinite concept which is the truth of those things called concepts in ordinary life.[32] Any finite understanding is not a true concept, or, rather, *the* true concept.[33] Anselm was as aware as any man that to possess a determination of the understanding is not to guarantee its existence; the concept of God

[28] VBS, p. 354.   [29] *Ibid.*, p. 363.   [30] HP, iii, 65-66.   [31] VBS, p. 363.
[32] VB, pp. 541-42 (VBS, pp. 354-55).
[33] VBS, p. 363: "The Notion which is only something subjective, and is divorced from Being is a nullity."

is the speculative concept, different utterly from the concepts of common usage, and to Anselm's proof one must only elaborate this identification between concept and infinity which allows being to become one of its internal determinations.[34]

The infinite with which the ontological proof should begin is the concept in-and-for-itself, the Universal which determines itself. In contrast to the static concept-analysis of Anselm and Kant, the Hegelian concept is dynamic. Motion lies at the heart of the concept. The universal particularizes itself through determination and determines itself through negation, posits finitude and then negates this finitude in its own infinity, being coincident finally with itself as this very movement itself. This is the actuality which the concept-in-general is; and this concept is the concept of God: "This is the Notion in general. This is just what the Notion of God, the absolute Notion, God, really is."[35] The fault of almost all previous thinkers was to remove movement from the concept, to fix the concept through abstraction and to maintain this abstraction through philosophies of understanding. The dialectical movement of scientific method identifies with the content of the concept only when negation, determination, and transcendence lie within the very definition of the concept. The true concept is essentially self-motion, self-mediation, and self-determination. Precisely because the concept has already been established as infinite, one can argue to its interiority in determination; to be determined by another—either to be or to act effectively— is to be finite, limited, in relation of dependence upon another. "It is in fact this and this alone which marks everything finite: —its being in time and space is discrepant from its notion."[36] The question of the ontological argument turns on another problem: What is Being?[37]

Being, as established at the initial moment of the *Logic*, was not the concrete actuality which the concept is. Being is

---

[34] HP, III, 66.   [35] VBS, p. 355.

[36] ELW, No. 51, pp. 107-108.

[37] VBS, p. 355: "The primary question is: What is Being? what is this attribute, this determinateness, namely, reality? Being is nothing but the unutterable, the inconceivable; it is not that concrete something which the Notion is, but merely the abstraction of reference to self."

mere abstract reference to self, immediacy without determination: "We may say, it is immediacy. Being is the immediate in general, and conversely the Immediate is Being, it is in relation to itself, that is, the mediation is negated."[38] Now the concept has been demonstrated as both necessary and as having life, as self-mediating. So, then, the weakest of determinations must also be within its determination. What can mediate itself must possess its own self-identity among its predicates. Being differs from the concept not as the Thomistic actualization of the total reality, but as part differs from the whole in which it is included. Being, as abstract self-identity, is a mere moment within the totality of the concept. Like any moment, being unites with the concept through mediation, and this mediation is the self-movement of the concept.

The Hegelian argument is basically: The finite has indicated that its dialectical truth is the infinite. This infinite concept cannot be merely subjective—that would constitute it as finite in form, and the truth of the finite in form is the infinite. The infinite concept, then, must generate its own objectivity, its own being, overcoming the finitude between concept and reality. This infinite concept is divine; the divine is its own process, its own movement. In the dialectical method of Hegel, the demonstration of the existence of God from motion identifies with the nature of God himself: "The Concept is this totality, the movement, the process to objectify itself."[39] Concept is *die Bewegung* and *der Process*. The fixed subjectivity which understanding postulates of the concept is false, essentially finite; "the very idea of the Notion implies that it has to do away with this defect of subjectivity, with this distinction between itself and Being, and has to objectify itself."[40] The dialectical method reformed the cosmological and teleological proofs by entering into contingency and limited life and following through to their infinite truth in necessity and universal life. Now the dialectical method enters into the infinite concept-as-

---

[38] *Ibid.*, p. 535.

[39] VB, p. 542 (m). The entire history of philosophy can be understood as drive of the infinite form to become subject. Schelling had begun to move in this direction. Cf. HP, iii, 516.

[40] VBS, p. 356.

such and follows through its self-production. The concept is its motion, just as finitude is its own denial. The concept "is itself the act of producing itself as something which has Being, as something objective."[41]

The concept has moved through successive stages of intense reflexivity. In logic, necessity was the reflexive identification of concept and actuality. In the science of nature, universal life was the reflexive identification of ends and means; now that the concept has passed beyond the immediacy of logic and through the mediation of nature, it can return to itself in consciousness. The concept can grasp the other as projection of itself. Now "the Notion shows itself eternally in that activity whereby Being is posited as identical with itself."[42] And this is the concept as entire freedom, the concept which identifies with God. The concept in itself was the idea reached through logic; the concept alienated or projected into finitude was nature; now the concept in-and-for-itself, as "the continuous act which abolishes differences" is the concept as spirit, as "the Notion of God in its entire freedom."[43] "What we call Soul is the Notion, and in Spirit, in consciousness, the Notion as such attains to existence as a free Notion."[44] And the movement which is this spirit, this concept returned to itself, is the synthetic conjunction of subjectivity and objectivity into infinity.[45] Just as the finite concept moves itself to its non-being, its contradiction, and thus to the assertion of the infinite whose being it possesses, so the infinite concept moves itself to its own being, containing this being as the most immediate of its many determinations.[46] It identifies with the movement to abolish the defect of subjectivity, with this distinction between itself and being, and in this mediation produces itself as objective. Within the concept as spirit, being is not added to the notion nor is there a third in which both unite. "The unity is rather to be conceived of as an absolute process, as the living movement of God, and this means that the two sides are distinguished from each other, while the process is thought of as

41 *Ibid.*   42 *Ibid.*, p. 364.
43 *Ibid.*, p. 365.   44 *Ibid.*, pp. 356-57.
45 VB, p. 544 (VBS, p. 357).   46 VB, pp. 550-51 (VBS, pp. 364-65).

that absolute, continuous act of eternal self-production."[47]

This speculative grasp of the divine as spirit is the Christian God.[48] The God of the dialectic is the God who reveals himself through action, through projection, becoming through this revelation more deeply united with himself.[49] This dialectical union of being with concept gives the initial being with which the logic opened a new status. Being is no longer the merest abstraction; it is the being of God, now concrete and absolute: "We have not to deal with Being in the poverty of abstraction, in immediacy in its bad form, but with Being as the Being of God, as absolutely concrete Being, distinguished from God."[50] For in determining himself to be, God determines the entire movement which he identifies with. God is process. The divine attributes are not destroyed in an abstract unity but designate moments within the process itself. "It is therefore the inner necessity of reason which shows itself active in thinking Spirit, and produces in it this multiplicity of characteristics, . . . virtual stages in development."[51] God is the process; his attributes are the moments of the process. And it is with this grasp of the concept of God that Absolute Idealism has reached full circle. "Absolute Spirit, which is found to be the concrete, last, and highest truth of all Being, at the end of its evolution freely passes beyond itself and lapses into the shape of an immediate Being."[52] Being was obtained from the concept of science at the initiation of logic; now this concept has reached full infinity in thought, seen to contain all its determinations as moments and all its objects as projections, and from this limitlessness issues its own foundation. What is critical for the dialectic was not that a purely immediate beginning be discovered—there is no immediacy that is in its truth unmediated—but that the whole form a system, a complete circle so that the first is last

[47] VBS, p. 366.　　　　　　[48] VB, p. 551 (VBS, p. 365).
[49] VB, p. 546 (VBS, p. 360).　　[50] VBS, p. 365.
[51] Ibid., p. 219.

[52] WLJS, I, 83; II, 484. This understanding of spirit as the ontological proof of itself is equally the conclusion of Ute Guzzoni, Werden Zu Sich: Eine Untersuchung Zu Hegels "Wissenschaft der Logic" (Freiburg: Verlag Karl Alber, 1963), pp. 27-30. Guzzoni lays great stress upon the reflexivity of the Hegelian principle and its ultimate merger with dialectical becoming as both Sich-Begründen und Sich-Gründen.

and that the last is first.[53] Progress is a return to the foundation, reflexivity within the entire movement as within the concept whose nature it is.[54] The beginning is one-sided, abstract, without this complete determination of its implications in motion, so that the dialectic away from the starting-point is actually a penetration into the starting-point, in the formation of the circular movement which is its truth and which is its actuality as spirit. "For the result contains its own beginning, and the development of the beginning has made it the richer by a new determinateness."[55] All expansion is movement, all movement is the concept, and the infinite concept as spirit is God. Thus the dialectic movement of the method identifies with the dialectical movement which is the spirit:

> Each new stage of exteriorization (that is, of further determination) is also an interiorization, and greater extension is also higher intensity. The richest consequently is also the most concrete and subjective term, and that which carries itself back into the simplest depth is also the most powerful and comprehensive. The highest and acutest point is *simple personality*, which, by virtue *of the absolute dialectic which is its nature*, equally holds and comprehends everything within itself because it perfectly liberates itself.[56]

It is this spirit as system which overcomes the provisional or hypothetical nature of the Anselmian form, while raising to the level of pure science the content of the ontological proof. The end and the beginning justify each other in a movement in which they both identify.

Hegel's God is thus a God of motion—not the God above movement as the pure act of Aristotle, moving and final cause of all change; nor Cicero's God reached by controversial consensus debating over movement in physics, ethics, and epistemology; nor the Newtonian God whose domination set up planetary systems and whose existence constitutes their mathematical coordinates. Hegel agrees with Aristotle that God is

---

[53] WL, I, 56-57 (WLJS, I, 83).
[54] WL, I, 55-56; II, 502-503 (WLJS, I, 82; II, 483).
[55] WLJS, II, 482.   [56] *Ibid.*, II, 483.

pure activity, not the abstract activity of the *Metaphysics*, but the concrete activity of dialectical movement: "In order that it [pure act] may appear as activity, it has to be posited in its moments or stages."[57] Absolute Idealism keeps the Aristotelian reflexivity of principle, but corrects its abstraction by lodging dialectical movement within God and deepens the truth of finite essences by generating all finitude out of the underlying infinity to which it returns. The comprehensivity which Cicero achieved by an interpersonal *mundus*, Hegel obtains through an assimilative method, and he specifically corrects the *De Natura Deorum* for a phenomenal representation of divinity and for its antinomic method: "This is the kind of reflection which institutes comparisons and in this way gives to the hitherto fixed forms of the gods a dubious and vacillating character."[58] Newton's focus upon the empirical rather than upon concepts as the proper study of philosophy prevented physics from ever attaining significant advancement, and his method turned him from true infinity: "Here the Idea in its infinitude is not itself the object of knowledge; but a determinate content is raised into the universal."[59] This led to a disjunction between exact sciences and religious piety, and thus he contributed nothing to the philosophic development of religion.[60] The only philosophic content in the Newtonian natural science lay with "the fact that the bases of both are universal, and still further that *I* have made this experience, that it rests on my consciousness and obtains its significance through me."[61] Hegelian Idealism will purify the science of nature from its sensuous orientation through a new focus upon thought-determinations, and through their finitude rise to the universal life which harmonizes the organic and inorganic.

The Hegelian God is demonstrated through motion, but, more profoundly, as motion, a single movement whose structure is dialectic, whose determinations are moments, and whose truth is the reflexive infinity of spirit.

[57] PR, III, 12.   [58] *Ibid.*, III, 308.

[59] HP, III, 162, 323-24.

[60] *Ibid.*, III, 162. While Newton figures in HP, his name is not even mentioned in PR.

[61] HP, I, 59.

Conclusion: *Theme and Pluralism*

After the *Summa Theologiae* had determined the nature, the subject, and the methods of its inquiries, sacred doctrine turned to the problems of the reality of God, rejecting three demonstrations of the divine existence and elaborating another five. One cannot pass from the meaning of God to his existence, for though it is evident in itself that God is, it is not evident to us. The proof cannot be a *demonstratio propter quid*, whose middle term would be the definition of the cause, but a *demonstratio quia*, an illation which proceeded from effect to cause. Among the five ways by which such an inference could travel, one stood predominant as the *prima et manifestior via*, the one which took its origins from sensible movement: "It is certain and sensibly evident that some things are moved in this world."[1] Aquinas ascribed this demonstration to Aristotle, and in commenting upon the *Physics* he stressed its preeminence over the other proofs: "This way of proving that the first principle is, is the most efficacious and cannot be withstood."[2] Again, in the *Compendium Theologiae*, the final and smallest of his summaries, the argument *ex parte motus* alone finds a place.[3]

Neither Thomas' separation of the a priori from the a posteriori nor his enthusiasm for the argument from motion could fix the career of either. Scotus thought *primum ens* a far better description of God than *primum movens* and built a correspondingly more appropriate argument from the possibility of being than from the movement of things. Cajetan claimed that from motion one inferred the divine only *per*

---

[1] *Summa Theologiae* I. 2. 3.

[2] Thomas Aquinas, *In Octo Libros Physicorum*. Lib. viii. lect. 1, sec. 991.

[3] *Compendium Theologiae* 3. *Opuscula Omnia*, ed. R. P. Mandonnet (5 vols.; Parisiis: Sumptibus P. Lethielleux, Bibliopolae Editoris, 1927), Vol. iii.

accidens, and in Suarez the rejection is total: "It is found in-efficacious in many ways."[4] On the other hand, the *Opus Oxoniense* and *De Primo Principio* revived the ontological argument and used it to color the a posteriori in an inference from *primum ens* as possible to *primum ens* as necessary, and René Descartes and Père Caterus would open modern philosophy with the discussions of Anselm and Gaunilon.[5] Finally, while successors would correct or reject the conclusions of Aquinas' argument as inappropriate or the distinctions by which he sets up the demonstration as invalid, a science of motion would emerge which denied any correlation between motion and mover. "Whatever is moved is moved by another" has occasioned as lasting a debate, as thorough a transformation, or as complete a rejection as either the *demonstratio a posteriori* or God as *primum movens.* The Thomistic synthesis served neither to isolate an argument nor to fix an understanding of movement, determine its application and define its source for all times; but it did draw into its unified inquiry diverse elements whose ambiguities, refutations, and transmutations affect a continuing problem within the history of philosophy: Can one prove the existence of God from motion?

What issues as question in Aquinas begins to develop as a connecting problem among philosophers howsoever diverse. This book originated with a difficulty about the *quinque viae* and its contradiction posed by the Newtonian axioms of motion. It was decided not to reformulate the Thomistic demonstrations—that would have been a question of inquiry—nor to isolate semantically each demonstration for a consideration of its patterns of meaning. Rather the attempt was to discover what was involved in the tradition of which Aquinas and Newton were but variant developments, a tradition which Thomas located in Aristotle and Newton in Pythagoras and which advances beyond either into almost every significant philosophical investigation. Both the career of the question

---

[4] For these texts and an historical commentary, cf. Owens, "The Conclusion of the Prima Via," *op.cit.,* pp. 33-37.

[5] Alvin Plantinga (ed.), *The Ontological Argument: From St. Anselm to Contemporary Philosophers* (Garden City, N.Y.: Doubleday, 1965), pp. 31-49.

and the antinomies within its solutions suggest that its course has not been simple repetition and resolution, but continuous adaptation and variation. Its content does not reappear univocally when the meaning of motion, the nature of mobiles, and the characteristics of God shift, and the entire structure of the problem hangs upon the significance of proof. The problem is a continuing problem, and this work attempted to treat it as such.

For this continuity is destroyed if one reduces the variations and complexities of its elements to a single doctrine or insists upon a single method for all valid demonstration. It is no great trick to read Thomistic *motus* as simple locomotion in space and to prove Aristotelian physics absurd, but this is to mistake one's own semantics for another's and to hammer down a complicated pattern of philosophic thought into a single, linear progression towards one's own philosophy. Out of this confusion stemmed objections such as those of inertia against a proof from motion, of inadequacy against a God as mover, of verification against a *demonstratio quia*. And the converse has been equally true. Maritain's dismissal of Teilhard as "theology fiction" repeats the perennial inability of the Peripatetic tradition to understand Platonic myth, and MacKinnon's reduction of Newton to Coulson's "god of the gaps" fails to account for what is a far more subtle theology.[6] The problem must be treated as a continuing problem, one which exists now in one variant and then in another, and the ambiguous recurrence of the problem must be carefully distinguished from its previous significance or its later development. "Can the existence of God be proved from movement?" is singular in its ambiguous formulation and can serve to connect discursively the most divergent philosophies, but it is multiple in each of its embodiments as the question is nailed down to a definite sequence of meanings and arguments. The unity of

---

[6] Jacques Maritain, *The Peasant of the Garonne*, trans. Cuddihy and Hughes (New York: Holt, Rinehart, and Winston, 1968), p. 119. For Aristotle's similar reduction of his opponents to πλάσμα, cf. *Ph.* viii. 1. 252ᵃ4. Edward M. MacKinnon, "Theism and Scientific Explanation," *Continuum*, v, No. 1 (Winter-Spring, 1967), 72.

the ambiguously continuous problem is that of a *theme*; its existence within any inquiry is that of a question within a system. Thus the difficulty which arose between problematic motion which needs a mover and inertial motion which denies a mover enlarges into a problem common to philosophic tradition, upon which philosophic semantics must be brought to bear to distinguish divergences and interrelations of meaning and in which a discursive unity can be discovered which is thematic rather than systematic.

Since the problem which issued from the confrontation was one of demonstration, the attempt to trace this theme concentrated upon its particularization through divergent methods. The selection of Aristotle, Cicero, Newton, and Hegel was dictated by the distinct method which each employed and by their collective exhaustion of the four possible methods within the semantic schema through which they were examined— philosophic methods either particularized for each problem encountered or universalized for every question posed or constructed to resolve wholes into components or systematized to assimilate all movements into their infinite truth. These methods distinguished the philosophies analyzed in each of the four parts of this work; the theme connected them.

What is immediately evident in Aristotle's problematic method is something curiously empirical. Words, thoughts, and things keep a distinction in kind, though the term possesses meaning and reference as well as verbal form. Thus one cannot move from the nature of thought to the existence of things, and a particularization of methods follows upon the distinct natures of their subjects. With this implicit exclusion of the ontological argument, problematic inquiry moves to the resolution of its questions through commensurate causes; and apodictic demonstration is only obtained when any fact is resolved into its proper principle. Problematic motion is a progressive actualization of the potential as such, a successive realization of ability; and motion is differentiated into a plurality according to the categories of which it is subject. Contradiction lodges at the center of such movement insofar as any change passes from a state of privation to that of its cor-

270

relative act. Aristotle's essentialist interpretation would predicate movement neither of underlying atoms nor of transcendent mind, but of organized entities, substances whose potencies
would be the subject of movement and whose natures would
be its internal source. Aquinas' ontological interpretation varies
this predication, for the movements of things and men reflect
the governance of God, as their substances result from the
divine ideas and their existences are a participation in the
divine *esse*. While both Aristotle and Aquinas refuse to pass
from meaning to existence a priori, both find the successive
actualization of substances pointing to the pure activity of reflexive thought as moving or final cause.

The operationalism of Cicero shifts the contradictions of
movement into the antinomies of statements, and the reality
or concept of motion is what men call motion. The plurality
is no longer a plurality of kinds, but a plurality of perspectives
as movement becomes successively within the ongoing rationality of the debate on the locomotion of atoms, the epigenesis
of mind, and the traditions of the body politic—all included
within the changes and interchanges of controversy. Problematic movement does not specifically appear within the positions
advanced since it differs from the Stoic only in expression, and
movement transmutes into that qualitative change which issues from diverse propositions or conflicting positions. While
the problematic used the opinions of men as a propaedeutic
to scientific inquiry, the operationalist adopted interacting formulations as the universal scientific procedure. This allows for
a restatement of the ontological argument, not as a synthesis
of other demonstrations, but as a perspective within the community, as a contribution to that community of actions and
discourse. Demonstration also shifts from a resolution in terms
of causes to a consensus in terms of community, and it is this
consensus which recognizes the gods as members with men
in that comprehensive society which is the order of the universe.

From this community, Newton's logistic mechanics takes the
Epicurean physics, eliminates the a priori ideas, and constructs
a Stoic a posteriori argument from design. Aristotelian motion

271

goes the way of occult qualities and Ciceronian method obtains only that movement which was relative, apparent, and common. The *Principia* fixes movement as the logistic translation of bodies in space and time, and the contradiction passes similarly from problematic privation and operational conflict to the imbalance of forces impressed and inertial. Plurality is obtained within movement neither of kind nor of outlook, but between the absolute and relative. Within the logistic method, motion becomes the property of bodies (masses) rather than of statements or potencies, and the entitative interpretation locates the mobile as neither substantial integrities nor human expressions, but the realities which underlie either phenomena. Newton's conjunction of the logistic with the entitative eliminates an illation from concept to reality, but Spinoza and Leibnitz could reintroduce the a priori argument by joining to the logistic method an ontological interpretation which found the final significance of what appeared in the transcendent categories of mind. The comprehensivity which Cicero achieved through community changes into the comprehensivity of forces transformed into gravity for astronomy and into domination as the proper characteristic of the divine. God authors movement by imparting those forces which balance out into a system and by constituting those mathematical coordinates which alone allow translation in space to be absolute.

Hegelian dialectic method determines movement neither as the qualitative predications of speech nor as the locomotion of bodies, but the evolution of thought. The entire universe is the concept in development, containing a movement which is only partially found in the transfer of bodies or the alterations of speech. Motion is most profoundly becoming, a generation or negation and the corruption of this negation through a deeper assimilation; and this becoming identifies with the movement of the thinker as he identifies with the total, thinking universe. Contradiction is within movement as its dialectical nature, a conflict neither in absence nor statement nor force, but between any concept and the implicit negation which constitutes the truth of its concept. The plurality of motions becomes the multiplicity of moments within the single circle of *Werden*, an infinity of progressive generation and corruption. The dialectic found any final distinction between symbol, thought, and thing ultimately false, and thus could reestablish the illation between meaning and existence in an ontological examination. Because Hegel, like Newton, found the ultimately real within the substrate of the given, the ontological argument could be corrected from its form in Anselm and Augustine, where it was the best among many, and made to evolve out of the other demonstrations as their completion and ultimate foundation. This evolution of the concept constituted dialectical demonstration, an internal process in which system, thought, and thing identified in movement and in contrast to the externalities of causal resolution, community consensus, or composite forces. Plato's ontological interpretation would distinguish the moving universe from the changeless ideas and locate the ultimate mobile as the world soul; Hegel's entitative interpretation puts movement at the center of the idea, reducing the world soul to a single manifestation of dialectical spirit. The operationalists had allowed the a priori arguments as opinions within a thinking community; the dialectician would elevate the a priori arguments as the ultimate proof within a thinking universe.

In following this continuous line as it shifted from method to method, this study focused upon the divergencies attained by the change in scientific procedure and concretized these findings through an interpretation of those things of which motion was predicated. But each of the methods would attain God as a different source by which to make its procedure objective, by which to set the discursive movement of statement or thing or thought or substance within a unity. Aristotle organized his universe around reflexive beginnings and found the final significance of the cosmos in the thought utterly commensurate with itself. Hegel took this reflexivity, making it concrete through its merger with the movement it authored, self-projection and self-assimilation. Using a comprehensive principle, Cicero placed actional gods within a single society with men, making this society dependent upon the gods as members. Newton took the infinity of force as comprehen-

273

sively identified with the divine nature and as author of the system of the world both in its origin and its mathematical constitution. All four of the authors studied used "holoscopic" principles. God transcendently energized the world in Aristotle, authored the system in the beginning for Newton, or ultimately merged with the universe as part or whole in Cicero or Hegel. For God figures as moving and final cause in problematic inquiry and as efficient in logistic mechanics, while the divine is an element of the interpersonal society for the operationalist and the world is a finite projection of the infinite for the dialectician.

The *theme* is never simply repeated; it runs through every philosophy, and with each inquiry it sets up its own distinct problems and works through divergent methodologies to idiosyncratic solutions. Even when an attempt was made to repeat a previous philosophy, repetition was not effected. Cicero professed to learn his method from Aristotle, but it was Aristotle become an operationalist. Hegel took over the Aristotelian principle of thought thinking itself—only to have that principle merge with its movement and with the potentiality moved. Just so one system does not refute another as the tradition alters from philosophy to philosophy. The dialectical method could be joined with simple principles to obtain a God as the Plotinean One or with an actional God whose creative decision determined whatever reality existed. The problematic method in the Stoics could join a comprehensive principle, finding the resolution of all distinct problems and methods within a single ultimate solution. The ambiguities of the theme and the infinitude of possible statements sustain the continuity of philosophy, and the dialogues of philosophers become the exploration and extension of the thematic concerns of men. The richness of the theme lies with its many metamorphoses, and shifts in the dynamics of semantics only underline a tradition that is part of the fabric of human thought. In this thematic predominance, the existence of God as demonstrated from motion stands as one of the overwhelming problems of philosophic history, pervading the experience of men, the procedures of their investigations, the significance of their discourse, and the commitment of their lives.

The theme which issued for this book out of a confrontation with medieval thought and which was traced within four major authors of Western philosophy is confined neither to the West nor to the past. It is the common heritage of men who think. Teilhard de Chardin spoke again for the dialectical embodiment of this tradition with a statement which summarizes the answer to the common problem with which this study was concerned: "I am not speaking metaphorically when I say that it is throughout the length and breadth and depth of the world in movement that a man can attain the experience and vision of his God."[7]

[7] Pierre Leroy, "Teilhard de Chardin: The Man," prefaced to Teilhard de Chardin, *Le Milieu Divin: An Essay on the Interior Life* (London: Collins, 1962), p. 36.

Index of Persons

INDEX OF PERSONS

278

Index of Subjects

accidental, 37, 58; dependent, 60-61; divine, 3-4, 108, 193, 237, 246; efficient, 84-85, 134-35, 150, 245, 274; essential, 37, 58; eternal, 29, 66-67; final, 7, 19, 29, 36, 61, 69, 75, 78-79, 82-85, 197, 199, 230, 245, 264, 271, 274; first, 7, 59-61, 63, 168, 193, 237; forming, 246; four causes, 16, 61, 195, 250; material, 61, 73; of motion, 3, 195; moving, 3, 7, 23n, 29, 36, 40, 42, 56-61, 62n, 66-70, 77, 84, 197, 199, 230, 245, 264, 271, 274

chance, 32, 36-37, 45, 82, 105, 111, 134, 150, 170, 196-97, 247, 250

change, 35-36, 44, 58, 162, 171-76, 188-89, 203, 229, 264, 271

choice, 52, 124, 197

commonplace, 98-99. *See also* topic

community, commonwealth, 104, 107, 146, 153-56, 211, 271-73. *See also* society

compositio, composition, 15, 136, 163-64, 166, 169, 188-90, 194-95, 203

COMPREHENSIVE PRINCIPLE, *see* principle

concept, 7, 21n, 81n, 108-10, 116, 125, 137-38, 145, 152, 214, 216, 218, 221, 224, 227, 229-31, 238, 240, 243-44, 247-51, 254-65, 272-73

concept, divine, 5, 118, 238, 254-56, 260-61

conjunction, 10, 16, 20, 45, 53, 55, 262

consciousness, 115, 210-11, 216, 223, 226

consent, universal, 102-103, 108-10, 112, 114, 116-19, 122, 125, 137, 145, 151-52, 233

constitutiones, 98-99. *See also* issues; rhetoric

construction, 89, 136, 163, 171, 213-14. *See also* logistic and operational methods

content, 31n, 110n, 215-264 *passim*

contingency, 209-11, 224-26, xx: 232-43, 244-57 *passim*, 261. *See also* argument from contingency

continuity, 42, 45, 47, 65, 67, 147

contradiction, 6, 12, 34-35, 43-44, 137, 210-262 *passim*, 270-72

controversia, 92-93, 95, 97, 104, 107, 121-22, 151, 161. *See also* controversy

controversy, 12, 86, 98-156 *passim*, 160, 169, 197, 203, 258, 264, 271

conversation, 96, 136, 146

coordinates, 6, 8-11, 23, 25, 27, 86, 96, 107, 146, 189, 199-201, 203, 236, 264, 272. *See also* interpretation, method, principle, selection

corruption, 33, 44, 50-51, 65-67, 69-70, 75, 77

cosmos, 4, 29, 50-52, 55-56, 67, 72, 84, 104-105, 113, 115, 127, 132, 155, 183, 207, 232, 245, 253, 273. *See also* universe

creation, 35, 51, 62n, 103, 106-107, 111, 113, 116, 126, 129, 135, 200, 247

criterion, 22-24, 26, 32, 99, 108, 110, 118-19, 172, 177, 226

criticism, 89-90, 103, 162, 208, 217, 235-36, 247-48, 258. *See also* judgment

culture, 93, 108, 113, 118, 137

debate, 6, 12, 92-156 *passim*, 178, 223, 225-27, 230, 234, 264, 271

deduction, 125, 165-66, 171, 236

definition: Aristotle, 17-20, 22, 24n, 30, 38, III: 39-43, 44, 71-72, 99-100, 171-72, 222; Cicero (*see* issue, definitional; question, definitional); Hegel, 218, 237, 241, 253, 257; Newton, XIV: 171-77, 182n, 187

demonstratio propter quid, 48, 267;

demonstratio quia, 48, 267, 269

demonstration: Aristotle, 22n, 28, 46, 49, 52, 56n, 80, 195, 199, 223; Cicero, 121-22; cosmological, 241, 258, 268, 270, 273 (*See also* argument, proof); Hegel, 211-13, 225-26, 234, 251, 254-55;

INDEX OF SUBJECTS